PRACTITIONER-BASED RESEARCH

Power, Discourse, and Transformation

edited by
John Lees and Dawn Freshwater

KARNAC

First published in 2008 by
Karnac Books Ltd
118 Finchley Road, London NW3 5HT

British Library Cataloguing in Publication Data

A C.I.P. for this book is available from the British Library

ISBN: 978 1 85575 538 3

Edited, designed and produced by The Studio Publishing Services Ltd
www.publishingservicesuk.co.uk
e-mail: studio@publishingservicesuk.co.uk

www.karnacbooks.com

CONTENTS

Ashwini Bhalla, MSc, MBACP, BSc, received her Masters in Therapeutic Counselling from Greenwich University, London. Her counselling training during the course at Deptford Drug Service and Greenwich Mind furthered her interest in addictive behaviours, mental health, and dual diagnosis. As a result, she subsequently started a practice in drug treatments for substance misuse clients at the Haringey Drugs Advisory Service (Barnet Enfield & Haringey Mental Health Trust) as a Shared Care Co-ordinator. She worked closely with GPs, delivering training and supervision on harm reduction and prescribing, and supporting the provision of drugs treatment for stabilized clients within the community. Currently, she provides counselling for the more chaotic substance misuse clients, with a dual diagnosis, at the Redbridge Drug and Alcohol Service (North East London Mental Health Trust). Her clinical approach combines motivational enhancement techniques, cognitive–behavioural coping skills, and psychosocial interventions. She is also currently studying the person-centred approach in Christian Counselling with the Orpington Christian Counselling Service.

Jeni Boyd works as a counsellor in Primary Care and in private practice. She has completed a Masters degree in Jungian Studies at the Centre for Psychoanalytic Studies, University of Essex, where her major dissertation was on accessing "the shamanic potential of the individual" through altered states of consciousness as found in the ritual of a Native American spirit lodge and through the Jungian process of active imagination. Her Research Masters degree at Nottingham Trent focused on another liminal space, that of the dream-world, and her interest in the use of dream-work in short-term therapy is being further explored through a PhD Research degree at the University of Manchester.

Christine Crosbie had a long career in journalism and research before training to be a counsellor. Difficulties in her personal life led her to seek therapy, aged thirty-seven, and six years of intensive psychoanalytic psychotherapy ensued. It was partly this experience that led her to undertake counselling training and start down a new career path. She gained an MSc with Distinction in Therapeutic Counselling from the University of Greenwich in 2006. She now works as a counsellor to university students. She lives with her husband, daughters, and dog in a village in Kent.

Geoffrey Denham, PhD, is Director of the Postgraduate Programme in Psychology at Auckland University of Technology. He is leading New Zealand's first professional training programme in Counselling Psychology at AUT (see talkingpsych.co.nz). His research is focused on language practices in psychotherapy, the consequences of medicalizing suffering for mental health management, and examining the psychotherapeutic benefits of various forms of representation and naming in psychotherapy. Most recently, he has developed a training package for transcultural counselling that draws on work in medical anthropology. He has written on post trauma recovery in *Gielen, Draguns and Fish* (in press). He is a practitioner researcher, a registered psychologist in New Zealand, a member of both the APS and NZPsS, and Co-ordinating Editor of the *Australian Journal of Counselling Psychology*.

Dawn Freshwater is Professor and Dean, School of Healthcare, Leeds University, UK. She is a qualified nurse, a psychotherapist, and a clinical supervisor. As Editor of *Journal of Psychiatric and Mental Health Nursing* and a dedicated writer and reader, she has co-authored/edited and authored over fifteen texts. Her interests lie in the area of reflexive research, transformation through reflective practice, and advances in knowledge development. She is a Fellow of the Royal College of Nursing.

Jana Helena initially trained as a psychodynamic counsellor, before undertaking further training at Masters level in integrative counselling and psychotherapy. She has been working in mental health and substance misuse since 2001.

Barbara Hunter, RGN, RMN, BA, MSc, is an integrative therapist and holistic health practitioner currently practising independently. She was born in Aotearoa (New Zealand). Her cultural and professional roots have influenced an interest in all cultures and their spiritual traditions throughout the world. With many years of experience in the Health Sector, as both clinician and educator/lecturer in the Faculty of Nursing, special interests have developed to include mental health issues and feminist ideology (particularly, education for women).

John Lees is responsible for developing research and curricula at the University of Leeds and for quality assurance, learning, and research at Crossfields Institute, Education, Training and Research inspired by Anthroposophy. He is also a BACP Senior Registered Practitioner. He has written numerous articles on clinical practice, practitioner research, and anthroposophy, was Series Editor of Routledge's "Clinical Counselling in Context" series and former Editor of *Psychodynamic Counselling*.

Roderick McKenzie has experience acquired through twenty-six years of practice across the broad spectrum of mental health nursing, including acute psychiatry, care of the elderly mentally ill, continuing care, and substance misuse. Roddy has had an interest in the spiritual dimension of nursing care for a number of years now, and has always been particularly intrigued by the gap that exists between practice and academe. His career focus now is on closing that gap, using practitioner-friendly methods, and he is using his own experience and research interests to explore the methods, possibilities, and reality of his aspirations. He lives in the Highlands of Scotland with his wife Jenni, two children Aidan and Niamh, two cats, a dog and a bicycle.

Sabi Redwood holds the position of Senior Lecturer at the Centre for Qualitative Research at the School of Health and Social Care, Bournemouth University, and is currently working on conceptualizations of "quality of life" as it is lived rather than how it is measured, and how qualitative methods can contribute to generating evidence for healthcare practice. He teaches qualitative research methods, research ethics, and practice development processes, and supports students' learning in research and practice development methodologies in health and social care. He previously worked in the NHS, managing children's nursing services, before starting a career in research and higher education. His interests include poststructural philosophy and critical theory and how these may be put to work in order to resist the search for simple answers and easily applicable solutions for policy and practice, the ethics of doing research with human beings, using the arts and humanities in research and education, as well as topics related to difference, diversity and intercultural sensitivity.

Tris Westwood has been fascinated by psychology for as long as he can remember, and wanted to "do" it. He believes that the word "reality" has an actual corresponding thing, and that between the experience of the word and the thing we have psychology and philosophy. However, he feels that few social science academics or academies take psychology seriously enough to risk disturbing the flow of funding from typically conservative organizations with vested interests in the results. Psychologists' vested interests closely follow those of funders and, as a result, Tris contends that we come to read elaborate psychological interpretations to do with issues consistent with funders' concerns but read no such treatments of far more pressing and real issues such as the almost limitless delusional features of all religions. His main interests are creativity, analytical psychology, and consciousness, and for him these three things are the stuff that existential novels, and other psychologically-minded symbolic fiction/art, bring together in a real way.

Introduction

One of our main reasons for editing, and contributing to, this book is to support the research that is undertaken by practitioners as a result of investigating both their clinical and professional and personal experience. The first chapter, by John, discusses, among other things, the prevailing academic culture which is increasigly influencing the way we think as clinicians. He also looks at the need, in the face of this, to promote practitioner-based approaches to research.

Tris Westwood echoes many of the themes of the first chapter. He steps outside the conventional ways of academic research that pervade most higher education institutions and professional life (and permeate into all aspects of society) and examines it with a broad lens. He views these conventions—and, in particular, the increasing reliance on abstract methodology—as an avoidance of facing up to the realities of lived human experience and the power of our creativity.

Barbara Hunter and John, who worked together as student and research supervisor on an MSc in Therapeutic Counselling course show, in their chapter entitled "A transformational dialogue between the fisherman and the gentle warrior", how the process of

teaching and learning is mutual and not just one way—as well as
tutors teaching students, students also teach tutors. It takes the
form of a dialogue between Barbara (the gentle warrior) and John
(the fisherman), and it describes a point at which Barbara had
become stuck with her Masters dissertation and John, as her
research supervisor, was unable to help her. It shows how they were
both stifled in their creativity for various reasons (connected with
the context and, of course, themselves), and how Barbara and then
John were able to awaken from this malaise. It is a story of awakening as a precursor to emancipation.

The work of Geoff Denham also questions the suitability of
established academic and professional healthcare structures for the
practice of clinical work (Chapter Four). In particular, he looks at
the way in which the medical model, with its emphasis on diagnosis, treatment, and procedures, is entirely unsuitable for the practice
of counselling and psychotherapy, with its emphasis on the talking
cure. The medical model "suggests that something is administered
to the patient following diagnosis" but this "makes little sense in
the psychotherapeutic context" since, as he says, it is not possible
to administer a conversation.

Tris Westwood, Barbara Hunter, and Geoff Denham, in different
ways, challenge the structures within which we have to work. In
order to make this point, both Tris and Barbara use creative writing
as a means of breaking free of the limitations of methodological systems, academic protocols and conventions.

Jeni and Dawn have shared many years of experience both as
practitioners and researchers. Jeni's work also breaks with convention. Her chapter entitled "And so the whirl owl flies: a Jungian
approach to practitioner research". Early on in the chapter she says
that she does not know why she wants to give the chapter this
name but, at the same time, says that, in her heart, she knows that
it is the correct title. She is aware that it symbolizes something
of central importance. She returns to the issue towards the end of
the chapter but, in the meantime, reflects on a range of issues,
including the fact that the use of intuitive perception (such as
knowing that the title is significant but at first not knowing why)
challenges what Hauke has referred to as "the hegemony of a dominant rationality". In order to do this, she surveys a range of fundamental Jungian concepts, such as the collective unconscious and

synchronicity, and such notions as subjectivity, hermeneutics, and phenomenology, which are implicit in the Jungian method, and argues, in effect, that although they stand outside the dominant thinking system, they can form a valid approach to research methodology. In effect, she demonstrates how we can use ways of conceptualizing clinical experience in order to provide an alternative to conventional research methodology and, in so doing, contribute to the broadening of the epistemological and ontological range of research.

Christine Crosbie was, like Barbara Hunter, a student on the MSc in Therapeutic Councelling course that John ran for twelve years. Furthermore, like Jeni Boyd, she uses myth and symbol as a technique in the narrative. Its central theme is an examination of the possibilities of despair and hope in the therapeutic relationship. On the one hand it examines concerns about counselling as a "pit of abusiveness that seemed to me to lurk within the therapeutic relationship"; on the other hand, it looks at the transformational possibilities of therapeutic work and research. She describes a journey through both of these possibilities and, in so doing, moves back and forwards in time and inwards and outwards. It surveys the complexities of therapeutic transformation in a way that is grounded and realistic.

The question of abusiveness and convention leads on to the chapter by Sabi Redwood, entitled "Ethics and reflexivity in practitioner enquiry" (Chapter Seven). She briefly traces the history of current ethical practices with their emphasis on autonomy and informed consent. She points out how generalized positivistic approaches to ethics see the individual as "an abstract entity transcending context and the specificity of experience". In contrast there is an approach to ethics where "concrete circumstances and relationships shape ethical decision-making"—where "receptivity, relatedness, and responsiveness become more important than rights, norms, rules, and ideals and in which we can create a dialogic relationship through adopting a reflexive stance". Indeed, this approach resonates with the ethical principles underpinning this book.

Roddy McKenzie, a dedicated researcher-practitioner, looks, in his autoethnographic study (Chapter Eight) at the spiritual dimension in nursing care and some of the complexities of this issue. He makes the important point that the worldview of nurses and patients usually differs from the worldview of the dominant discourse. And, whereas the worldviews underpinning the latter almost invariably remain opaque and hidden, he argues for transparency. In order to emphasize this point, he includes a moving and powerful personal narrative that brings transparency to bear on the evolution of his own spiritual view. He speaks about how, for many years, he stared across the River Clyde at the Argyll hills from his home town of Port Glasgow. He then goes on to describe how "taking to the mountains was one of the major transitional episodes of my life, if not *the* one". In contrast to the "unemployment, sectarianism, violence, and alcohol" of his home town, he was introduced, through mountain walking and climbing, to "more than a few immeasurable elements in my life: mortality, impermanence, time and timelessness, sacred space and place".

The question of personal narrative and transparency is also central to the subsequent two chapters of this book, both of which were, again, based on MSc dissertations. In Chapter Nine, Jana Helena shows how she was able to use research as a means of bringing about personal transformation. This is an important aspect of practitioner research that has been discussed by, among others, Ellis (2004) and Etherington (2004). Jana addresses her own traumatic experiences, "a space where nothing holds any meaning any more and where despair and confusion take over", which incorporates a fear of falling apart and breaking down. Yet, in so doing, she is also able to move beyond the personal in order to use her own experiences as a means of challenging some commonly held assumptions about psychiatric distress and madness. Ashwini Bhalla (Chapter Ten) also explicitly describes a journey of self-discovery and transformation. It was stimulated by a critical incident on the training course in which she was witnessing a discussion between a friend and a tutor. While the friend was "relaxed, carefree", and was able to tease the tutor, she noticed that her own response was "stiff, frozen". She was struck by her "rigid state" and realized that it had been "persistently present throughout my life, passing off as 'normal and natural' ". The ensuing narrative describes her search for her voice. It describes a painful struggle that moves seamlessly through memory, present incidents, outer events, inner experiences, and the broader cultural implications of the research. It both describes the method of personal inquiry research and demonstrates it.

The question of communication and dialogue with you, the reader, is taken up in particular by Dawn in Chapter Eleven. We are interested, as Dawn says, in "what you have done to the words you have read, how you have interacted with them, interpreted and translated them . . . how you have participated in the process of this book".

In this sense, the book is not finished.

John Lees and Dawn Freshwater
June 2008

CHAPTER ONE

A practitioner researcher's view of academic life, emancipation, and transformation

John Lees

My main interest in contributing to this book is to develop the research undertaken by practitioners as a result of investigating both their clinical and professional and personal experience. In saying this, I am writing as a practitioner who has, in recent years, become an academic and a researcher. Put differently, I think that research based on the skills of the practitioner can supplement conventional research methods as a result of incorporating personal experience into the research process and questioning premises and assumptions, including his/her own. Such researchers might, but do not necessarily, work in an academic institution. In contrast, more conventional approaches to research emphasize the importance of generating knowledge in a specialist area but, in so doing, usually exclude personal experience from the process. They rely on pre-designed methodological systems and may be undertaken by practitioners who have become academics or by pure academics. Indeed, this aspect of academic life has been strengthened in recent years in the healthcare professions as these professions have become academized.

My reason for emphasizing the work of practice-orientated researchers (whom I will now refer to as practitioner researchers) is that their work is under-represented in research communities. This book is thus meant to contribute to supplementing the evidence that is produced by conventional researchers in professional discourse (henceforth academic researchers). Indeed, I believe that the so-called hierarchy of evidence does not sufficiently recognize the evidence that is produced by practitioner researchers. For instance, it privileges the "meta-analysis of randomised controlled trials" over and above the "evidence from expert committee reports or opinions and/or clinical experience of respected authorities" (Geddes & Harrison, 1997). As such, it does not give such a high status to the evidence that practitioners gather as a result of their clinical experience, by placing their work at the bottom of the hierarchy. In spite of this, the evidence that practitioners produce when they examine their ongoing engagement with real clients and patients has always been, for many practitioners, a source of inspiration and support in their work, and we would like to augment the further development of this approach to research.

I have valued practitioner research ever since I began working as a counsellor in the late 1980s. In more recent years, as I have undertaken a research training, I have begun to clarify and consolidate my views about the value of practitioner research and to write about it. I now want to help to disseminate the views of practitioner researchers and thereby contribute to the development of a pluralistic research community in which the evidence generated by both types of academic activity is fully recognized and given equal status. Having said this, my own work incorporates both practitioner and academic research elements. On the one hand, I adopt the outlook of the practitioner, and like to identify myself as such. On the other hand, I incorporate some of the characteristics of the academic researcher.

In the next section I adopt an autoethnographic perspective in order to show how I have worked with, and related to, both practitioner research and academic research throughout my working life in the healthcare professions. In subsequent sections I continue to examine the two perspectives, maintaining the autoethnographic focus throughout. Thus, I adopt an "ethnographic wide angle lens, focusing on social and cultural aspects" (Ellis, 2004, p. 37) of my personal experience while also looking inward to expose a "vulnerable self that is moved by and may move through, refract and resist cultural interpretations" (*ibid*.). A central reason for writing the chapter in this way is that I believe it will help to demonstrate some aspects of the culture of practitioner training and academic life.

The autoethnographic approach

My interest in practitioner research stems from my original clinical training. I was trained to value my direct experience of working in the consulting room and to reflect on these experiences. I came to believe that it was the most useful way of undertaking research. We were encouraged to develop a variety of skills, such as working with the counselling relationship, using our selves as a tool of knowing, reflecting on our practice, and developing reflexivity. Indeed, I wrote a few articles from this point of view (Lees, 1994, 1997, 1998). So, my preferred research method for many years was the case history or case vignette based on such reflections on clinical experience in the light of theory. But then my career took an unexpected and unplanned turn in the mid-1990s, when I began to work in academic settings. In so doing, I gradually became aware of a different way of thinking. I had several experiences that confronted me with this, but will mention just one for the time being: my experience of running a postgraduate counselling training course.

I originally designed the course in the mid-1990s and it ran for the first time in 1996. I adopted the same training principles that I had learnt on my own training (which have been well-described by Noonan [1993]). These included an emphasis on group work. It was difficult at first to hold the new cohort together, as there were some powerful group dynamics and I was not sure whether we would be able to continue from week to week. But I had learnt about group and institutional dynamics on my own training course, and so I adopted these methods. They incorporated Kleinian psychoanalytic views about primitive psychopathology. I find these theories to be of limited value in my clinical work, as they do not take into account my predominantly humanistic and spiritual beliefs. However, I think we all become a bit "mad" in group situations, and so I found such methods helpful for managing the difficult group dynamics on the course. In particular, the group interaction seemed to promote a culture or "lifeworld" that emphasized extremes of emotion. I actually felt as though my state of consciousness was constantly changing. Sometimes I was living in a world that resembled the world of my day-to-day experience, in which my emotional reactions were familiar and manageable; at other times I was living in a world of movement and inner activity in which my emotional life became unstable and ever changing. Overall, we encouraged the students to place themselves at the centre of the learning process and develop the capacity to constantly reflect on their experience. They felt engaged and involved in the process.

I then experienced a major change in 1998, when the first cohort of students reached the final year of the course and began to embark on their research projects. At that time I had not undertaken my research training and had very little experience of academic research. Hence, it was quite understandable that the co-ordination of the research was undertaken by an experienced academic researcher. However, I gradually began to realize that we had entered into a different lifeworld and that it was quite different to the clinical training lifeworld that I had been used to. There were many aspects to this. The students had to focus on a research question rather than their experience within the lifeworld, to suppress their emotions rather than focus on them, to remove themselves from the research process rather than put themselves at the centre of it, and to distance themselves from their experience rather than examine it. The emphasis was on logic and rationality rather than their direct capacity for knowing and emotion. They had to take a neutral rather than an engaged standpoint, and create experimental conditions rather than work with their experience. In retrospect, it seemed amazing that, although I had been working in academic environments since about 1994 (and had been trained in them), I had not been fully conscious of the essentially different nature of this lifeworld. Up to the time that the students began their research projects I had, for the most part, viewed the academic lifeworld through the lens of the clinic. But we now had to move back and forth between a world of movement, inner activity, and reflexivity and one in which movement and our inner responses to phenomena were discouraged.

Since that time I have also realized, much to my surprise, that my own profession of counselling and psychotherapy has been developing, over the past few years, a research culture that adopts the thinking of the academic lifeworld rather than the thinking of the clinic. The reason for my surprise is that I had assumed that counsellors and psychotherapists thought similarly to me, and would want to maintain their clinical perspective even when they entered the academy. Indeed, I thought, at first, that it was supremely ironic that such a quintessentially reflexive profession was transforming itself into a research community in which reflexivity did not have a place and that the profession which is concerned with personal transformation and growth was fostering a research community that was more concerned with the aims of conventional academic research, such as replication and generalization, than with transformation.

Ever since my experience on the training course and my experience of the lifeworlds of practitioner training and research, and academic research, I have tended to think about them as a polarity of different ways of thinking. I have also had to deal with the fact that I have a preference for the practitioner approach to training and research. Indeed, I have spent a great deal of time over the past few years developing my own particular form of practitioner research. However, I am now trying to develop a perspective which sees that polarization is an abstraction from reality, since it does not take into account the complexity and fluidity of human experience. Instead of thinking in terms of polarities, my current ideal would be to promote healthcare research communities in which the practitioners were able to move seamlessly between both lifeworlds and see the inevitability and purpose of both of them. So, my aim is to achieve balance. However, this is not easy to do. Essentially my way of dealing with the situation has been to build on practitioner methods and also learn from the ways of thinking of academic research in order to develop new approaches to practitioner research.

In the next section I look further at my reasons for stressing the importance of balance. I do so by discussing the problems that arise when we do not achieve balance. I take the view that academic research can become too constraining when it is not sufficiently fructified by practitioner research, and that practitioner research can become too chaotic and personalized when it is not sufficiently fructified by academic research. My overall question, thus, is: what will be the consequences for human beings if we do not establish a balance between the two ways of thinking? In order to address the question, and in spite of the fact that imbalance can occur in a number of ways, I approach the matter by concentrating on a more specific question: what will happen if the methods of academic research are not fructified by the methods of practitioner research? My reason for doing this is that these methods currently constitute the dominant discourse in healthcare research and, in view of this, are currently in danger of unbalancing healthcare research communities.

The academic approach: the importance of balance

My reflections on these questions are influenced by my beliefs and my views about the status of methodology in academic research.

With regard to beliefs, I have a long-standing interest in the evolution of consciousness (and philosophy). This derives from an interest in the work of Rudolf Steiner, who, among other things, wrote (and spoke) extensively about how human consciousness changes over time (Steiner, 1909, 1914, 1923). In fact, you could say that this notion underpins all of his work (including its practical applications in such fields as education). According to this view, it is important to remind ourselves that we are experiencing a particular way of thinking today that did not exist in the past and will not exist in the future. So, this perspective pervades the way in which I view contemporary healthcare research.

With regard to methodology, the dominant research discourse at this stage in the development of our consciousness emphasizes pre-designed methodological structures. The researcher decides on a research topic or question on the basis of having conducted a literature review, then designs the methodology, and only engages in the fieldwork once this has been completed. However, this process does not always work for me, since I often undertake research that involves the examination of fieldwork which has already taken place and, in some instances, happened many years ago. My approach to research actually arises out of my interest in the case study method that has developed in the counselling and psychotherapy profession, starting with the case histories of Freud, and the notion of reflection on practice that has always been a central feature of clinical thinking in this profession. So, it emulates the way in which I think and work as a practitioner. Having said this, I do, of course, attempt to develop these methods further in the light of my research training. But, essentially, I try to avoid designing the methodological process in detail at the beginning of my research. I will have some methodological ideas, usually of a subjective, phenomenological, narrative, autoethnographic, Steinerian (or anthroposophical), and/or heuristic nature. But I do not elaborate on them too much at the outset, as I find such a process stifling and detrimental to the way in which I do research. None the less, it is still important to establish rigour, and so, as the research proceeds, I will typically bring methodological thinking, structures, and perspectives to bear on my research.

I see research that emphasizes a flexible approach to methodology as providing a counterbalance to the dominance of academic research methods in healthcare research. I also see it as providing an opportunity for academic researchers to question the basic tenets of their approach to research, including its epistemological and ontological premises, and as an opportunity to establish more equitable research communities. At the moment, research methods, which resemble practioner methods, such as autoethnography, narrative, and heuristics, are frequently questioned and challenged in a way that can create anxiety and uncertainty among its proponents. As the autoethnographer, Sparkes (2002), has said, "such narratives are treated with deep suspicion and hostility within the academy" (ibid., p. 214). Having said this, he also argues that we attempt to "listen carefully and to attempt to grasp what is being expressed and said in research traditions different from our own" (ibid., p. 223). (In my case, this involves a struggle to prevent myself from polarizing and criticizing other approaches.) In order to illustrate these points, he describes, in the course of his article, an exam board meeting in which, in view of his previous experience about the way others viewed his preferred autoethnographic methods, he experienced a great deal of tension: "In the days leading up to this meeting, I feel the defensive posture I'm so used to taking seep into my bones ... I'm tired, my lower back aches more than normal" (ibid., p. 225). Yet, he then goes on to discuss how the external examiner, against all his expectations, poured praise on a student dissertation that used autoethnographic methods. The examiner, who was an academic researcher, concluded his report by saying,

> this dissertation had a big impact on me in a lot of ways. Even though I'm not sure how to judge it, I'm happy to judge it as a first-class piece of work, and support the grade that it has been awarded. [*ibid.*, p. 228]

It was a wonderful example of being able to "grasp what is being expressed and said in research traditions different from our own".

I shall now return to the issues that I introduced earlier: the dangers of imbalance within academic and professional life, particularly due to the dominance of methodological structures, and my tendency to create unhelpful polarities between practitioner research and academic research. In so doing, I shall redress the imbalance in my own perspective, since, in spite of my concerns about an excessive reliance on methodology, I accept the need for introducing methodological thinking in my own work for the purposes of increasing rigour.

All methods are inadequate and it is more useful, in my view, to see the inadequacy in one's own method than to concentrate on that of others. My own approach involves returning at an early stage of the research to my previous experience in order to discover new aspects of it and/or to engage in the research writing from the outset in order to see where it leads me. I see this as helping to develop an approach to research that can provide a counterbalance to academic research. I invariably find then that I am surprised by what I discover in my experience. I begin to awaken to its liminal, contextual, and previously unknown aspects and I am inspired to achieve new levels of creativity and understanding.

Many of the authors in this book demonstrate the liminal and contextual in a variety of ways. They also prioritize their experience over and above methodological structures. Rather than engaging in an approach to research in which everything revolves around the methodological design, they develop ways of doing research that revolve around their lived experience.

To return to the question of the evolution of consciousness I would argue that such an "experiential turn" has much to offer to our healthcare research communities, since the dominant academic researcher approach, if it remains unfructified by another approach, will have, in my view, certain deleterious evolutionary consequences. Indeed, I cannot shrug off the sense that such processes constitute a way of thinking that, in view of its formulaic aspects, carries the danger of developing an automaton consciousness—a way of being that Erich Fromm foresaw many years ago:

> In the nineteenth century the problem was that *God is dead*; in the twentieth century the problem is that *man is dead*. In the nineteenth century inhumanity meant cruelty; in the twentieth century it means schizoid self-alienation. The danger of the past was that men became slaves. The danger of the future is that men may become robots. [Fromm, 1956, p. 360]

I am concerned that, in evolutionary terms, such tendencies will increasingly permeate culture and society over a period of time as a result of limited ways of thinking in the academy. The way of thinking that has been developed in the academy over the past four hundred years—and represented today by what I have referred to as academic research—has now influenced all aspects of human consciousness. It is based on the scientific experimental method which, four hundred years ago, began to replace other states of consciousness. In medieval times, people thought that they were connected with the world and with each other. They saw the stars and the planets as being intimately connected with their lives. And then came the Age of the Enlightenment. Those intellectuals and philosophers who were the originators of current forms of academic thinking—such as Descartes at the beginning of the seventeenth century—rightly took exception to the excesses and narrowness of the medieval mind, which promoted superstition and which gave a great deal of power to the church. Yet, in wanting to wake people up from the religiously dominated "dark ages", they went to the other extreme. They concluded that the direct experience of human beings is too unreliable to have any value. As a consequence of the development of this way of thinking, it has become increasingly difficult today for us to trust our experience.

We are all affected by the legacy of Descartes. However, the evolution of consciousness moves ahead and, just as medieval consciousness was affected by the scientific method, so our future consciousness will be affected by an excessive reliance on the methods of academic research (using linear and experimentally-orientated qualitative and quantitative research methods). This is why I think it is important to counterbalance these methods with practitioner researcher methods. If we fail to do this we will, in my view, accelerate the decline of our ability to trust our experience and a result of this will be a profound effect on our thinking and way of being in years to come. I am concerned that, due to our reliance on protocols, procedures, criteria, and mechanical ways of thinking, our lived experience will increasingly become an irrelevance and we will eventually become reliant on "evidence-based experience"; that is to say, we will be told what we should be doing and experiencing. As a consequence, we will lose touch with our natural faculties and capacity for tacit knowing, with the result that our actions will become programmed, thus promoting a form of robotic behaviour. So I agree with the views of Erich Fromm and others who have written about similar things, such as George Orwell, Aldous Huxley, Friedrich Nietzsche, Rudolf Steiner, and many more.

Personal experience of the two approaches

There is another aspect to Erich Fromm's quote. In view of the pervasiveness of the way of thinking of academic research based on the scientific method, I have realized over the years that the points that Fromm makes also apply to me. So, in quoting Fromm, I am also describing certain aspects of my own experience. In view of the fact that I have been brought up, and currently live and work, in a culture that is influenced by such ways of thinking, I am inevitably influenced by these tendencies. I have been permeated by such ways of thinking throughout my life by a process of osmosis, since they have formed the basis of my education from the nursery to my postgraduate research training. So, I have built up strong habits, and am now subject to self-alienation and habitual programming tendencies. Like other people, I am in danger of becoming a robot and am subject to abstracting tendencies in my work. Although I try to put myself at the centre of my research, I often find this very difficult to do. So, whereas I originally saw the clash of paradigms as an outer issue (for instance, when I encountered the two paradigms on the course that I am running), I now also see it as an inner issue. In this sense, I incorporate elements of both the standpoint of the academic researcher and the practitioner researcher.

I just want to pause for a moment and think about the previous paragraph and the process of thinking about my own text, and say, in the first instance, that in thinking about my work in this way I am adopting a technique that arises out of my training and experience as a counselling practitioner. One particular skill that many counsellors develop is to be able to work with their internal supervisor; that is to say, to reflect on what they are doing as they are doing it. Put differently, they develop the capacity to supervise themselves. The notion of the internal supervisor was first used by Casement (1985). He referred to it as a process by which practitioners "learn to watch themselves as well as the patient, now using this island of intellectual contemplation as the mental space within which the internal supervisor can begin to operate" (*ibid.*, p. 32). So I am now transferring this skill to my writing, using my experience of writing this chapter as an opportunity to develop my internal supervisor and "watch" myself as I am writing by creating a "mental space" that enables me to reflect on the way in which I am constructing my text as I am constructing it.

In thinking about my own narrative, I am already beginning to reflect on my reflections; that is to say, to turn my "thought or reflection back on itself" (Freshwater & Rolfe, 2001, p. 529). But I am not just doing this as a reflective exercise. Such reflections enable me to go "beyond the usual introspective focus of reflection to consider the wider social and political context" (*ibid.*, p. 530). In particular, it enables me to become more conscious of the extent to which I am influenced by dominant discourses; the way in which the social systems and ways of thinking that permeate my environment create a sense of alienation and a tendency to become robotic and indulge in abstraction, and to manifest these tendencies in my text, even though I am trying to break free of them. However, this then poses the question: what do I then do as I develop this awareness? Drawing on critical theory, Mezirow (1981) refers to this as a process of developing "perspective transformation":

the emancipatory process *of becoming critically aware of how and why the structure of psycho-cultural assumptions has come to constrain the way we see ourselves and our relationship, reconstituting this structure to permit a more inclusive and discriminating integration of experience and acting upon these new understandings. [ibid., p. 6]*

Indeed, this is how I see reflexivity. It does not involve only a process of reflecting on reflections and then raising our consciousness of our "psycho-cultural assumptions", but also "acting upon these new understandings" in order to bring about what Freshwater and Rolfe (2001, p. 530) refer to as "politically-informed action or 'praxis'". For example, in response to developing my critical awareness of the imbalance in healthcare research communities, I changed the course that I ran for many years, as described earlier, by promoting an approach to research that does not create a split between the clinical training lifeworld and the academic lifeworld. I have also, as a result of this, contributed to constructing this book.

In saying all of this, I also want to make the point that it is not easy to stand outside my own point of view and to change my habits, and so I often need the help of others to help me to do this. A recent example of this was in the construction of this book. I wrote to Dawn suggesting a running order for the chapters. I then rationalized the order on the basis that they could be divided into the three following areas:

- challenges to the academic box;
- ways of breaking free;
- emancipation and transformational processes.

In saying this, I was dimly aware that by making such a distinction I was failing to do justice to the complexity of each chapter, and so also, as a result of this, managed to say that, in spite of the division, the chapters covered all of the areas to some degree. However, I still went ahead and divided the chapters into three themes in an attempt to give structure and order to the book. But I then reflected on the matter in the light of a brief conversation with Dawn, and it became clear that, in trying to put order on the book and seeing the narrative in terms of certain themes, I was at the same time creating an abstraction and reduction from the reality and that I could equally well have chosen other categories. I was trying to fit the chapters into "boxes", even though I was trying to escape from boxes.

In reflecting on the way in which we constructed the book, I am highlighting another aspect of practitioner research that runs through it: the principle of researcher transparency. There are many aspects to this. For instance, it should be clear by now that I, and other authors in the book, have made our preconceptions, beliefs, and experience transparent rather than attempting to bracket them as is often the case in research.

Earlier in this chapter I spoke about the two lifeworlds which I encountered in my work as a counselling trainer - the world of clinical training which I had cultivated ever since my own experience of training and the world of academic research which came into clearer focus as the students progressed. I then referred to how this experience prompted me to find ways of working towards a balanced approach to research and overcoming the gap between practice and research. Indeed, this has been a central professional concern ever since, and this book constitutes, for me, one of the fruits of this work.

The chapter has discussed, among other things, how I have been helped by others in this process, including the students that I have taught and some of the people who have contributed to this book. I have also introduced an approach to research that is concerned with communication rather than providing attempts to represent reality. In autoethnographic terms it has not only meant to "portray the facts of what happened" but also "to convey the meanings" (Ellis, 2004, p. 116) that I have attached to my experience. Indeed, this principle applies to the book as a whole. It attempts to "evoke readers' responses . . . open up the possibility of dialogue, collaboration, and relationship" as well as promoting "social justice and equality" and thinking "through consequences, values, and moral dilemmas" (*ibid.*, p. 195).

Restraints and limitations

By way of conclusion I shall mention one consistent theme, which also pervades the other chapters. In one way or another, the chapters explore the process of emancipation from restraints and the limitations of various aspects of our society and culture, including our upbringing, our professional socialization, and our educational and academic systems. In this sense, all of these articles are "searching for a voice"—trying to face an internal, rather than an external, locus of evaluation.

When I contributed to our original proposal for this book, I had just been thinking about the work of one of the earlier critical theorists, Antonio Gramsci, since I thought he echoed my concerns. So I introduced his ideas in the book proposal: in particular, the distinction between the conventional intelligentsia who reproduce the "ideas and systems of beliefs which enable the masses to be dominated by a small minority" and the "practitioner" intelligentsia (Holmes, 2002, p. 74). I was aware that academics prioritized conventional academic research. But I also took the view that this carried the danger of failing to recognize the value of practitioners' experience and research. Thus, I saw the book as an opportunity to acknowledge the importance of practitioner research with a view to disseminating the views of those intellectuals who are involved in everyday practice and experience: practitioners themselves.

Roddy McKenzie specifically takes up this theme and makes the important point that there is a type of intellectual—whom Gramsci refers to as organic intellectuals and I have referred to as the practitioner researchers—who, as a result of their professional work, are experts in the "messy complexity of social life". Indeed, the book is anti-hegemonic in the sense that it challenges the power of the conventional intelligentsia and emphasizes the importance of the contribution of the "organic intellectual" who is not recognized by the conventional intelligentsia, but who

> [carries] on some form of intellectual activity: that is, he is a "philosopher", an "artist", a "man of taste", he participates in a particular conception of the world, has a conscious line of moral conduct, and therefore contributes to sustain a conception of the world or to modify it, that is, to bring new modes of thought. [Gramsci, 1971, p. 9]

I believe that such intellectuals can contribute to providing a countervailing force to the dominant mode of thinking in professional and academic life by writing directly out of their experience and inspiring other practitioners to value the research that they are doing from day to day and to continue to research into their valuable and mostly unheard and unrecognized experiences. In so doing, they form the basis, in my view, for meaningful social change based on the liberation and transformation of the practitioner or the practitioner researcher. Such intellectuals can "bring new modes of thought" and they have the ability to overcome the research–practice gap. In disseminating their work, this book addresses the vital need to acknowledge that the research undertaken by practitioners constitutes a form of evidence that should play a more central role in healthcare research discourse. In order to achieve this, we thus want the book to have a broad appeal which can speak to all those who engage in research, including both academics and practitioners.

As I have indicated, the work of practitioner researchers has a lot to say to people involved with all aspects of professional life. It can help academic researchers to broaden the ontological and epistemological perspective of their work. It can support the work of other practitioner researchers. It can also encourage healthcare practitioners who may not have an academic training to develop their research skills and to realize that they are actually researching into their practice on a day-to-day basis. Finally, it can provide a certain degree of transparency to help clients and patients to see aspects of professional practice and professional development that are usually hidden from them. Indeed, one problem with much academic and research discourse is that it is difficult for many practitioners to understand it. I would, therefore, like to promote a way of writing that is clear and accessible to as many people as possible; to make the point that *academic writing does not have to be obscure and inaccessible*.

By emphasizing the value of the work of the organic intellectual or practitioner researcher, we want to develop a form of discourse that concentrates on fitting the principles of the academy into the clinic, rather than the principles of the clinic into the academy. In contradistinction to many academic researchers in healthcare, who tend to link healthcare research with positivistic psychology research, or medical research, or mathematics, I am linking with those approaches to research that are based on human experience and that have been developed in sociology, anthropology, literary studies, and the arts. My reason for doing this is that I think these disciplines have developed research methodologies that closely resemble the methods developed by practitioners. They also produce research that is both readable and moving and informative about the work of practitioners and academics. I am thinking here of recent developments in narrative, heuristic, and autoethno-graphic research and, in particular, the work of such pioneers as Etherington (2004), Ellis (2004), Frank (1995), Freshwater and Lees (2009), as well as Laurel Richardson, Andrew Sparkes, and many more. It is providing us with a much-needed and coherent alternative to the dominant paradigm of academic research. This is particularly important because it offers the readers the possibility of reflecting on the pervasiveness of the dominant paradigm (that is to say, the way in which our healthcare professions are underpinned by it) and to see how it affects all aspects of our lives. Without an alternative voice there is no possibility of doing this, and this creates a tendency towards onesidedness. So, by providing an alternative, we have the opportunity, over time, to counterbalance the onesided tendencies of the dominant discourse and transform its exclusiveness and tendency to deny points of view that are different to its own. We can help it to reflect on, and question, its premises. In so doing, we then have the opportunity of developing a pluralistic healthcare research community that is both unified and diverse (which, on the one hand, is "cohesive" and, on the other, can contain a "multiplicity of valid approaches" [Samuels, 1989, p. 4]). In order to achieve this, it is essential that an alternative to academic research comes into clear view. We hope to contribute to the development of this alternative.

References

Casement P. (1985). *On Learning from the Patient*. London: Tavistock.

Ellis, C. (2004). *The Ethnographic I: A Methodological Novel about Auto-ethnography*. Walnut Creek, CA: Altamira.

Etherington, K. (2004). *Becoming a Reflexive Researcher: Using our Selves in Research*. London: Jessica Kingsley.

Frank, A. (1995). *The Wounded Storyteller*. Chicago, IL: University of Chicago Press.

Freshwater, D., & Lees, J. (2009). *Practitioner Research in Healthcare: Transformational Research in Action*. In preparation.

Freshwater, D., & Rolfe, G. (2001). Critical reflexivity: a politically and ethically engaged research method for nursing. *NT Research*, 6(1): 526–537.

Fromm, E. (1956). *The Sane Society*. London: Routledge & Kegan Paul, 1963.

Geddes, L., & Harrison, P. (1997). Closing the gap between research and practice. *British Journal of Psychiatry, 171*: 220–225.

Gramsci, A. (1971). *Selections From the Prison Notebooks*. Q. Hoare and G. Nowell Smith (Eds.). New York: International Publishers.

Holmes, C. A. (2002). Academics and practitioners: nurses as intellectuals. *Nursing Inquiry, 9*(2): 73–83.

Lees, J. (1994). On becoming a psychodynamic counsellor: learning about countertransference. *Counselling, 5*(4): 299–301.

Lees, J. (1997). An approach to counselling in GP surgeries. *Psychodynamic Counselling, 3*(1): 33–48.

Lees, J. (1998). From consulting room to institution to society. *Psychodynamic Counselling, 4*(2): 221–236.

Mezirow, J. (1981). A critical theory of adult learning and education. *Adult Education, 32*: 3–24.

Noonan, E. (1993). Tradition in training. In: L.Spurling (Ed.), *The Words of my Mouth* (pp. 00–00). London: Routledge

Samuels, A. (1989). *The Plural Psyche*. London: Routledge.

Sparkes, A.C. (2002). Autoethnography: self-indulgence or something more? In: A. Bochner & C. Ellis (Eds.), *Ethnographically Speaking* (pp. 209–232). Walnut Creek, CA: Altamira.

Steiner, R. (1909). *Occult Science*. London: Rudolf Steiner Press, 1963.

Steiner, R. (1914). *The Riddles of Philosophy*. Spring Valley: Anthroposophic Press, 1973.

Steiner, R. (1923). *The Evolution of Consciousness*. London: Rudolf Steiner Press, 1966.

CHAPTER TWO

Real bodies of knowledge

Tris Westwood

H aven't you all got homes to go to like this recently renovated flat in immaculate decorative order and ladies and gentlemen, boys and girls, by the left let us pray because in the beginning there was nothing so taking two eggs carefully separate the yolks and capitalize on this unprecedented offer with smiles of satisfaction on their faces they left the words contempt of court in that decaying building designed and built by Lord so-and-so in the mid eighteenth century with deepest regret this application did not satisfy the regulations and therefore could not be considered . . .

My points are that language has styles—shapes—and that it, and they, *do* things. The shape and rhythm of the language reveals the form and flow of the consciousness responsible for its inception and use: language is a product of consciousness so, when so very much is possible, the boundaries and prohibitions, answers and tones, customs and meanings of any language paints a picture of the thinking that made it.

Each Language Method (languages themselves are methods and share many of the qualities we find in various research methods in soc-sci) has a concomitant consciousness; it is connected like the skin of a fruit cleaving to the flesh beneath, integral to it, the outer presentation of it—look at that plumply glistening nectarine (we see the skin—the skin is plumply glistening but we call it the nectarine because we know the two go together as one) and you know it's going to taste good, but that other dull one, not. Computers foam-stuffed in boxes on trucks or unwrapped and plonked under your desk, ugly mechanical lines in plastic and metal also talk about skins presenting and being part of the body beneath, but here carries a different value.

When a skin and the body can move and express and show us experience then its connection is even more intimate; we can read it and feel it. In dealing with human experience, our stories move faster and are more immediate than waiting for the ripening of a fruit. Both, though, are to do with surfaces and contents, and contents within contexts, and this also comes back to how I am writing these words here and how they look and what they hold.

And, like anything living, responsive, sensate—the nearly black cat sheltering under the clematis watching keenly but softly as the rain peters out and then half picks and half skips in that curious cat-on-a-dubious-surface way back to the kitchen's (those little damp footprints along the hall) warmth and dryness and the plate about to trill with the hypnotic dance of the spoon and smell that food— it interacts and so affects back in its turn the shape of consciousness and experiential possibilities within consciousness.

Consciousness starts whole and has vast possibility. As we learn language it seems these possibilities diminish, and then, as we grow further from the ground and become more invested in any particular language method(s), the more reduced our possibilities yet become. Very dogmatic language methods have the effect of reducing possibility to probability or, worse still, the seductive but very unnatural (in the vast majority of cases) straight line of certainty. In these systems life and being have become artificially polarized, and this serves many ideological functions necessary for the smooth and profitable continuance of those dogmas.

What happens to us and our real experience and process when we do our research or try to think or talk or write? Where do we go? Does our journey allow us to reach the page, or are there too many hurdles, gates, the names and dates and jargon and the delusion of being clear or precise or objective or selective or proper or clever or right, or do we just need to hide . . . yes, I think "hide" for the most part. How, though, and from what?

This is how and what I want to write for my chapter. There are many other ways I could write it but none of those would present for you my real attempt to do what I feel is genuine regarding how I have found research and researchers to be. Now, if I decided to go with the usual academic style and drop some well-known names in and some long technical words, how would I be doing what I set out to and what would that look like?

Maybe I should give it a go and start right here and then tell you the many experiences I have in doing something false; something that would stand mostly as a sign to the academic community that "I'm OK aren't I? I know what I should say and how I should say it." How would this feel and what would I experience being left out, ignored, denied, covered-up, glossed-over, fabricated, insinuated, manipulated, pressed into the sordid shapes of my sentences.

I am not going to do that quite yet, but will play with it a little later. The language methods of religion and research are similar— Let us pray and Let B equal the square of A amen—and so is the peculiarly reductive consciousness that comes along for the ride. I find it very interesting that the things supposing to offer *Answers* and *Truth* are actually so reductive. I had thought that these methods that offer "forever" would be radically expansive, but actually they are paltry, predictable, misogynistic orders written in dust.

Many of the seemingly open, dialogic, and embodied research methods used in soc-sci are simply well camouflaged, watered-down versions of the above.

Any tool we make can expand or contract our potentials and boundaries, or indeed our physical shape: a scalpel, a chisel, a mallet, a new nose. In a way similarly as concrete but hard to see or experience as such, our consciousness changes, and this is how real learning through using language, through reading, writing, and speaking can happen.

Naturally, you do not need me to tell you this; you already know it, but might not be aware of the great significance this rather obvious fact has on our lives and, in this particular case, on research and what we loosely call "education".

The changing shape of my consciousness stirs new syllables around my mouth and now I am hearing different sounds and sighs and promises and excuses crafted in the instant (see below why "in the instant" is part of our story) and pushed out into the air and the ears of another for whom those sounds might become something of their most recent journey in the course of their experience of consciousness. "Do you fancy a cup of tea?" probably won't do it, "Did you see the film last night?" is unlikely to do it, but "Why are you afraid to tell the truth?" might, sooner or later, do something but because none of this is linear (because it is real) and because it is symbolic (because it is real) there are no firm answers. I have found that firm answers are usually symptomatic of falsehood.

Firm answers generally are the domain of the crippled mind and the violent body: in short, of males. In the academies there are a lot of females, and many of them unfortunately have that reduced type of male consciousness due to plying their trade in the academies where these particular language methods and dogma are currency. So, what I'm talking about is not actually males and females, but rather masculine and feminine ways of experiencing and communicating.

In psychology, in particular, it is far more likely to find people to ask searching personal questions than have the stomach to answer them. Part of the psychologist's training is learning to hide among the constructs and theories and the turning around of difficult questions so they don't have to DO psychology themselves.

Consciousness is an experience, and because it is, language has a body. What any language method does to this body has real consequences.

This language here is doing something, I do not know what yet, but it is doing something. More than that, language is something. It isn't intangible, as some people like to think, not that concepts cannot be concrete—language has some excellent qualities which I am trying to write into the two or three stories in my chapter.

One of these qualities we have already touched on, languages' interactive relationship with consciousness; another is the non-logical way language happens that tells us, with each word springing up by itself, something important about how consciousness itself works. Then there are the words that we know we should say, that we need to say but don't, the ones that get stuck in our throats, unable to get past the feelings we are experiencing. We have some idea what these words would sound like because they are a direct expression of something immediate. Language is the sound of consciousness and not all such sounds are equal.

Another of the many qualities of language is that it can be very rigid and narrow in its form and content and then its interaction with consciousness is that of repressing it (the tool controlling and then changing the craftsperson, a bit like how we have created computers to be labour-saving devices but now seem to have less time and space because of them). This aspect relates to the usual disembodying procedure of method.

It is easy to use the word "disembody" and not see the actual processes and consequences this word indicates when we *do* it in reality. This stops us becoming aware of the very poor quality of the consciousness that requires such a dislocation and denial of the body.

When I was a child, my life was like a dream because, like most children, I had not yet been taught to lose myself in religion and education. My experience of the days and the nights was largely indistinguishable because I was whole and thinking and experiencing in that "magical" way children do. Those marks appear because that magic is simply being whole and is a natural state; one that we are in from our beginning.

The sadness is, of course, that when we are taught to "grow up" we throw the magic away, and while as a researcher it's good not to believe in Santa, or gods come to that, we also throw away a type of experiencing that we end up sorely missing and mourning, perhaps without even knowing it.

That we can be unaware of things that work through/on/in us and affect our perception and behaviour is something that points to psychology meaning something. Everyone must be aware of something that they only became aware of after much time going round and round in unpleasant circles.

Becoming aware of such things is often easier than changing those old orbits and not replacing them with another piece of revolving damage. Anyway, we must all have the feeling of becoming aware of something that we were not aware of before and that was having a big effect on us and on the people who we were relating to at home, at work, at school, alone.

This shows us that the implicit is powerful and we do not have to be immediately aware of something for it to be having an effect on us. This poses the question that if something we are not aware of can do this in a consistent and persistent way, then mustn't it have its own awareness; i.e., it has meaning to itself and is working autonomously?

Many people feel uncomfortable about this point: this "unconscious" behaviour had awareness of itself because it kept exerting its influence on me; it was something in me, part of me, but happened to me without the "me" part understanding. Consciousness works on many levels and we are aware of some, semi-aware of others, then vaguely aware of some, and unaware of others, can learn some things and forget others, but they are all working consciousness.

Method usually treats human consciousness as explicit through an over-estimation of the face value of our behaviour and also avoiding the sorts of conversations that will reveal the activity of the implicit. By doing this, very explicit, or exteriorizing, methods can allow researchers to find their results both reliable and valid without these significances having any bearing on the reality of the situation.

How does this work, then? How can we have this relationship with our own consciousness, the thing that is our "On" switch? It's odd, isn't it, and interesting too—at least I think so. This is where language methods come in. When we have an ambiguous, symbolic, and incomplete relationship with our own consciousness, we typically compensate by looking for answers exteriorly, and this anxiety for answers is forged into the language method as above.

Sometimes I think of psychology as being the study of things that we identify in the outside world that actually point to, or are symbolic of, our inner experience or activity, usually laced with fear. So pervasive is this exteriorizing of our consciousness and infatuation with surfaces that we have even invented gods and might think that a new car or house or chair will make us happy.

This is what happens when we do not understand where our thoughts come from. We do not usually understand where our words come from either. They seem to just keep dropping out, and although we may have a suspicion of what is coming next, we do not really plan it. When people do plan their speech—as in . . . errrm . . . speeches and presentations—they usually come across as extremely wooden, and anyone who has been to academic conferences will be painfully aware of this type of robotic communication.

If language does not happen in the moment of its creation then it is robotic, pre-programmed, and this means something regarding following the prescribed language methods of research and education. If your own words written just the other day turn you into a robot, then what is that dusty old method doing to you?

Talking of robots, if language and consciousness did not work in the way I am suggesting (I suggest it because I'm aware of this process every day and every night), then the billions that have been poured into and spent by the best brains in the business to make computers talk all by themselves would have come up with something by now. If language was "logical", then the computers, which I am told work logically, would not only be able to use language by themselves in a meaningful way but would be gabbling along and our problem would be to shut the darn things up, not to get them talking in the first place.

Computers are not alive, of course; they do not have bodies and so they cannot have real language. Language has some logic of its own, but for the most part acts non-logically; which, of course, is different from saying "illogically". Something else I have noticed with academics is that when you say, for instance, you want to remove the constraints of Method, they often assume this means that chaos will ensue; likewise, if you say something doesn't work "logically", they opine that it must therefore be "illogical" (rather than non-logical or having its own form of logic/meaning which cannot be freeze-dried and pinned out on paper for passive consumption).

Thus proclaimeth the learned man. Thus it is written. Thus it will be done.

There is also that awful thing called Logic that, like religious dogma, constitutes the most oppressive and unreal forms of consciousness and language.

Does any of this matter? I guess it does because the interactive experience of consciousness and language is something that can result in communicating the sound of reality. Some writers have really tried to form these sounds and senses, such as Virginia Woolf and George Orwell. They have tried to make the language a presentation of the way consciousness is. This is a great feat, and one that we can learn more from in respect of psychology and philosophy than from a skip-load of disembodied academic texts on the subjects.

Subjects like psychology and philosophy, which are about human experience and understanding, should, of course, be written from the most . . . errrm . . . human perspective, and the taut, fusty, reductive, brittle, "logical" way most academic texts are written says to me that they have very little to offer except as indicators of how far gone into a disembodied inhumanity the authors are; how shut off from reality their method of consciousness has made them.

Fear. Fear and dread of "not knowing"—this is the fuel which we add to our oddly ambiguous and symbolic relationship to our own consciousness. When these two experiences occur, then all sorts of methods, recipes, laws, oaths, prayers, gods, come along to try to stem our deep insecurity. And once we have established the lie and it is making money and gives us power, then how do we get beyond it?

The parable of the miracle of the stone

And they heard from the people that one had found a stone, at the foot of the great mountain, which could become changed and they said that they would leave their high tower of knowledge that toucheth the clouds and travel to that place and these two wise men and one wise(ish) woman shall test this stone and name it in its true way according to The Lord and His true teachings.

Praise the Lord for he is Truth and in the Lord ye shall find Truth.

They travelled two days and two nights to the place of the stone where they found lowly people in hovels and this affronted their goodly ways and finery and around one such place a motley crowd gathered and a ragged woman collecting petty alms from those others so that they should touch the stone and be cured of their poverty, plight and misery.

Praise be to God for only in Him is true salvation found.

The wise ones drew their goodly robes close about them and descended into the hovel and sent away the beggars and the sick and the needy so that they could test the stone. They chided the lowly woman for collecting the petty alms and took the stone as theirs and left the woman cast to the ground in woe and unseemly affect for her sins and her filthiness.

Sickened by the woman's manner and her hovel the wise ones said unto themselves that they should return with the stone to their high tower that touches the beard of God (praise be to God). This they did and decided that not until they be back should any of them look upon the stone so it was placed in a silken purse and the purse placed in the wisest one's silken pocket for the whole journey.

Having not left their tower for many years the journey was hard for the wise ones and they grew tired; the woman more so for she was a woman and was weak. The Lord hath made her so and her kind. So say the Lord.

In this needful time a potent wind blew that pushed them onwards on their donkeys that they gathered great speed and left behind the servants and novices bearing their food and bedding and tents and books and chairs and robes and jewels. The wise one praised The Lord for the wind and cursed the servants for their sloth.

Praise be to God for He rewards the just.

And when they did come unto the high tower a strange lightness appeared in their hearts as they were carried up the many stairs to the very summit that verily did touch the sky. And very verily the top of the high tower touched the sky and the Lord said that this pleased Him for the wise ones were close to Him and were good. Praise the Lord for He is Truth.

The wise ones gathered round the great table and then the oldest and wisest of the three took the silken purse from his silken pocket and from it removed the stone for them all to gaze upon. The stone was . . . the stone was . . . the stone-like object was small and dark and smooth like a stone. They gazed upon it with great concentration.

"What are you?" demanded the wisest of the stone. Nothing. "By God in Heaven, what are you?" he demanded. Nothing. "Then I shall break you asunder and force you to yield to the glory of God in Heaven our Father and Creator of all things!"

With this he took up a hammer from beneath the great table and cast a blow with it directly upon the stone. Sparks flew but the stone remained and the wise man had hurt his wrist. "This object is hard and spiteful," spake the wise man who had just now dropped the faulty hammer in pain.

"This hammer and this stone are in league with the Devil!" exclaimed this wisest of men and with that took up his pen and began to write in the great book of laws just like his blessed forebears before him.

"We must test the stone," said another. "Yes," rejoined the third and with that they began to talk as to the best way to test the object and write its law. Soon they began to argue and feel vexed and the wisest said that this is the malevolence of the stone clouding their goodliness.

"It is small and round and flat and cool and dark and hard, this stone. It weighs two ounces and measures one and a half inches long and wide and three quarters of an inch deep. It is dark grey, a grey before charcoal and after slate. It is cool to the touch and makes a sound thus when tapped and thus when struck and thus when spoken to. Praise be to God for he is the measurer of all things!"

"No! It is a world! It is no small thing this stone. It is vast and light and hot and it breathes and sees and touches whatever touches it. This is a magical stone and we must find the quality of this magic! Be it for the good or for the bad! Praise be to God for He moves in mysterious ways!"

"No! No! This is what was spoken of about this object. It changes. It finds in the eye of the beholder something new each time. I behold it and I see a tablet inside and on this tablet is written something in the language of the angels and by finding the tongue of this goodly script we shall become as God. Praise be to God for He has given us this Approbation."

The three then sat in silence, each believing they each to be right and each unwilling to speak for the vexation of not being able to make the stone give up its secret so that all shall know theirs is the correct answer. They sat in gloom and bitterness.

"Remember the blessed parable of the Enunciation of the Blessed Jargon? Remember how those wise men were saved from the quickening sands by chattering the blessed jargon (hot air doth rise) and how they learnt that everything is nothing in the world of men and how the wise should pay their taxes no more for having found this truth?

"We must seek the answer in the blessed tomes!"

Then from behind them came a voice. It was the beggar woman that first had the stone. They had not seen her follow them back to the high tower these two days past, so fixed was their gaze ahead.

"You say you are wise and yet you find no answer in the stone," she protested.

"Be gone beggar woman, this concerns ye not and your presence here next to God the Mighty Father is a damnable crime!"

The beggar woman began to speak but the wise ones had summoned their servants and before the wretched creature could make any sense she was taken off to be flogged for her crimes. As she was dragged down flight after flight of stairs towards the dungeon she wept and thought on how she knew the stone and in knowing it didn't know it and in this found something from herself in the stone's lustrous surface reflected in the light of the land and her eye which belonged to the land and the mud and the rain and the sky.

I can see the sense in some methods and in some parts of most methods, but don't really know of any that are commonly used in social science research that are, well, real. I am pleased that there are methods for drilling and pulling out teeth, for making samosas and roasts, for building hospitals, for making ceramics, music, and painting, and making films.

All those methods, and ones like driving a car and forming orderly queues at bus stops are great. That does not mean, though, that they can be written into how we do research. Things may be different in the Sciences, but when we come to developing and using methods to describe and explain human experience, then we are in a very different situation.

When we are dealing with human experience, then we need a likewise experiential method, and this is nowhere to be found. Instead, we social scientists have a litany of methods that are reductive and "logical," therefore not just missing how the human landscape actually is, but damaging it.

Those "academic sentences", look at their shape; are the words still there like crouched and bowing figures fearfully honouring some falsely emboldened god or another?

When I talk about method it is fairly clear to most that there are things called methods in research and that someone developed each one and each is supposed to be good for collecting, describing, analysing, and explaining information that we get from people. Where the concept of method starts to become pretty hard to "see" in action is when we talk about our writing style as method.

This seems to frustrate people, maybe because the apparently "neutral" way they write is very much like their apparent understanding of how consciousness and language work. I do not understand the sort of person who responds to this sort of question defensively, because to me in this question is the fascinating possibility of finding out about the least known entity in the world: consciousness.

But many huff and puff and roll their eyes skyward and tighten up and yawn and go and make a cup of tea or cry or lash out or laugh because they just want their writing to be just writing. It's neutral and objective and in that style because that is the best way to impart information without "contaminating" it. You must understand we really have more important things to do than to waste time talking and thinking about such things.

Psychologists, in particular, are never so keen to "not waste time" as when you are asking them to do some real psychology. Strange, I know, but this is the way I've found them. It does matter and it does mean something and it does carry value statements, and it is something and it does affect how we do things and it does send out messages to those reading our work to Obey and it is . . . errrrrm . . . largely inconsistent, and often contradictory, to what we like to say we are doing when we do research.

I am not expecting researchers to write like Golding or Plath: no, I am rather thinking of them simply and honestly describing their research process. There was a time when to be a scientist you wrote down your smallest thought or sensation about things, your most fleeting impression or association and you described these in very personal terms. By "personal" I mean that there is an "I" in the sentences rather than the dreadful "It appeared that . . .", etc.

This was fine, and those scientists were really trying to understand things and knew that the vehicle for doing so was their self— all of their self. They would be dedicated to the closest detail or fluctuation of whatever it was that they were observing. Then came the rise of method, on the back of things that the good scientists may have found and conceptualized into stratified forms, and then came shortcuts to doing the close observations and one of the first things that was pruned away was "I"—it cast too long a shadow.

Now, if I follow X's method I just do that and then get the answer and none of this needs to involve me as a person; I can use the third person and instead of the reality of that being a false thing to do I can say, in reverence to Method, that it is more OBJECTIVE. I find it odd that soc-sci researchers will feverishly say of this or that study that the results cannot be extrapolated to other populations, times, areas, and cultures because things naturally change, but at the same time these researchers think nothing of using and reusing and reusing again the same tired methods, written ages ago, to get those ungeneralizable results.

Other method makers have gone to great reductive efforts to make the results gained from the method generalizable, but mostly, within soc-sci, this is a con that fits the business model that gets the funding from the reductive-minded organizations and establishments who pay the wages of the people doing the research and those educating others to become researchers.

I had no idea what trouble I would get into by wanting to think for myself in a social sciences research dept. I had thought that the primary skill needed to be a researcher would be to be able to think freely, creatively, and analytically. Not so. I have learnt that the actual most important skill is that of obediently mumbling names and dates and at all costs not upsetting the people funding the research. Researchers do, after all, find just what it is that they are paid to find.

And how many times have I heard researchers talk about not being part of the mainstream, about "pushing the boundaries", about "being radical" (I think they mean by this "thinking and writing down their own thoughts") blah blah blah, and then when I read their research . . . errrrm, how shall I put it, it's dead, disembodied and therefore disowned in the sense of taking any real responsibility for it. After all, Heidegger made me do it! Giorgi (or any other of a raft of dismally regurgitated names) made me do it! It's all written on some stone somewhere . . .

Ah yes, stones. "Relative"—I've been wondering what that means. It has a few meanings; it has a real meaning (I am not now scrambling anxiously through a large dictionary to tell you all about its etymology like a good robot who thinks true meanings are handed down from clever people with beards), well there's my aunt—she's a relative; there's stuff like distance covered relative to speed or velocity or whatever and time; then there's a (pseudo-) philosophical use (which is actually political) and it is this meaning that relates most to what I am saying.

Let's have another look at that stone. Only this time with researchers, so we are being more literal this time. One, a very scientific sort, asserts that by knowing the stone's dimensions and weight, its geological data, its type of matrix, its origin, the types of tools used to mine or fashion it, the period it has been around, we can come to know the stone. They then say, with a quaint smile, that then . . . then . . . by using the power of science we can look at (representations of) the atomic structure of the stone and that will unlock all there is to know about it.

Then there's this long-haired but uptight type who goes on about "style", and says that if we have read and properly understood what those great figures have told us about style, the aesthetic, the Renaissance, we can say that this stone, the one right here, is ugly.

Now this last word works like a trigger on the third researcher, who pipes up, irate, and proclaims that not only is the stone beautiful but that it isn't a stone because to them it's aaaaaaaaaaa, er, a plug for a bath! They maintain that any judgements on the stone are relative and no one interpretive value has more value than any other.

This sort of nonsense actually reverberates around some research departments, though not usually about stones; usually about concepts, behaviour, or people, which is worse. The problem all of these people fail to see is that they are all wrong. I know people hate to be told they are wrong, especially if they have become very attached to assuming they are right, but never mind.

The stone exists in itself. It exists. It wouldn't matter if a million earnest professors shuffled past it and proclaimed it to be beautiful or ugly or flint or coal, because none of that has anything whatsoever to do with knowing the stone in itself. It isn't there as some magical thing shaping itself into the form of whatever noises this person or that person makes about it. Those noises are just that—the sound of someone wanting to say something about the stone so that they can fit it into the sense that they like to make of the world . . . now it has a place and everything is peaceful once again.

The truth is the stone exists in itself and despite our best efforts WE DO NOT KNOW IT. This is the problem—NOT KNOWING. There is nothing quite like the uncertainty of not knowing to make people spout out names, dates, theories, and any other type of quantifying data . . . George said that professionals resort to scrawling this anxious sort of jargon like cuttlefish squirting out ink.

Why is it too much to say that, in the case of the humble stone, the pebble, the piece of grit, we do not really understand it and cannot know it. Ah, I think I've just worked it out . . . if we do not really understand a piece of grit what are we to do about bricks and paving stones . . . and people, and ourselves, and life?

As I said before, I had thought that, this being the case, researchers would respond by taking seriously the thing closest to themselves and therefore the most possible to understand: themselves, or rather, their own consciousness. I had thought that taking the experience of your own consciousness seriously and doing things with it would be what research was about. I was wrong.

The insecurity of not knowing grit doesn't make most researchers want to boldly go into inner space, it makes them want to meekly and sycophantically hide behind the armour made by some great man (no doubt) and pontificate about outer things. We are the inner, the integument, the radiating warmth and experience of being.

Without a body, the researcher becomes brutally numb and masculinized. They seek not to become genuinely involved in the research process. They run no risk of asking ill-fated questions. They avoid real issues of ethics—"I do these experiments on primates because I can and because there is a market for it". They see themselves sitting on a nice chair with Professor written on the back. Without the body they can join the abstraction and dislocation of research; they can enter the Business. They can say everything is Relative so they do not have to really think about ethics in case that disturbs their sleep.

Ah, but this may just be the bitter swan-song of someone leaving soc-sci research. It may have no more currency than that. And anyway, what would it matter if things are as I have said? The mortgage gets paid at the end of the month (if you remain obedient) and you get your nice trips overseas to attend conferences—funny, among the researchers who are so concerned about the environ-

ment I have never met people who have collected so many air-miles! They love to globe trot and talk with rushed and hushed concern about "global warming". In the twenty-first century—the internet age—is there any justification apart from a prurient vanity for academics to be jetted off to this conference and that symposium? I think not. How can these people be so disconnected? Ahhh
. . .

This sort of disconnection, this ability to say or write words and NOT BE PRESENT and not have to DO the concomitant BEHAVIOUR is what happens when people take their body out of their method of consciousness and language.

I never realized that faithfully reporting my experience in a research department would cause such trouble.

CHAPTER THREE

A transformational dialogue between the Fisherman and the Gentle Warrior

Barbara Hunter and John Lees

T his chapter describes some aspects of the development of our tutor–student relationship on a Masters in Therapeutic Counselling course. (At the time of writing John was the course leader as well as a trained practitioner and an academic and, at the time of writing, Barbara was a student in training in the final year of the course whose research dissertation John was supervising.) In addition to our different roles, there were some other essential differences between us that we believe had a bearing on how the relationship unfolded. There was obviously a gender difference. However, there was also a cultural difference. Barbara is a *pakeha* from New Zealand (or Aotearoa), which is a country that is unique in fostering bi-cultural relations between the indigenous Maori people and the pakeha, the white population. The bi-cultural nature of her upbringing enabled Barbara to develop a spiritual perspective on life that incorporated a love for, and connection to, all things pertaining to the Earth. John, meanwhile, was born into Anglo-Saxon British culture. Having said this, he had a long-standing interest in different spiritual traditions; in particular, Rudolf Steiner's anthroposophy.

The core of the chapter consists of a written dialogue that took place between us and was focused on Barbara's experience of being John's research supervisee within a university. The dialogue took place at a point in the supervisory relationship when Barbara's work had begun to flounder and John's supervisory input had become counterproductive. Barbara had chosen to do her research using learning by inquiry methodology (Clarkson, 1998). She incorporated elements of autoethnographic research, narrative research, and heuristic research. Over the years, John has variously referred to the method as reflexive action research (Lees, 2001), psychotherapeutic research (Lees, 2003), as well as learning by inquiry, but now prefers to call it practitioner research (Freshwater & Lees, 2009). It focuses on the self and the development of the researcher, and so it is a demanding and challenging methodology and it is not unusual for students to experience difficulties at some stage of the research process.

In view of the fact that Barbara's work was floundering and John's supervision was not helping her very much, we could say that the written dialogue arose out of a crisis situation. In spite of a great deal of struggle and effort, Barbara was unable to give focus to her research and we were both frustrated. Yet, the dialogue provides an account of how we began to wake up from the malaise. It explores, first of all, why the relationship had reached an impasse and then shows how first Barbara, and then John, were able to engage in a transformational process by exploring the dynamics of the supervisory relationship. The turning point was a letter that Barbara wrote to John (whom she named the Fisherman), to which she gave the title "The lost soul in the research process". John felt that the letter was quite different from anything else that Barbara had written up to that point. It enabled him to understand the context in which their supervisory relationship was taking place. He was inspired to respond in a similar dialogic form ("The fisherman responds"), in which he referred to Barbara as the Gentle Warrior.

The bulk of the chapter is taken up with the Gentle Warrior's initial letter, the Fisherman's response and the Gentle Warrior's response to the response ("Well now, fisherman"). These constitute the next three sections of the chapter. We have made some minor editing alterations to the dialogue but, essentially, the text accurately conveys the content of the original letters. We consider that the dialogue is a narrative analysis that gives an account of what happened at this crucial transformational point in their work together. As such, it is a form of cognition that "operates by combining elements into an emplotted story" (Polkinghorne, 1995, p. 1) and is "concerned with the overall narrative itself and the meaning which it conveys" (Blumenfeld-Jones, 1995, p. 25). In other words, the narrative constitutes the "analysis". It is, in effect, an organization of "the data elements into a coherent developmental account ... [it is] ... a synthesis of the data rather than a separation of its constituent parts" (Polkinghorne, 1995, p. 15). What we have written resembles a particular type of narrative, what Ellis (2004) refers to as an "unmediated co-constructed narrative" (p. 75). This means, in effect, that it is unmediated by a researcher expert. It simply emerged out of our interaction in relation to Barbara's research. In many respects, the dialogue blurred our respective roles of tutor and student—so-called tutor expert and so-called student.

As in any good narrative analysis, our particular story gives some information about the cultural context in which the story takes place, the nature of the protagonists, the role of any significant other people in the narrative, the choices and actions of the protagonists, the historical perspective of the story, the outcome, and the plausibility of the story (Polkinghorne, 1995, p. 17). To some degree, these points have already been touched upon. We have noted the (academic) context, said something about the protagonists (the Gentle Warrior and the Fisherman), hinted at the fact that there is a historical perspective in as much as we brought different cultural perspectives to bear on the dialogue, and we have also mentioned the transformational outcome. We have not identified any other protagonists apart from the two of us—apart, that is, from noting that, in terms of the principle of intertextuality, our experiences were influenced by the work of others such as Steiner, one of the founders of autoethnography (Carolyn Ellis), the work of Polkinghorne, and so on. But, as narrative research is more about communication than representation, then its plausibility depends on the opinion of you, the reader, and whether it communicates anything of value to you.

The following three sections correspond to the three letters that we sent to each other at this crucial stage of the research. The final section highlights what we see as the value of the dialogue. In that section we reflect on the narrative to consider some of its key features. In particular, we will attempt to identify what it is saying about academia, research, research supervision, culture, and human relationships generally.

The lost soul in the research process

I have taken a journey and have felt like the alchemist, forever searching. Has the journey, however, honoured the soul?

Today this is the story of the *lost soul*, the self in the research process. This is just the narrative and for this exercise will be devoid of academic rigour, definition, qualitative data, and books.

It is really a long journey beginning with an intense interest in the spiritual self and my spiritual being. Why was I so interested in the spiritual? The magic of the moments captured me and lifted my spirit. I observed recovered addicts and admired their integrated persona with what appeared a deep internal glow. It was a state I wished to attain.

Why was I so interested in the spiritual? I stem from a heritage that is bi-cultural where there is something unique, ultimately linked with the power of *te whenua*, the land. From professional and cultural roots I have developed a belief in the holistic self, which incorporates body, mind, and spirit realizing the importance of this towards a healthy being, and important to my thinking and philosophical orientation is a psycho-spiritual integration.

I was stimulated and enthused on entering the counselling course when I discovered that the reflexive process was an approach that could be utilized for the research component. As a professional I had worked in this way for a number of years, developed a very strong belief, and had gained much satisfaction and enlightenment from engaging with such a process. I was also passionate about research.

I was also interested in the space of the therapeutic relationship. Past clinical encounters had been stimulating and thought provoking, especially as to what transpired in the space between two people.

It was a shock, however, to find that I had become so enmeshed in the process. Perhaps that was a journey in itself, and to reflect on this may assist with a transforming element. Maybe the research then becomes an exercise to find the meanings and make connections with the journey to date. How could someone who was so passionate about reflexivity not even use the process, not even ask why?

How did I get so lost in the self? Was I so lost within that I could not even find a way out, that my magical moments and spiritual solace became my source of comfort, as they did, with much meaning found in the ritual involved?

I began the third year of the programme with an academic supervisor I have labelled "the Fisherman", an old name that had been attached and used over the years. As I went my merry way I thought very deeply about this name, but no other came to mind. Why did I call him the "fisherman"? Reflection took over. What do fishermen do? They sit, on the beach, beside some water, or in a boat, and fish with a fishing line, some bait on the hook at the end, and wait for the fish to bite. Sometimes, if they have to wait too long, they despair, or frustration sets in. Indeed, if they have to wait too long and get no fish, no bites, they will give up, pack up and go home. (In symbolic terms it was an image of the Fisherman waiting beside the pool of water/the unconscious.)

Supervision is, I believe, paramount to the journey of a student, therapist, or a professional working within a helping relationship, and it is a process that I have always immensely valued. In supervision at the commencement of the research year, I related to the Fisherman an experience which I thought had been very connecting and one that had focused me back on my research during the summer break.

> I spoke about a most beautiful warm summer night. The magic of the moment filled my body and connected with my soul. I sat at the open window at times and revelled in the beauty, the whispering trees, the soft, swiftly moving water, Big Ben, which chimed each quarter hour, a magical sound with a mystic hue of blue and yellow light around the magnificent buildings across the water. The movement and sound of boats in the early morning hours was music to my soul and connected with much warmth back to my cultural roots. Utter peace and tranquility.

> *The fisherman stated*: That was about your self.

> I felt gutted, the inner voice saying "hello, have you not been sitting in research lectures, reading papers from William West and others which

cite putting the 'self' at the centre of the research?" The outer voice found no place and on reflection was a parallel to those whom I was working with at the time, the chronic Eating Disorder. I was the "deflated balloon" and I felt robbed.

"Dried up old Hu Hu bugs on the fishing line."

With a grim set face he stated: You need to ground it in something, ground it in your experience of working with addiction (as this was the topic of my research). I am getting directive now.

"Dried up old Hu Hu bugs on the line."

Regression to a state of Piaget's concrete thinking, confusion and chaos ensued. The fisherman is very open with very expressive non-verbal reactions. I went into a hyper-vigilant state of constantly observing with enormous eyes, watching for anything at all that might tell me "I was doing it right". I watched his reactions towards other students as they presented their research. Those who had done well was expressed very clearly, the face shone and the chest seemed to swell with pride. I noted that many spoke about their own process, but for me it seemed it was a no, no. What was that all about? I wondered. Keep to the boundaries of the profession, only discuss the work.

What unconscious processes, thoughts, was I connecting with, I wondered. Were the constraints too containing/not containing so that I could not see the wood from [*sic*] the trees?

Did I in fact become lost/enmeshed in the organizational/course anxieties about the reflexive methodology?

The theoretical perspective of addiction became the focus of my research and this coincided with my professional clinical self working in the addictions area. I was stuck within by the research and desperate to finish and move on. I remained intensely focused on the "Spiritual" concept in regard to recovery.

A year ago, the Fisherman seemed to me to begin to have doubts about my work, which was always to be forthcoming but never amounted to much. It seemed all chaos, chopping and changing methodology and fluctuating from one idea to the next, reflexivity to case study, to reflexivity and around and around. Very little work was forthcoming and I was asked to present a summary and a time management plan for the next tutorial, which I duly gave. The

Fisherman appeared dubious in regard to the time restraints, stressing yet again the importance of leaving time for reflective thinking. He then announced that he would be going on a working trip for several weeks:

> *The fisherman, appearing anxious and exasperated, said*: I am going away, a long way away, I will not be here for many weeks next year.
>
> *I responded*: That is all right—I will work around it.
>
> *My determination was very strong and what is the anxiety I wonder? I can work by myself.*

I booked to present my "research in process" for a classroom presentation, and this proceeded. Feedback from the students was enlightening: four students referred to being confused, one said it felt cloudy, another said it was fragmented, others said they would have like to hear more about my process, one said "I kept expecting you to say you were a recovering addict", one advised me to look at my own journey and process in order to bring it all together and make sense of my own magical experiences, one said that she was fascinated by the way the world of the addict had got inside me, making me confused, some referred to parallel process, some to the need to be more reflexive, some to my cultural roots, some to the transpersonal elements, some said they were touched and moved, one said she was inspired, and there were many more as well. During the presentation I was astonished and surprised to feel an intense grief very deep within. This occurred when I was talking about the *Marae*, and the *Te Whare Nui*, the house at Auckland University. I reflected on this very deeply.

I had always loved school and thrived on my university education. I had worked hard as a student, performed well and felt nurtured and stimulated from teachers and lecturers. My high school was an all girls' school which fostered very free and creative thinking. Young women were enabled to engage with tasks and activities that were progressive for the time. Likewise, my university days were full of creativity with freedom to express thoughts and ideas.

Where had my *Pakeha* Feminist Spiritual self vanished? Had I submissively succumbed to a patriarchal white middle-class establishment?

The Fisherman, during the presentation, appeared "cut off", no eye contact, staring at the paper that I had handed out. As other students gave feedback there was a smile on his face which I read as "I told you so". The inner voice within stated; "What a disastrous student".

Comments from the Fisherman following the presentation were valued, although there was an apology in relation to the limits of these due to scanty notes taken at the time. Where was he then, what was he thinking when students had been so enlightening? Comments included:

My observations about addiction needed to be focused on.

I need to look at different approaches to addiction and my reason for using the transpersonal, including my cultural roots.

There was confusion in data collection and analysis.

The presentation mirrored the addictive process.

The methodology included existential phenomenological principles.

I was discovering something about relapse.

What does it mean to find a connection with the spiritual/transpersonal?

I noted that the comments were different to student comments in that there was academic structure, located in addiction and methodology, in comparison to students being more reflexive about the process of the self and the journey. Very much within the male–female discourse, I thought.

I began to feel very desperate and decided to "just begin searching for some academic who could help me". Although this was constantly on my mind it never eventuated.

Coinciding with the classroom presentation was my personal therapy space where my addict self was being explored: initially a co-dependent, manic compulsive helper in an alcoholic system, leading to a workaholic. At this point the workaholic was being used in systems in a way that was destructive and abusive to the self. I made a decision to give away the madness and abuse of the workplace.

In the New Year at the first Tutorial I related to the Fisherman that I believed my research was focusing on addiction and was far away from the concept of "Space" that had been my initial vision.

"Yes," he replied with a look of steel on his face.

Dried up old Hu Hu bugs.

It seemed to me the Fisherman was beginning to think about packing up and going home, although I believe he was somehow "holding things in mind". I seemed to be getting into trouble now. An angry retort.

Fisherman: It's all about self, self, self.

Little Lucifer and the Devil.

Anthroposophy—mm

But the inner silent voice told me:

—*Does this mean I should be thinking this way?*

—*I have insufficient theoretical knowledge in this direction to go this way at the moment.*

—*Was he trying to reach me somehow? The frustrated Fisherman.*

—*Whose research is this anyway?*

—*What about "my space"?*

—*Shame Shame Shame! I felt.* Not much like the character I thought I was-far related from the compulsive helper who never thought about self.

Fisherman: You will need to look at egotism in this too.

What utter horror I felt at that—I have a big ego? All I was wanting was to throw some light on process of the recovery of addicts and, in particular, the role of the spiritual within that process. The recovery rates for addicts are poor and I believed treatment programmes were limited in terms of what they offered to individuals. I was concerned about the increase of addiction globally and much money is being given out in the marketplace, but I have some concerns that institutions are out to capitalize on this without thinking about the whole complex process for individuals.

Confusion and chaos. How could someone who is so passionate about research and reflexivity become so enmeshed in "the swampy lowlands".

In February of this year, in my personal space, I stood on a wooden floor and worried about my research—an anxiety was setting in because I seemed to be getting nowhere. I looked down at my books and papers from where I was standing, an organized mass of paper, books, and folders.

A thought came into my head: "Things just have to change". Immediately following this my inner body became "exceptionally still". This was followed by a sensation/feeling of "an energy, a slither of silver/yellow light, like a rod" that passed through the centre of my body—this could only be described, I felt, as spiritual. I remained standing on the floor, deep in thought about this; I felt the chaos dissipating from my body, leaving my body and vanishing up into the air. This, I felt, had implications for the concept of addiction, as, despite much research, it is not really known why/how an addict chooses to recover.

I was rooted and gutted. I had given head space to my being "an addict" but had never felt it internally before. Clunk, not a very nice feeling, rather painful and embarrassing. It was, however, accompanied by an internal centredness—I could now focus on what I was doing.

The swampy lowlands of my research continued though. Where had all my insight gone?

An enormous grief, like something I had not experienced ever before, took over my being. In conjunction with this the addict physical destruction began to take its toll on the body, requiring exhausting integrative treatment. The words in my mind were, I felt, imprisoned within.

Supervision was a priority now, I felt, but I needed to wait my turn.

In the last supervision the Fisherman remarked: "There is something addictive about this, no new words, going around in a circle."

Later, with a grim expression: "What is going on here?"

Yes I thought angrily, what indeed is going on here?

A wonderful huge succulent crayfish on the end of the line.

I reflected on two issues:

- The addict EXPOSED. A very sophisticated junkie. From a co-dependent, manic compulsive helper, to workaholic, to the current the addiction and pull to the spiritual, an obsession with seeking spiritual solace to escape my emotional pain. I was now at the bottom of the pit, there was only one way now: UP.

● The TRANSFERENCE in supervision.

I wondered what the Fisherman meant to me. As far as I was consciously aware, the only connection I had with the Fisherman was professional-teacher/tutor–student, and this I felt was very boundaried.

I reflected very deeply.

Nothing, but . . .

When the Fisherman sent me an email that was work-orientated, usually with feedback, I would look at the address,

FRANK Fj

Looking at this gave me a warm, fuzzy, and I thought "most interesting" sensation, but thought no more. It was quite detached from the work. This went on for months.

I reflected now . . .

My father was Francis John: FRANK, he was called. He was a professional businessman working very hard and keeping long hours. He died at a young age and I had had a very special relationship with him, although time with him was often limited due to his working hours. I have never grieved for him, rather keeping with me a wonderful warm memory in my mind, identifying with, idolizing, idealizing, and always incredibly loyal towards him.

Frank was a highly intelligent, creative and spiritual man, his spiritual thinking many years ahead of his time. He would help me with my homework at times, this usually being the creative aspect in projects, and we would create together. Sometimes he would sit on the edge of the bed at bedtime and have intellectual debates, often asking questions to stimulate the mind, these often focusing on music, literature, the arts, and spiritual issues. Ironically, one of my most favourite outings with him was to go fishing in the boat. Sitting in the boat was a time of quiet and peacefulness and I saw my father so immensely happy here, very patient, just waiting for the fish. In turn I was immensely happy to be spending this time with him, the two of us together.

In the context of supervision I had been unconsciously keeping alive the relationship of my father and the Fisherman: two men with similar attributes, same physical size, intelligent, creative, spiritual, gentle, and kind. In my deprived childhood I had two sources of comfort—school and the relationship with my father. In the current deprivation of addiction I had two sources of comfort—school and the re-creation of my Father's memory in the supervisory process.

Following my reflection on the supervision session, and the revelation of the transference, I had a very powerful feeling of an umbilical cord being cut.

I have an absolute feeling of freedom.

No academic mark will ever surpass the release of the self.

The fisherman responds

Your letter has given me a lot to ponder. It resonates powerfully—a welcome break from the stilted and deadening conventions of academic and clinical writing conventions that have engulfed me and which Tris, in a recent issue of *Psychodynamic Practice* that I co-edited with Dawn, has rightly ridiculed (Westwood, 2005). Of course, many people will not understand him and may also feel antagonistic. Yet these things need to be said. I hope we can contribute to the debate.

The direct comments about me in your piece make me feel self-aware but excited at the same time. I have the strong impression that I am meeting you in the piece—I will call you the Gentle Warrior. The self-awareness that your letter evoked in me was mildly uncomfortable, but any self-knowledge is useful. It shows a great deal of astuteness of observation on your part. I cannot deny what you say. So thank you. It motivates me to find new ways of grappling with The System that we were working in. Over the centuries it has taken its toll: Socrates having to take hemlock, the Inquisition, and many more. At least they don't kill us today. So what to do? Hieronymus Bosch, wary of the Hounds of the Inquisition, expressed the absurdity of it all in "coded" form in his paintings. So did Shakespeare [in his writings], I think. People today tend to give up, stifle their creativity, and the few who maintain their beliefs and still try to grapple with the System remain very bitter and angry. I met three of the latter recently, two in Australia and one in this country (four if I include you). I suppose it's my karma at this moment in time. The Australian referred to the "violence of modern epistemologies" and, I think, felt abused by the System. Another—a New Zealander living in Australia—was nearly ousted from her senior academic post. And then there was Tris, who wrote his struggles with the Research Degrees Committee into his doctorate (Westwood, 2004) and in which he challenged the views of the Chair of the Research Degrees Committee from a position of intellectual superiority. And you, an unfinished story . . . Anger seems to be the response of many. Read the work of Richard (House, 2003). He rails against the System. I have dialogued with him about this, since we share a lot in common apart from the course of action. I think anger just creates anger and so it just ends up in an endless cycle of attacks on each other. But I respect his standpoint and admire his work.

Others adopt a less aggressive response. For instance, Roddy told a human, vivid, and moving story about the death of his father and then added an appropriate level of academic concepts in order to get his Masters (Mackenzie, 2002). As regards me, the Fisherman, I haven't yet broken away from Convention, but am trying to develop ways of dialoguing. I consider, ultimately, I am a Manichean. Mani, who lived in the third century AD, developed a way of life that was concerned with helping people to strengthen their capacity to connect with others and the world around, irrespective of their point of view. After his death, Manicheanism flourished until about the twelfth century, by which time it stretched from the West of Spain to the East of China, when it began to face persecution and was eventually eliminated by the eighteenth century. There is a great need for it today, in my view. The world is so troubled. Rudolf, fully aware of what was going on, referred to the fact that we could soon be facing the "Grave of Civilization" if we didn't get our act together (Steiner, 1924). Are we on the way to doing this or aren't we? The Manichean strives to find a path of inclusivity. So, for me, it means agreeing, on the one hand, with all these people who have been hurt or damaged by the System and, on the other, finding a way of loving the persecutors (in fact not even calling them persecutors, but fellow human beings) and trying to maintain a dialogue with them, whatever they say and whatever they do.

So, the essential question, Gentle Warrior, is what are you going to do about your dissertation?

Let me know when you've thought about it. Just one parting thought. I have been grateful recently for reading Colin's piece about Antonio Gramsci's distinction between the conventional intelligensia who reproduce the "ideas and systems of beliefs which enable the masses to be dominated by a small majority" and the intelligensia who are not recognized by the conventional intelligensia since they are, ultimately, a threat to their *raison d'etre* (Holmes, 2002). The latter group, in Antonio's own words,

> carries on some form of intellectual activity, that is, he is a "philosopher", an "artist", a "man of taste", he participates in a particular conception of the world, has a conscious line of moral conduct, and therefore contributes to sustain a conception of the world or to modify it, that is, to bring new modes of thought.   :

But such people rarely hold positions in universities. They are probably just going about doing their daily business, say, as a practitioner, as conscientiously as they can. I actually think that you are one of these philosopher/artist/practitioner/intellectuals. If so, how can your work be of benefit to others?

Well now, Fisherman

We have dialogued and so much food for thought, wonderful glorious food.

Wonderful succulent crayfish on the line.

I feel very empowered, my *pakeha*, feminist, spiritual self once more returning, what wonderful freedom.

There is a need, however, to say goodbye to some old and bring in the new; to separate this I feel [it] is necessary to continue with the work that is to come.

You once stated to me in supervision "cross over the Bridge". These words are very true, now I am crossing the bridge but in doing this I bring my *pakeha* spiritual self.

> Hello River
>
> Today I have come from Pouihi
> Standing tall not far away

Pouihi from the mighty Totara
Sailing seas from Land of the Long White Cloud
Now with spirit in London town
Connecting souls from far and near.

I have come today river
Big Ben in all his majesty rules over
Gives forth his magic chime
My soul connects
You understand river
So patiently you have waited and waited
You know the connecting and disconnecting.

I connected one warm summer night
Long months ago
Music, magic and warmth you gave
Whispering trees, soft moving water
Mystic light
Utter peace and tranquility
A soul well fed.

Today I come river
Soul and spirit connect
The power of Te Whenua
You understand river
You wait with great patience.

The fern, the rose, integrate within
But do not forget scotch thistle
We all are one
A long time river—but it is one.

Some sadness river
A need to say goodbye
To Father Father
Father Frank Father Fisherman
Some tears to join your water river
Gently flow away.

It is different now river
It is to be
Goodbye Father Frank to the place of one to one
Goodbye Father Fisherman, his line to take
Will he come River?
With his line to give.

But hello, Fisherman Mani

Will he but come river
To join with Te Whenua
Soul and spirit

River 2

Hello River

I have come from Pouihi
Standing tall not far away
Connecting souls from far and near
Much spirit in London town

A grey windy day River
Whatever, you're always here
Water flowing strong River
Like energy within
Flowing flowing strong

Time is moving on now River
I give you line of Father Fisherman
The hook I keep, you know, safety River
Will you take to Rangitoto
Ruling Gulf with might and majesty

Big Silver Bird is waiting River
To connect with Aotearoa
To say goodbye to Father Frank
Good bye to fishing boat
All is peace

A line for Fisherman Mani River
To find and bless Down Under
Where will it be River?
River, mud pool, sand or sea
Now, different it is to be

Fern, Rose and Thistle, all are one
Now to bring out mortarboard
To guard a head of academia
What is research with no soul?
It is to be
Research with soul.

Discussion

In this final section we analyse our own narrative in order to identify what it is saying about academia, research, research supervision, culture, and human relationships generally. We do this from three points of view: identifying what we view as the two primary discourses that underpin the narrative, looking at our narrative, and saying something about the nature of dialogue.

Our narrative is influenced by the dominant academic and research discourse, but also by a less obvious discourse. The problems that we describe arose in the first place because we were both trapped within the former, although John was more trapped than Barbara. This is probably because of his position as an academic and his Western upbringing and education. His narrative is still stuck in the language of academia, whereas Barbara has managed to free herself from it in her narrative. As a result of this, she was able to initiate the transformational process. When she did this we were able to bring the other, less dominant and less obvious, discourse into focus. We now look at these two discourses in greater detail.

The dominant discourse provides the background to our dialogue. It is the knowledge system that dominates Western civilization and, as a result of this, contemporary academia. Like most people, we find that this way of thinking is so pervasive that it is difficult to avoid, since we have been educated according to its values. In fact, for much of the supervisory relationship we did not particularly reflect on its pervasive influence. It was only when Barbara wrote "the lost soul in the research process" that we became conscious of how it influenced both of us and underpinned John's remarks and attitude to Barbara's work. We then became aware of how our work together was influenced by its tendency to seek for "physical, explicit, scientific" proof and its emphasis on seeing knowledge generation as a quest for objectivity (Poonwassie & Charter, 2005, p. 17). You could say that, in philosophical terms, we then became aware of the fact that we were embroiled in a world that was dominated by a "Newtonian cause-and-effect conceptual structure" and, as a result of this, we were subject to this world's "Cartesian dualistic split between mind and body". As a result of this, we tended to get bound up in "reductionistic, analytic" nature (Clarkson, 1995, p. 184) in our work together. As our consciousness of the power that this discourse exercised over us came more clearly into focus, we realized that our experience was being influenced by another discourse that, in fact, we both find inspirational.

This less obvious discourse is based on a way of thinking and being that we both believe is *always* on the margins of our awareness but is usually unnoticed and unobserved. In fact, we think this way of thinking and being brings us into contact with a spiritual world that is not remote but is always present as it interweaves with our everyday existence. We have a glimpse of it when we experience the unexpected, the liminal, the remarkable, the unsystematic, and the unpredictable; that is to say, "many of the most significant and exciting life events and extraordinary experiences— moments of clarity, illumination and healing" (Braud & Anderson, 1998, p. 3). Yet, as we worked together, we found it difficult to grasp for much of the time in our joint work as a research supervisor and a research supervisee in view of the fact that we were influenced by the norms of the academic environment. As such, we did what most other people in that environment do: we "systematically excluded" our living and dynamic experience of the spiritual world from our research process, "along with the ways of recognizing and encouraging these exceptional experiences" (*ibid.*). In order to become aware of these liminal experiences (which have also been variously described as the numinous, the transpersonal, and the supersensible, as well as the spiritual), we had to raise our consciousness and become more alert than we usually were. However, this is not easy to do. The late Petruska Clarkson, who refers to this aspect of our experience as the working of "physis", was fond of quoting Heraclitus in order to make this point: "Research *means* to search again. Into many things. 'People who love wisdom must be good inquirers into many things indeed' (Fragment IX). Why? Because '*physis loves to hide*' (Fragment X)" (Clarkson, 2000, p. 67). In other words, she was confirming that such liminal experiences are quite elusive and easily ignored.

Another way of thinking about such experiences is to refer to them as the extraordinary in the ordinary. We are actually arguing that such experiences pervade our lives to a much greater degree than we are conscious of; "not a day passes without a miracle happening in our life" and that "if we do not discover a miracle in our life on a particular day, we have merely lost sight of it" (Steiner, 1918, p. 34). But we also think that we have to work very hard in order to recognize the existence of such phenomena. Indeed, such an awakening is often very difficult—even life-changing or painful—as we have tried to demonstrate in this chapter. Fortunately, Barbara was sufficiently in touch with this aspect of her experience to be able to initiate our dialogue and our subsequent transformational process. In Clarkson's terms, she managed to perceive "physis" in spite of the fact that "physis loves to hide". This resulted in an upsurge in energy and creativity for both of us.

We hope that our narrative incorporated the elements of a good narrative analysis. Our intention was to reveal some of the qualities of our cultural background and the context in which our dialogue took place, and also to say something about us (the protagonists). We have also included the voices of significant others in the narrative, mainly in the form of references to relevant literature, and have tried to place our story within a historical perspective. But, more importantly, we have tried to write the narrative in such a way that it exposes some of the characteristics of the two primary discourses that affected us and, in so doing, we have attempted to give a picture of what can happen when they come into contact with each other. Put differently, we see our narrative as providing a commentary on our higher educational systems and the ways of thinking that underpin them. We also hope that it demonstrates the importance of working with cultural difference and diversity in professional life today and, in particular, with the way in which contemporary Western thinking needs to be fructified by other ways of thinking in order to initiate change and transformation. We realize that it is not feasible to replace academic and professional systems, and so we do not think that it is of any value to just critique them. The Romantics did this in the early nineteenth century, and the critical theorists did it in the 1930s, but, in spite of this, it is still here, is here to stay, and will grow and continue to prosper for many years to come. We are, however, saying that it will be of great value to all of us if the dominant discourse can be fructified by this other discourse (and by other ways of thinking and being generally) and if a dialogue can take place between the two ways of thinking and being. We all have limited points of view and yet, in our view, our perspective can be enhanced if we allow it to be fructified by different viewpoints. This can enrich our experience and transform our lives for the better. However, this involves the transformation of the participants. We hope that our dialogue represents a small step in this direction.

We would like to finish by saying one more thing about the nature of dialogue and, in particular, draw on the dialogical ethics of Martin Buber. Once we can begin to make the spiritual world more conscious in our lives, we realize that it is also a world in which everything is interconnected including human beings. And, of course, Buber, who was a deeply spiritual man, was fully aware of this and the possibilities inherent in it. It was for this reason that he made a fundamental distinction between an I–Thou way of relating and an I–It way of relating (Buber, 1961). An I–Thou relationship is

> a relation of person to person, of subject to subject, a relation of reci-procity involving "meeting" or "encounter" as opposed to I–It which is a "relation of person to thing, of subject to object, involv-ing some form of utilization, domination or control". [Herberg, 1961, p. 14]

Furthermore an I–Thou relationship is one in which we are able to come into contact with this world of interconnectedness and see the other person in Divine terms; that is to say, as a manifestation of God. And this, as he realized, opens up a limitless world of possi-bilities. It helps us to move into a way of being which "has no bounds" (Buber, 1961, p. 45). So, in terms of our own relationship, you could say that we started out in an I–It mode in which John was the "tutor" and "expert" and Barbara was the "student" and "non-expert". We were still in a subject–object way of relating, with all the dangers of domination, control, and separation that are inher-ent in this. In this respect, it conformed to the usual pattern of acad-emic and professional relationships. But, although we were trapped in a system that promulgated "ideas and systems of beliefs" as a means of domination, and John was not able to recognize Barbara's potential as a member of the "intelligentsia" who was able to bring about "new modes of thought" and thus bring about change (Holmes, 2002), we were fortunately able to change this. The dialogue became counter-hegemonic. It developed into an I–Thou relationship in which, in some respects, there was a higher degree of mutuality than is often the case in a tutor–student relationship. This enabled us to humanize our relationship and, we hope, produce something of interest and value for the professional community.

References

Blumenfeld-Jones, D. (1995). Fidelity as a criterion for practising and evaluating narrative inquiry. In: J. A.Hatch & R.Wisiewski (Eds.), *Life History and Narrative* (pp. 25–35). London: Falmer.

Braud, W., & Anderson, R. (1998). Conventional and expanded views of research. In: W. Braud & R. Anderson (Eds.), *Transpersonal Research Methods for the Social Sciences* (pp. 3–26). Thousand Oaks, CA: Sage.

Buber, M. (1961). I and Thou. In: W. Herberg (Ed.), *The Writings of Martin Buber*. Cleveland, OH: Meridian.

Clarkson, P. (1995). *The Therapeutic Relationship*. London: Whurr.

Clarkson, P. (1998). Learning through inquiry (the Dierotao programme at PHYSIS). In: P. Clarkson (Ed.), *Counselling Psychology: Integrating Theory, Research and Supervised Practice* (pp. 242–272). London: Routledge.

Clarkson, P. (2000). Review feature. *European Journal of Counselling, Psychotherapy and Health*, 3(2): 307–321.

Ellis, C. (2004). *The Ethnographic I: A Methodological Novel about Auto-ethnography*. Walnut Creek, CA: Altamira.

Freshwater, D., & Lees, J. (2009). *Practitioner Research in Healthcare: Transformational Research in Action*. In preparation.

Herberg, W. (Ed.) (1961). Introduction. *The Writings of Martin Buber*. Cleveland, OH: Meridian.

Holmes, C. A. (2002). Academics and practitioners: nurses as intellectuals. *Nursing Inquiry*, 9(2): 73–83.

House, R. (2003). *Therapy Beyond Modernity*. London: Karnac.

Lees, J. (2001). Reflexive action research: developing knowledge through practice. *Counselling and Psychotherapy Research*, 1(2): 132–138.

Lees, J. (2003). Developing therapist self-understanding through research. *Counselling and Psychotherapy Research*, 3(2): 147–153.

McKenzie, R. (2002). The importance of philosophical congruence for therapeutic use of self in practice. In: D. Freshwater (Ed.), *Therapeutic Nursing* (pp. 22–38). London: Sage.

Polkinghorne, D. (1995). Narrative configuration in qualitative analysis. In: J. A. Hatch & R. Wisiewski (Eds.), *Life History and Narrative* (pp. 5–23). London: Falmer.

Poonwassie, A., & Charter, A. (2005). Aboriginal worldview of healing: inclusion, blending and bridging. In: R. Moodley & W. West (Eds.), *Integrating Traditional Healing Practices into Counselling and Psychotherapy* (pp. 15–25). London: Sage.

Steiner, R. (1918). *The Work of the Angels in Man's Astral Body*. London: Rudolf Steiner, 1972.

Steiner, R. (1924). *Karmic Relationships, Volume III*. London: Rudolf Steiner, 1977.

Westwood, T. (2004). Creative reading/writing as processes of transformation and empowerment in thinking/being. Unpublished MPhil/PhD upgrade.

Westwood, T. (2005). Academics' dynamics: re-writing referencing. *Psychodynamic Practice, 11*(2): 165–176.

CHAPTER FOUR

Refiguration in counselling and psychotherapy

Geoffrey W. Denham

I

How are we to articulate the common core of psychotherapy? How can we describe it in a way that transcends argument about this or that approach? That is the primary question of this chapter.

Wampold's recent meta-analysis of the psychotherapeutic effects literature has demonstrated support for the contextual model of psychotherapy or counselling and has found little support for a medical model of psychotherapy or counselling. These abstract descriptions are of interest because they are contrasting meta-models of psychotherapy. While a medical model of psychotherapy posits disorders, illnesses, or complaints, a psychological explanation for them, a mechanism of change, specific ingredients in treatment, and specificity of effect of these ingredients (Wampold, 2001, p. 14), the contextual model provides a contrasting view of psychotherapeutic engagements. The contextual model draws on Frank and Frank's (1991) work; it posits "an emotionally charged confiding relationship ... [in] a healing setting in which the client presents to a professional who the client believes can provide help" (*ibid.*, p. 25). A further feature of the contextual model is that there is a plausible explanation offered for the client's predicament and the articulation of some means of resolving the issues; that is, a rationale exists for a procedure that will address the problems and that makes sense to both therapist and client. Last, the contextual model posits an active participation of both client and therapist in the ritual or procedure recommended.

The contextual model descriptions attempt to conceptualize the special kind of conversation between patient and health professional, client and counsellor, client and therapist (I will use the client–therapist terminology in what follows), that constitutes psychotherapy.

In the West the understanding of this process of professional helping is infused with the language of biomedicine, with therapists frequently having connections with biomedicine through practice locations, referral networks, and the locations of their schools of training. It is not surprising, then, that there is a persistent tendency to employ terms like *treatment, diagnosis, procedures,* in describing psychotherapeutic encounters. On the one hand, this language of the familiar has the value of making psychotherapeutic work accessible to other health professionals, but on the other, it has the drawback of overshadowing a core feature of psychotherapy: it is, after all, a *talking* (language term) cure[1] (medical term) as Freud recognized. It is a special kind of professional conversation.

The medical model of psychotherapy (a meta-model in Wampold's 2001 usage) leads us away from this fundamental aspect of psychotherapy. To describe psychotherapy as a treatment for disorders of the mind invokes biomedicine and suggests that something is administered to the patient following diagnosis. While this model makes sense in the context of medical practice (the patient is given the injection or the surgical procedure is performed following a diagnosis), it makes little sense in the psychotherapeutic context. If psychotherapy is a talking cure, can words or a dialogue be administered? Can clients be given their weekly dose of admonition and persuasion? It is bordering on the incoherent to talk in such terms. A process of professional help is cloaked in biomedicine's familiar language register, obscuring essential features of the professional encounter. Better to see the queen with fewer of her biomedical robes if research effort is going to investigate psychotherapy in ways that advance our knowledge. Frank and Frank's meta-model of psychotherapy begins this derobing. Their use of the word *confiding* reveals the act of imparting in confidence, but also invokes having faith in, or entrusting something to, another person.

Wampold found empirical support for the contextual model and a lack of support for the medical model of psychotherapy. The commonly circulated idea that one form or "brand" of psychotherapy is superior to all others finds no place in the conclusions Wampold draws from his extensive meta-analysis of the research literature. All of the *bona fide* "brands" of psychotherapy are superior to no treatment (Wampold, 2001, p. 210).

Wampold's findings can be read as a caution against a muddle-headed conceptualizing of psychotherapy driven by attempts to position it in a biomedical discourse. It is situated there at great cost. In misconceptualizing psychotherapy as *treatment* or *intervention* (Pawson, 2006), resources have been wasted in trying to prove that the effective component of psychotherapy (the treatment or intervention) can be discovered and separated from the psychotherapeutic relationship in much the same way that effective active ingredients of a new drug can be separated from their placebo effects. As Wampold (2001, pp. 15–16) points out,

> . . . the specific ingredients cannot be delivered without the incidental ingredients. A therapeutic relationship is always present in psychotherapy and affects the manner in which the specific ingredients are delivered . . .The fact that the effects due to specific ingredients and common factors are psychological makes both of these effects interesting and relevant to psychotherapists.

Psychotherapy belongs as an adjunct to biomedicine, not within its borders. Much thought and research has been devoted to thinking of psychotherapy as treatment; far too little thought and research has been devoted to considering psychotherapy as a language event and a particular kind of dialogue. This chapter traces some of the implications of this turn-to-language model of psychotherapy.

II

While recognizing the importance of overwhelming emotional experience and distress to many therapeutic sessions, it is the quality and nature of therapeutic representation (talking, writing, drawing, sandplay) that gives psychotherapy its unique character. It is also psychotherapeutic representation that gives psychotherapy its potency in addressing human suffering and pain, and in opening the possibility of a different future. When Ricoeur (1984) notes that the artistic work (the poem, the novel, the play) extends an invitation to the reader/audience to occupy a world, a similar invitation comes from all *bona fide* psychotherapy. All psychotherapy offers the client a refiguration of life's problems and suffering. Some psychotherapy offers a constrained vision: an invitation to occupy an impoverished world with little possibility to do much more than cope or adjust; other psychotherapies extend their vision to both an individual and a world in need of repair. The capacity to represent and re-present is, none the less, crucial to therapeutic benefit. A refigured world is the result of effective psychotherapeutic work.

The notion that psychotherapy can be reduced to a venting of one's feelings, or anonymously writing about emotionally upsetting experiences is profoundly misleading. In short, the "venting thesis" misinterprets the crucial importance of finding a manner of representing suffering and misery as a means of transcending it, and the "disclosive writing" thesis (see Pennebaker, Colder, & Sharpe, 1990; Pennebaker, 1996; Pennebaker & Seagal, 1999) forgets that writing anticipates a readership, and hence at the very least is premised on a potential or mediated relationship of some kind. Writing appears to be private and occurring in moments of solitude, but always has communicative intent. Writing is profoundly dialogical, as Bakhtin (1981) recognized, and is premised on the assumption of a reader, even if only potential, virtual, or removed in time. And a reader is required for writing's communicative intent to be realized. This introduces two dimensions of psychotherapy: the relational dimension (therapeutic alliance, working alliance, dialogue, conversation) and the representational dimension (thoughts, words, images, writing, inscription, speaking, interlocutors, dialogue, conversation). Psychotherapy is both relational and representational. It is this relational and representational dimension of psychotherapy that I wish to lay out in the form of a dialectic.

III

My psychotherapeutic work with children in sandplay prompted me to consider the contribution their play made to the composing of their dilemmas, and to the finding of resolutions to them. If it can be said that the children taught me about the importance of representation, then this is a practice-based learning. Other play-therapists (Axline, 1993; Kalff, 1980) have submitted to this practice-based learning and reflection. However, I wish to extend the argument for the potency of properly conducted play-therapy to consider a theorizing that brings play-therapy and adult forms of psychotherapy under the one auspice. My purpose here is to offer a model for understanding play-therapy (using the example of sandplay) and then to suggest that the model is applicable to all psychotherapy.

Play-therapy is often misrecognized as an expressive therapy, in much the same way that representation in psychotherapy is misrecognized as "venting" or giving expression to feelings. Play-therapy is much more than expressive therapy and should not be separated from the rest of the therapeutic enterprise. The key to this new understanding of play-therapy is to recognize the sophisticated representational and relational processes taking place within it.

(What should be acknowledged here is a practitioner–research orientation. The impetus for this theorizing comes from my participation as a therapist in play-therapy. This practitioner–researcher is not on the other side of one-way glass! Nor does this reflective practice require a researcher outside the therapeutic relationship.)

At a minimum, sandplay (following Kalff, 1980) has textual features that allow children to inscribe their predicaments and, in so doing, explore them in a productive fashion. Textual features appear through symbolization in sand and through the dialogues that ensue with the therapist. Jungian-inspired therapists like Kalff focus on the symbolizing aspect of sandplay, but it is the representational aspect of the play I want to highlight. Through inscription (making a mark in the sand) children come to consider the family or school they belong to, their place in this community, and the meaning of their predicaments in a novel way. When they cross the threshold of the sandplay work, they represent a world in the sand, and in the process talk to the therapist about what they are doing, particularly as the relationship with the therapist builds and becomes robust. The indirectness of a typical dialogue in the context of the child's sandplay apparently takes the pressure off them to make themselves directly accountable to an adult person, and certainly I have discovered the importance of refraining from cross-examining children as they work on their productions. I might add that many children are quite adept at blocking or refusing the offers of help from "concerned" adults.

In therapeutic sandplay children can make statements, but in a figurative, metaphoric way. Each time I engage with children in sandplay I become aware of a great gulf of communication that lies between us, and wonder how it might be spanned. To the extent that I am able to respond meaningfully to their representations, I can develop a collaborative working relationship.

In sandplay I have identified three important points of reference: the work (representation, inscription, the sandplay), the relationship (child–therapist, therapeutic alliance, working alliance), and the child's world (of experience beyond the edges of this sanctuary, the world of action the child inhabits, the world beyond the artist's canvas).

The work is a creation, and, no matter how grand or how small, is something that most children produce with the utmost care and thought, apparently investing it with their very being. Countless times, I have wondered at the deliberation involved in the selection of play items, with the often agonizing placement decisions that children make, and with the degree of absorption they demonstrate in performing their self-imposed tasks. So, here is a special transitory work. The production of the work in the therapeutic context constitutes the crossing of a threshold from the inchoate to that which has form. It is not yet the indelible inscription of the familiar adult world, but is often made so by the therapist (e.g., photographs, detailed notes in case files, video recordings, etc.).

Simon,[2] an eleven-year-old only child, lived with his parents who both worked full time for the defence forces in Australia. One or the other of his parents was frequently absent from the home. His grandparents provided most of his before- and after-school care. He came to see the play-therapist in a school setting because of difficulties with his teacher, who had been insisting that all students in her class write a "true story". Simon refused, saying that if he couldn't write fiction he wouldn't write at all. At age eight, he had been referred to a psychiatrist because he had difficulty distinguishing reality from fantasy. At the time he said he could see through his skin; he made up stories about going to Africa with his dad; he said that his mother had lost some babies. He had spoken about cutting his arm off. In recent weeks, prior to the play-therapy session, he had spoken to his mother about killing himself. He said, "Why did you bother having me? I shouldn't have been born."

The child's relation with the play therapist is one that might develop. The therapist must be tested for trustworthiness and a capacity to understand what the child is doing, saying, and representing. There is a crossing from the solitary "world" of the child's experience of trouble to a social world through disclosure mediated by play. "Trouble", for the child, is often in form of thoughts or musings, too scary to contemplate. The developing relationship between therapist and child is a crucial part of enabling the representational process. Without it, the therapeutic activity disappears. There is no witness to the work and nobody to collaborate in its production as representation. Representation in therapeutic sandplay is to be understood as both an attempt to communicate *and* an attempt to refer to a world. This is the relational–representation dialectic of psychotherapy.

In his first sandplay, Simon made two mounds in the sandtray closest to him, and placed a baby in a snake's mouth at the summit of each mound. He then removed the snakes and pushed down into the sand. The babies were placed in holes he had made in the sand and completely covered. In his second sandplay, he constructed a battle-field: "The Uriki are deadly. They eat men." He arranged battalions of Uriki and men. The two armies were arranged on either side of the sandtray. They appeared evenly numbered. "It actually turns out that the men have a secret army coming up," he said. Using holes made in the sand, he depicted the secret army. "They cornered the Uriki. The Uriki are trapped by eighteen different armies. But one army of Uriki attacks and destroys a whole squadron." And later, "One group of men make a stupid mistake and wipe out half their army. The Uriki survive, and the men don't, except for one person. The Uriki eat him." And later again, "Then the Uriki grade the land and plant people, hoping they will come back. That is just plain stupidity"—the last sentence was spoken with great conviction and emphasis.

The third element—the child's world—is what remains beyond the sandplay and the therapeutic event of discourse. This is the child's world of action and ritual. The practical value of considering it separate from the relationship on the one hand, and the work of sandplay on the other, is to remind us of the interpretive work required to make connections from the security of the dialectic of therapeutic relationship and representation to the world beyond. The child's world of trouble is often difficult for therapists to access, and, as some referral process has occurred, will probably not be accessible by parents or teachers either, so the notion of it being "out of reach" is likely to be a sound premise on which to build play therapeutic work for two reasons.

The first is that representation performs an almost magical function of both referring to a (realistic) world and imagining a better one (not yet in existence). To conflate the work with the child's world is to come to a premature closure. To do so is to deny the child's acts of exploration and discovery as worlds are imagined, contemplated, reassessed, and re-proposed. The importance of the sand medium to refiguration is its compatibility to this process. Leaving aside our cultural preoccupation with inscription in all its forms, the sand allows itself to be remoulded and remodelled in endless ways and defies a sense of permanence.

The second reason is that experience of the other remains profoundly out of reach, but the bridges we build through this mutual meaning-making allow for moments of mutuality mediated by representations. As the child develops confidence in the representational practices of sandplay, supported by the therapist, representations become more, rather than less, make-believe. This is the antithesis of the teacher's instruction: *today we will only write true stories*. Furthermore, psychotherapeutic representation is dialogical in its character.

When mother came to pick up Simon from his first play-therapy session, she remarked that she had not seen him so happy for years.

The other danger is to conflate the child's world with the other element, relationship. If this path is followed, the child's world is then constellated solely in relational or psychological terms; e.g., as evidence of transference, or as indicative of the quality of the relationship with parents, peers, or family. There is nothing intrinsically wrong with the making of interpretations that give prominence to the therapeutic alliance. The danger is in not seeing that children might also be addressing matters outside the immediacy of the relationship: their place in the universe; their relation to the planet; their thinking regarding the sun, the moon, the stars, the planets, the waves and the tides, dinosaurs, insects and flowers; their quest; and their thirst for knowledge, adventure, action.

The work in sandplay is neither a self-portrait, a portrait of the therapeutic relationship, nor definitive representation of the child's world. The establishment of these points of reference, however, does create a space for hermeneutic activity. Therapists and clients make sense of representation and also look for the way in which representation points to the extra-linguistic, in the sense of what it reveals of the person and what it has to say about the world inhabited.

When I have presented Simon's case, intern therapists have recognized the implicit meanings of his invisibility, his fantasy trip to Africa with his father, his feeling of the failure of nurturing in the family, and the value of his fictional world. They can answer the question: "What did his playtherapy provide?"

IV

In the beginning of psychotherapy is the poem, the work of art, the thing made, the work of representation. Clients cross a threshold as they enter a therapeutic dialogue. They move from an inchoate, ineffable world of private experience to the language event of a therapy session, speaking with a professional, perhaps for the first time, about distress and suffering. This is both a relational and representational crossing. Children in play-therapy cross a similar threshold, in forming and making with sand and play materials. There is something made in a psychotherapy session—a work of some kind: a sandplay construction; the giving of an account; the construction of a dialogue; the production of something textual; something that can be read and interpreted, worked and reworked. There is an important movement from the prefigured, the not-yet-said, the tumble-dryer–of–thoughts–and–emotions–in–my–head, to that which has form, shape, substance—a configuration. In turn, what is produced can be modified and reinterpreted by both client and therapist in acts of refiguration. And refiguration encompasses the return of the work to the world of action through the actions of those who created it. This describes an arc central to representation or mimesis, according to Ricoeur (1984), from prefiguration through configuration to refiguration—a threefold mimesis. It also highlights that participants in therapeutic engagements are changed by these engagements and that the process of change takes place through this participation in acts of representing.

Psychotherapy provides a special setting for discourse. Discourse, in Ricoeur's usage is to be distinguished from language as system (*la langue* in de Saussure, 1959).

> [Ricoeur] defined discourse as occurring when some person A says p about x to some person B in accordance with phonetic, lexical, syntactic, and stylistic rules. That is, discourse always involves a speaker or writer and a hearer or reader as well as something said about some topic. It follows that full interpretation of discourse requires both the objective sort of analysis of which structuralism is an example and an appreciation of the self-understanding of the discursive partners (*Stanford Encyclopaedia of Philosophy*, 2007).

To illustrate: when a client speaks, there are two aspects of the speaking we respond to as therapists. On the one hand, clients put forward propositions: *I can see through my skin*; on the other, it is a particular person speaking—Simon, an eleven-year-old schoolboy. The forming of sentences in speech presupposes an identity or person speaking and some kind of proposition. In speaking, the client links together the proposition with his person. Speaking is grounded in being and we speak to say something about something. There is a connecting here of the world of experience and a wider world. The first point is that in speaking, clients put forward propositions about the world.

In our client's speaking, two fundamental avenues of meaning can be recognized. There is what the client intends or means to say, sometimes called the *noetic* part of speaking, and there is what the uttered words mean, the *noematic* part of speaking. The latter is focused on the propositional content of the speaking(Ricoeur, 1976); to engage with this aspect of meaning we need to *make sense of I can see through my skin*. With the exception of the setting of Simon looking at his own X-ray, we would challenge this proposition as being decidedly irrational. However, the utterance also refers back to the speaker and so is connected with the issuer of the statement. Simon extends an ambiguous invitation to discuss the noetic part of his speaking. To summarize, there is both a noetic aspect (what the client intends by speaking and how speaking works reflexively) and a noematic aspect (what the uttered proposition means). As psychotherapists, we acknowledge what the client means to say and what the words mean. In paying attention to the former, we enter the realm of the personal and often quite private aspects of the client's experience; in short, there is an engagement that draws on each interlocutor's reflexive understanding, whereas the latter gives opportunity for a dialogue whose underpinnings are contradiction, coherence, sense and nonsense, and bring the client into the world of what is reasonable, rational, or consensual in our culture.

Psychotherapy and counselling is a special communication context. It is an opportunity for clients to bring their concerns, issues, and worries into an illuminated space. Often clients are bringing matters they have previously not disclosed to anyone else. Speaking itself, when addressed to at least one other person, is a social act. Thus, the client's speaking is a communication or the sharing of something private.

As psychotherapists attempt to respond to their clients, they negotiate both the noetic and noematic aspects of the client's speaking. The less hazardous part of this meaning-making, concerns the noematic aspect, or the propositional content of the client's talk. How can we characterize this part of communication between client and psychotherapist?

The noematic side of speaking can be considered in two ways: it is the "what" and the "about what" of discourse. The latter refers to reference: what are you talking about? What happened in your world? The former refers to the *sense*: how is all this talking connected? What narrative coherence or incoherence am I hearing? As a listener, the psychotherapist contributes to the making of meaning that is here understood as emerging from the therapeutic dialogue. Something passes between me and you, as I listen to you, and that something is the sense conveyed through your words, and enabled by my capacity to share your world of reference. Meaning-making here builds on the noematic features of speaking: the "what" and the "about what" of discourse.

Simon's utterance might now convince the psychiatrist that he has considerable difficulty distinguishing between fact and fiction, but only if the psychiatrist ignored the noetic aspect of speaking.

Communication is less certain as it negotiates the noetic aspect of speaking. There are three basic elements to consider: the manner in which speaking is self-referential or self-reflexive (speaking reveals something about the speaker); the illocutionary act of speaking, and the intention of recognition on the part of the psychotherapist.

Language is self-referential in both simple and quite complicated ways. Clearly, when we use the first person singular pronoun "I", we are linking our statements to some authorial anchor, the "I": it is me that is talking, not somebody else. But psychotherapists sensitized to the noetic would recognize the multiple projections and displacements allowing clients to approach their issues obliquely, as Simon does with his "invisible man" statement. Presentation of self in psychotherapeutic sessions brings with it attendant hazards and risks. What will the therapist think of a client who says *I can see through my skin*? This hazard is tempered in psychotherapy by a certain tardiness on the part of therapists to formulate such assessments of the client's character and the general injunction for therapists to hold a non-judgemental view of the client, or at least suspend the making of judgements for as long as possible. The client's talk in psychotherapy is inevitably self-reflective and reveals their understanding of themselves. How this aspect of talk is negotiated by psychotherapists is likely to be quite important for therapeutic outcomes.

Will the therapist "get" what Simon is saying?

Illocutionary acts were first described by the ordinary language philosopher Searle (1969) as features of speaking. The locutionary aspect of speaking ("the what" and the "about what" already mentioned) is delineated from the illocutionary act of speaking, which is to say that in their speaking, clients (and all speakers) make requests, plead, implore, demand, question, assert, interrogate, promise, order, wish, assert, etc. As psychotherapy begins to address human suffering, pleading, questioning, promising, requesting, demanding, and other illocutionary acts will be evident in the dialogue between client and therapist. How do therapists respond to the illocutionary force of clients' statements?

The illocutionary force of a client's talk and the therapist's response to it has not received as much attention in theories of psychotherapy as the propositional content of a client's statements. Perhaps this is why the most widely distributed and well-known forms of psychotherapy place emphasis on "faulty" or "irrational" cognitions, on the readily identifiable shaky propositions that are alleged to inform clients' thinking. It is far less easy to identify the illocutionary force of a client's statements, and, even if correctly identified, a competent therapist does not always meet the client's questions with answers, or their demands with concessions, or accedes to their requests. The manner in which the illocutionary force of clients' statements are addressed effectively in therapy is a crucial area for investigation, and may well prove crucial for psychotherapeutic outcomes.

Both interpreting and responding to the illocutionary force of statements acknowledges para-verbal features of utterance (shrugs of the shoulder, voice intonation patterns, sighs and gasps) whose codes are more unstable, and which are capable of being concealed or faked. With an emphasis on cognitive behavioural approaches to therapy (CBT) in university training programmes, research examining how psychotherapists respond to the illocutionary force of their clients' statements has been missing. Much research has assumed the value of challenging the propositional content of alleged "faulty" thinking. There is an unfounded optimism in the value of challenging these propositions in CBT theorizing, but, as Wampold (2001, p. 9) points out, it may be more productive for psychotherapy research to focus on strategies common to all psychotherapies, as the evidence for the specific ingredients thesis is lacking empirical support.

All psychotherapists must deal with both the noetic and noematic aspects of client communication. Many questions come to mind. How do psychotherapists address the illocutionary force of statements presented by clients in psychotherapeutic dialogue? What responses to the illocutionary forces of client statements are therapeutically productive and which are therapeutically harmful? Do some psychotherapists completely miss, or misconstrue, the noetic aspects of communication so eloquently illustrated in Simon's three fantasy themes?

Last, the intention to recognize something of the client's experience must lie at the centre of psychotherapy. This is not the time or place to review such an extensive topic. All I can say in passing is that, given the research finding that some therapists consistently produce excellent outcomes with their clients and some consistently produce little change (Wampold, 2006), it is tempting to speculate that good therapists have an intention to recognize something that perhaps clients do not even acknowledge as they begin in therapeutic dialogue, and that ineffective therapists fail this assignment. Could we give them the "Simon Test" to check?

In summary, in speaking, clients put forward propositions about the world and possible worlds. As psychotherapists we acknowledge in various ways what the client means to say (noetic part) and what the words mean (noematic part). Meaning-making in psychotherapy is a public and dialogic activity that builds on the noematic features of speaking—the "what" and "about what" of discourse—but this has been over-emphasized in recent research and writing. Clients' talk in psychotherapy is inevitably self-reflective, and how this aspect of talk is negotiated by psychotherapists is probably quite important for therapeutic outcomes, but little examined in a systematic way. How therapists respond to the illocutionary force of clients' statements, and more generally to noetic aspects of communication, would seem to be at the centre of potent psychotherapeutic dialogue. Practitioner–researchers are well-placed to notice and research these interesting and productive relations.

Note

1. A website now celebrates this. See talkingcure.com
2. The author acknowledges Keith Baker, who supplied the case notes on Simon (not his real name).

References

Axline, V. (1993). *Play Therapy*. New York: Bantam.

Bakhtin, M. M. (1981). *The Dialogic Imagination*. Austin, TX: University of Texas.

de Saussure, F. (1959). *A Course in General Linguistics*. New York: McGraw Hill.

Frank, J. D., & Frank, J. B. (1991). *Persuasion and Healing: A Comparative Study of Psychotherapy*. Baltimore, MD: Johns Hopkins University Press.

Horvath, A. O. (2000). The therapeutic relationship: from transference to alliance. *Journal of Clinical Psychology*, 56(2): 163–173.

Kalff, D. M. (1980). *Sandplay: a Psychotherapeutic Approach to the Psyche*. Santa Monica, CA: Sigo Press.

Pawson, R. (2006). *Evidence-based Policy: A Realist Perspective*. London: Sage.

Pennebaker, J. W. (1996). Cognitive, emotional and language processes in disclosure. *Cognition and Emotion*, 10: 601–626.

Pennebaker, J. W., & Seagal, J. (1999). Forming a story: the health benefits of narrative. *Journal of Clinical Psychology*, 55: 1243–1254.

Pennebaker, J. W., Colder, M., & Sharp, L. K. (1990). Accelerating the coping process. *Journal of Personality and Social Psychology*, 58: 528–537.

Ricoeur, P. (1976). *Interpretation Theory: Discourse and the Surplus of Meaning*. Fort Worth, TX: Christian University Press.

Ricoeur, P. (1984). *Time and Narrative*. Chicago, IL: University of Chicago Press.

Searle, J. (1969). *Speech Acts: An Essay in the Philosophy of Language*. Cambridge: Cambridge University Press.

Stanford Encyclopaedia of Philosophy (2007). Paul Ricoeur. Accessed 27 June 2007 from http://plato.stanford.edu/entries/ricoeur/

Wampold, B. (2001). *The Great Psychotherapy Debate: Models, Methods and Findings*. Mahwah, NJ: Lawrence Erlbaum.

Wampold, B. (2006). What should be validated? The psychotherapist. In: J. C. Norcross, L. E. Beutler, & R. F. Levant (Eds.), *Evidence-based Practices in Mental Health: Debate and Dialogue on the Fundamental Questions* (pp. 200–207). London: Sage.

CHAPTER FIVE

And so the whirl owl flies: a Jungian[1] approach to practitioner research

Jeni Boyd

W riting in 1931, Jung identifies four stages in therapy, "namely confession, elucidation, education and transformation" (Jung, 1954, par. 122). These stages co-exist and are not necessarily sequential, but characterize aspects of the dialectical relationship between therapist and client at various points in the work together. Readers may like to consider whether these stages could be said to characterize aspects of the dialogue between the researcher and the researched and the dialogue between the author, through this text, and themselves, the reader.

To this end, I begin with a confession.

"And so the whirl owl flies": I confess I have no idea what this means, but I "know", in my heart, it is the title of the work. This may seem totally illogical (it is) but carries an emotional valency that cannot be ignored. There is some deep and, as yet, indefinable meaning; a meaning so strong it has not only a psychological effect, in that I am fiercely moved, but also a physical effect: it is the title of the chapter. Jung insisted that it is highly important to admit lack of understanding from time to time (Jung, 2001, p. 9). However, the passionate and provocative author Ben Okri cautions, "Accidental perceptions can sometimes be profound", but it is always best to make this "into a leavening agent, to extend its radiance and influence throughout the texture of the work" (Okri, 1998, p. 20).

Accidental perceptions, if that is what this is, challenge what Hauke calls "the hegemony of a dominant rationality . . . characterised by its intolerance for ambiguity and by its single-minded, phallic assertion of the Truth" (2000, p. 141). Freshwater and Rolfe (2004, p. 96) see the dominant discourse of research in the caring professions as favouring positivistic "scientific" formulations and granting "authority" to those who conform. There is a long history of challenging the dominant discourse; Paracelsus (1493–1541), the forefather of chemical pharmacology, pioneering the use of chemicals in medicine, could only do this by pitting the authenticity of his own experience against the authority of tradition at that time (Clulee, 1980, p. 74). *Plus ça change, plus c'est la même chose.* Jung, too, offers an early critique of the dominant rationality of his day, challenging epistemological and ontological assumptions, and offering a chance to rethink. He advises the researcher that:

> he will learn next to nothing from experimental psychology. He would be better advised to put away his scholar's gown, bid farewell to his study and wander with human heart through the world. [Jung, 1953c, par. 409]

Emotional, the subject and the post-modern self

"Love and friendship in their various forms—are at the centre of most of our stories" (Hopcke, 1997, p. 49) and love and compassion are at the "heart" of many caring professions. The idea of "emotional intelligence", popularized by Goleman (1996), has been further explored by Damasio (2000), the Portuguese neuroscientist, who argues that emotion is central to the process of reasoning, when balanced with rationality (*ibid.*, p. 41). A case is made for including the heart—i.e., emotions—in nursing practice and training (Freshwater & Stickley, 2004), which I would extend to research: without heart, without passion and interest, we are unlikely to survive the vicissitudes of practitioner research (or of our practice). As Polanyi (1958, p. 300) observes, the personal participation in the search for knowledge occurs "within a flow of passion". The emotional charge must be consciously kept in mind, as it is only too easy to lose this value, because "thinking and feeling are so diametrically opposed that thinking almost automatically throws out feeling values and vice versa" (Jung, 1964a, p. 99). A point echoed by Freshwater and Stickley (2004, p. 96), who affirm that rational and emotional are both "essential to intellectual functioning and indeed to healthcare practices". Although emotional valence is not in itself enough to make the research "worthwhile" on a wider scale, that the work has a deep meaning to the researcher "increases the likelihood that it may have some meaning and value to others" (Coppin & Nelson, 2005, p. 127). However, to own our heart-speak is to "move from a monologic interpretation of the world of practice" (Freshwater & Rolfe, 2004, p. 104), and the acknowledgement of one's own individual difference "means becoming visible and being seen as separate from the others" (*ibid.*, p. 94).

Leaving the security of an established methodology, of the familiar and the known, feels risky, but Jung never shied away from risk. The postmodern stance challenges fixed ideas such as "reality" or "truth", promoting a plurality of viewpoints, and Jung, from a surprisingly postmodern viewpoint in 1929, concurs.

> I think it is best to abandon the notion that we are today in anything like a position to make statements about the nature of the psyche that are "true" or "correct". The best we can achieve is true expression. By that I mean an open avowal and detailed presentation of everything that is subjectively observed. [Jung 1961, pars 771–772]

As early as 1934, Jung acknowledged his own subjective viewpoint, identifying the "subjective premise as a psychic idiosyncrasy" (Jung, 1964c, par. 1025) seen as conditioned by the individual, by the family, by the nation, race, culture, climates, localities, and history, thus contextualizing his work and his research. More recently, Hauke claims that one important aspect of the postmodern condition is a recognition that "the individual and the subjective is a valid position from which to know the general and apparently 'objective' " (Hauke, 2000, p. 85).

As Avis and Freshwater (2006, p. 221) point out, subjectivity needs to be acknowledged: "it is having a theory in mind that makes particular features of experience apparent". Jung went on to argue that by owning our personal prejudices we are actually contributing towards an objective psychology (Jung, 1977, par. 275). Viewing the human psyche as, "the most challenging field of scientific enquiry", Jung also suggests that we be modest "and grant validity to a number of apparently contradictory opinions" (Jung, 2001, p. 58).

The practice of psychotherapy is based on intersubjectivity; the therapist and the client are both "in" the work and both are influenced and changed by it. There is no distanced impartial objectivity, yet much psychotherapeutic research is still conducted along the lines of classical science in the form of RCTs, as if independent from any subjective influence, in a particularly inhuman and mechanistic way. McLeod, when writing about qualitative research in counselling and psychotherapy, states that "not just *any* methodology is appropriate" and circumambulates his own epistemological beliefs when he writes:

> the process of knowing involves employing a practical method, that is derived from an epistemology [theory of knowledge] which is in turn grounded in an ontology [set of assumptions about the nature of life]. [McLeod, 2001, p. 55]

He then identifies phenomenology and hermeneutics as the two epistemologies, within the tradition of Western social science, that have informed research practice. The fusion of phenomenology and hermeneutics, that McLeod sees at the heart of Heidegger's work (*ibid.*, p. 62), integrating the two approaches as complementary aspects of knowing about human existence (*ibid.*, p. 59), can also be seen in the work of Jung. John Beebe (2004, p. 179) roots Jung's hermeneutics in the pragmatism of William James and suggests that this predates Heidegger, Gadamer, and Ricoeur. Jung describes the essential character of hermeneutics as a "constructive process of interpretation" (Jung, 1953b, par. 131) resulting in a complex picture of possibilities (Jung, 1953d, par. 495). These cannot be proved, but their validity is seen in their intense value for life. Jung also states categorically, that he is "an empiricist and adhere(s) as such to the phenomenological standpoint" (Jung, 1958a, par. 2). He acknowledged the work of Fechner and Wundt who initiated a "drastic revolution in methodology" in order to "make clear to the scientific world that psychology was a field of experience and not a philosophical theory" (Jung, 1959, par. 111). However, in his view, theory still played too great a role. "Learn your theories as well as you can, but put them aside when you touch the miracle of the living soul" (Jung, 2001, p. 120).

On a personal note, I find that when theory emerges through practice or research, the theory–practice gap is breached and objective or external knowledge morphs into internal or subjective understanding.

The objectivity of scientific research is no longer sacrosanct and it is recognized that a totally objective position is impossible to achieve. Braud and Anderson (1998, p. 20) identify "expanded" methods of research in social sciences that highlight or emphasize the influence of the researcher. The "unscientific" inclusion of the subjective has been countered by an emphasis on the role of critical reflexivity in research (Etherington, 2004; Lees, 2001, 2003) and in identifying, acknowledging, and valuing bias. Mantzoukas (2005, p. 292) cautions against attempts to exclude bias from reflective and reflexive studies, which he sees as both artificial and contradictory, weakening their usefulness. I doubt if the bias of a researcher can ever be fully negated, for this presupposes that we are completely aware of our bias; perhaps as Freshwater (2005, pp. 311–312) suggests, bias can never be fully known, and although what is conscious can be articulated it will always be only a partial view. This she regards as inevitable (*ibid.*, p. 311), words foreshadowed by Jung, writing in 1933:

> Even when I deal with empirical data, I am necessarily speaking about myself. But it is only by accepting this as inevitable that I can serve the cause of man's knowledge of man. [Jung 1933, p. 120]

A Jungian approach to practitioner research goes beyond conscious bias, adding an extra dimension in terms of awareness of the unconscious processes. This is viewed not only as part of the bias to be acknowledged and explored through critical reflection, but also as a huge potential. Alongside the suggestion that bias can never be wholly known (personal unconscious) is the idea that bias can never be wholly expressed due to the unconscious dynamics of the specific context (cultural and collective unconscious). Within the National Health Service, where I work, the twin behemoths of "clinical governance" and "targets" cast unseen ties around the practice of many healthcare professionals.

Between worlds

It is to the unconscious that I now turn. One of Jung's fundamental beliefs is in the existence of an "unconscious", perhaps partly to counteract the popular attitude of the time. In 1927 he wrote, "There are, as we know, certain views which would restrict everything psychic to consciousness, as being identical with it. I do not believe this is sufficient" (Jung, 1960, par. 295).

Jung made a clear distinction between the personal unconscious, which contains lost memories, painful ideas that are repressed, sense-perceptions not strong enough to reach consciousness, and finally, contents that are not yet ripe for consciousness (Jung, 1953a, par. 103), and the collective unconscious: a structural layer of the human psyche containing inherited elements, distinct from the personal unconscious. The collective unconscious contains the whole spiritual heritage of mankind's evolution, born anew in the brain structure of every individual (Jung, 1960, par. 342). Of course, the contents of the collective unconscious require the involvement of the personal unconscious in order to manifest, but the concept of the collective unconscious, alongside collective consciousness (or *Zeitgeist*), helps therapy and research move beyond personal experience to a wider perspective.

One example of the collective unconscious, made manifest through the personal unconscious, happened in the second cohort of my dream research when a young woman brought a dream of two birds falling into flames. Nicole's dream had many layers: it was indeed about her immediate circumstances, but the day that she dreamt this was 11 September, though she was not consciously aware of the date until our exploration of the dream. My own therapist also reported a time when "Osama Bin Laden" figures were appearing regularly in the dreams of her clients. I note, too, dreams of suffocation, gasping for air, which coincide with worldwide concern over greenhouse gases and carbon emissions. We are suffocating our world. The dreams, of course, also have a strong personal layer, which, in my research into dream-work in short-term therapy, usually becomes the focus.

The title of this chapter came from my unconscious in a dream the night I was invited to contribute. As my research concerns the value of dreams in counselling and psychotherapy, if I am to remain congruent to my beliefs, I cannot ignore my own dreams. For Jung, "dreams are the direct expression of unconscious psychic activity" (Jung, 2001, p. 2). He questions Freud's causalistic approach, which focuses on "why?" and asks "what for?", recognizing that the dream is not an isolated psychic event cut off from everyday life. "And so the whirl owl flies" was an expression, in my dream, of something not yet consciously recognized or conceptually formulated, but none the less real to me, and left me wondering "what for?"

The unconscious psyche as a source of knowledge is not an illusion, as our Western rationalism might suppose. All knowledge does not come from without and Jung points to investigations of animal instincts to support his claims. Jung was influenced in his conceptualizing of the unconscious by three factors: his personality, his interest in physic phenomena, and by Nietzsche (Hauke, 2006, p. 59). He also conducted experiments in 1909, using word association tests, to establish "scientifically" the concept of the unconscious and its processes, in which, according to Papadopoulos (2006, p. 28), he "almost accidentally stumbled across" the phenomena of "shared unconscious structures" that led to his formulation of the concept of the collective unconscious. Jung saw the ego as the centre of consciousness, but the unconscious was a creative force that influenced conscious thinking and was often "truer and wiser" (Hauke, 2006, p. 66).

At this point my ego consciousness was still trying to make sense of what I wanted to say and I was struggling against many opposing forces, both internal and external. The next morning . . .

. . . waking early to the half-shadows that precede dawn, I saw close by the ghostly shape of a young barn owl battered by the high winds, struggling. Transfixed, I watched, knowing that somehow my presence was necessary to the moment. In a liminal space, where time had no dominion, I stood at a threshold, feeling the tension of separation and connection. The excitement of the unknown, of great potential, was beating like strong wings, in my heart. I was the owl.

Deeply moved, I recognized at once the significance to myself, to my research and my attempt to communicate my ideas, a significance that is hard to put into words. This is the raw data, this is my thought, my belief, my passion. *This is Jungian research methodology.*

I invite you, the reader, to close your eyes and dwell upon the image, challenge it, dispute its significance, "read" it your way, and then together we can explore it further.

Jung did not use the word "ontology" and Shamdasani, writing about the scientific status of psychology, states, "given the sacramental significance of the word 'science', it may be fruitful to speak more generally of ontology-making practices" (Shamdasani, 2006, p. 2).

Embedded throughout Jung's writing are ontological assumptions that contribute to his conception of the nature of reality. One such idea is that of the *unus mundus*, or unitary world, "towards which the psychologist and the atomic physicist are converging along separate paths" (Jung, 1964b, par. 852). The *unus mundus* is concerned with an interconnectedness between each stratum of existence that is "essentially at odds with causal explanation" (Samuels, Shorter, & Plaut, 1986, p. 157). This led to his development of the idea of synchronicity as an acausal connecting principle referring to events connected in a meaningful but not causal way. Holding synchronicity in mind can protect the therapist from "feeling that everything is due to fate, or falling back on purely causal explanations" (*ibid.*, p. 147), which can undermine the client's experiences, or therapist's experiences.

Papadopoulos writes that:

> once this "meaningful connection" is established then a certain pathway is created, a new context is construed as an active process, a living experience begins which could lead gradually to the emergence of a new awareness. [2006, p. 37]

This also highlights an important facet of Jung's epistemology that it is "knowledge in the making" (*ibid.*, p. 31). His explicitly stated teleological attitude (Jung, 1956, par. 332) suggests that knowledge is related to a future purpose and goal rather than simple explanations in terms of causalities.

I remember, early in my career, commenting to my supervisor about the fact that so many clients were presenting with issues that paralleled mine. I was concerned about the effect I was having. It was gently pointed out that I was not that powerful. I was not "causing" these events, but was perhaps part of a wider pattern of relationships, which would help me work with my clients towards their goal. I was part of the *unus mundus*.

Using a broken shell during counselling, the work resulted in the following poem: creativity and imagination helped meaning-making for therapist, client, and supervisor.

> imperfect beauty, if you had not
> been broken, how could I have seen
> the soft rose that gently unfolds
> inside your hard defensive shell,
> *or know. . . that I am beautiful too?*

(Mishka)

More recently, in my research, a client presented me with a dream about a baby born in Poland, the day after I had watched an animated short film, *Harvie Krumpet* (Elliot, 2004), that also begins with the birth of a baby in Poland. My heart "flipped" as she spoke, which confirmed to me the relevance of the "coincidence". Harvie's struggles as an immigrant helped inform my understanding of the client and the synchronous event aided our understanding of the dream and (later) of my own struggles as an "immigrant" into the world of research.

The sight of the owl struggling when I was struggling with the title of this chapter, with my practice in the current climate of the NHS, and with my research was, to me, also an example of this connection. In trying to understand my reaction to this vision, the "strong wings beating in my heart", I found comfort in Jung's words: "The very enormity of the experience gives it its value and its shattering impact. Sublime, it is pregnant with meaning" (Jung, 1966, par. 141).

Jung's writing is full of contradictions and paradox, which at times both annoys and fascinates me, and yet defends against hagiography. Papadopoulos (2006, p. 46) identifies two conflicting epistemologies in the writings of Jung, which he calls "Socratic ignorance" and "Gnostic epistemology" or "positivist stance" (*ibid.*, p. 43). Dehing (1990, p. 393) sees Jung as an empiricist who "every now and then turns into to prophet", and his search for proof to validate his personal quest for meaning as occasionally "interfering with his hermeneutical methods" (*ibid.*, p. 391). Papadopoulos places this in the clinical context and contrasts Jung's Socratic openness with his Gnosticism, which resulted in him being, at times, explicitly prescriptive in terms of specific actions and directions (2006, pp. 44, 47). I acknowledge that this contradiction is present in my own writing: I am open to the new "knowledge" that emerges from experiencing the *unus mundus* but state, rather dogmatically, "this *is* Jungian research methodology". However, like Dehing, I "prefer the perplexed Jung to the one who enunciates and proves" (Dehing 1990, p. 393).

I experienced the owl not as Athene's owl of wisdom, but as *my* owl: the ghostly owl of moonlight, of intuitive knowledge rather than direct perception. The intuitive aspect of knowledge is important, but intuition is not enough. Critical reflection is necessary to "explicate the tacit knowledge that informs our thinking and decisions when we act on the basis of gut instinct or intuition" (Avis & Freshwater, 2006, p. 223). This critical reflection is heralded by Jung, who recognizes the need for both intuition and intellect, united in a creative act (Jung, 1971b, par. 541). I also note Jung's caveat "I must prevent my critical powers from destroying my creativeness" (Jung, 2001, p. 120).

Jung writes of two kinds of thinking: directed or logical thinking, linked to language and directed to the outside world, and fantasy thinking. "Directed thinking or, as we might also call it, *thinking in words*, is manifestly an instrument of culture" (Jung, 1956, par. 17), which he values as having produced "modern empiricism and technics". He extends William James' idea of nondirected thinking, which is seen as merely associative, to include thinking that leads us away from reality into fantasy, where "thinking in verbal form ceases, image piles on image, feeling on feeling" (*ibid.*, par. 19). This kind of thinking he equates with the imaginative play of children and the kind of thinking exhibited in dreams. Non-directed or fantasy thinking is subjectively motivated, not altogether by conscious motives but also by unconscious ones.

Whereas directed thinking is an altogether conscious phenomenon, the same cannot be said of fantasy thinking. Much of it belongs to the conscious sphere, but at least as much goes on in the half-shadow, or entirely in the unconscious (*ibid.*, par. 39).

I simply note here that, although the concept of the unconscious can be a difficult one to grasp (or "prove'), so too is the concept of the wind. The wind itself cannot be seen or touched and can only be measured by its effect on other things, e.g., an anemometer or *a young barn owl* seen in the *half-shadows* struggling to cross a field . I am also aware that it was the struggle against this invisible force that held the owl in my view for so long, allowing a deeper engagement. "It is only with awareness that a new, useful and illuminating order can emerge" (Boyd, 2007, p. 63). So, I reflect now upon my own "struggles" in my therapeutic work and in my research, which at times drain my energy and frustrate me, yet, paradoxically, allow a deeper exploration and involvement, with the accompanying possibility of new understandings.

The emphasis, in science, on conscious, logical thinking to the detriment of fantasy thinking has, Jung believes, led to an imperviousness to new ideas, "we have become rich in knowledge and poor in wisdom" (Jung, 1956, par. 23), an idea explored, through the concepts of bios and zoë, in relation to research by Boyd (2006, pp. 72–73). However, both call for an inclusive approach, and Jung cautions that fantasy thinking alone "is bound to produce an overwhelmingly subjective and distorted picture of the world" (Jung, 1956, par. 37). Understanding, for Jung, is connected to the individual and unique, and is opposed to knowledge, which is concerned with the general. For the scientist, the individual is a unit, stripped of individuality, but it is those individual factors that interest the psychotherapist and which can provide understanding (Jung, 1964b, par. 497). Shamdasani (2003, p. 97) suggests that this has strong echoes of Dilthey. Jung recognizes the danger of over-emphasizing the subjective element creating social isolation and calls for a balance between understanding and knowledge, but, as Shamdasani points out, how this is to be achieved is not made clear (*ibid.*, p. 98).

Creating isolation

The view from my window, my world, is, as Noel Coward (1930, p. 28) once said of Norfolk, "very flat": a vast expanse of space, land, and sky, unfamiliar perhaps to those of you who live in urban areas.

Many of us fear an empty space, thinking of it as a vacuum, or a negative force, yet space offers us potential, free from the strictures imposed on us by others (Boyd, 2007, p. 63).

Perhaps because of this space, my eye was drawn immediately to the owl, just as your eye may be drawn more to the words of Jung rather than my words, "the flatlands, either side of great mountains?" (Westwood, 2005, p. 174). And yet, I recognize that *my presence is necessary to the moment*, just as yours is to this text. My involvement in research is as necessary as my involvement in my practice. There are flatlands and peaks, the seemingly ordinary and the unique in everything, but I value both, in their own right and in dialogue with each other, in the internal landscape of thought and the external landscape of research and of written text. Jung's approach to psychotherapy, like his approach to research, is closely linked to everyday life. "We have no Laboratory equipped with elaborate apparatus. Our laboratory is the world. Our tests are conceived with the actual day-to-day happenings of human life" (Jung, 1954a, par. 171).

These are the flatlands of practitioner research, but above them, the vast expanse of sky.

The space before me was not just a frame or background, but a dynamic experience. I became *transfixed*. Bachelard's phenomenological approach claimed that space was understood through the body, not just through vision and rationality, suggesting that "by leaving the space of one's usual sensibilities, one enters into communication with a space that is physically innovating. For we do not change place, we change our Nature" (1964, p. 206).

Together with Merleau-Ponty, Bachelard challenged, as Jung had done, the Cartesian split of mind and body, which allows us to objectively observe the world from a "safe" distance (Boyd, 2003).

According to Jung, the tension of the opposites, of mind and body, of inner and outer, can produce a new uniting function that transcends the opposites themselves, producing a new and vital agent in the symbol (Jung, 1971a, par. 479). One of the difficulties of any discourse is the limitation of language, and much of our thinking is based in the world of space, time, and causality. Peat writes of Bohm's "Explicate Order" and his proposition that a radically different "Implicate Order" exists.

Within this order the duality of matter and mind obtain their resolution. What appear as distinct objects well separated in space and
time are, within the Implicate Order, enfolded each with the other.
What at one level appears an object at another becomes a process.
[Peat, 1995, p. 4]

Peat continues, citing Jung as making the division between the
personal unconscious attached to "an individual brain and body"
and the collective unconscious, "shared by all people in the form of
symbols" (*ibid.*). The relevance here is that . . . within the Implicate
Order it is not objects, but processes that are the focus, and process,
rather than objective outcome, is the focus of my research'.

What we are dealing with is an "imaginal world, a 'mundus
imaginalis' that has its own process and can also transform" Field
(1991, p. 97). *I was the owl.* Field, and Schwartz-Salant (1998), are
writing about the therapeutic encounter, but the idea of an imaginal world, an alternative dimension of knowing and being, can be
useful here in terms of our consideration of what is happening
between the viewer and the owl, and what I believe happens
between the researcher and the researched in my research into
dream-work. The idea of the *mundus imaginalis* was a concept
developed by the French philosopher Corbin, who, drawing on his
study of the writings of Persian mystics, suggests that between the
"sensible" world of phenomenon and the "supersensible" world of
the Soul is an intermediary world of image, a *mundus imaginalis*.
"This world requires its own faculty of perception, namely imaginative power" (Corbin, 1972, p. 7). Samuels (1989, p. 163), using
Corbin's ideas to explore the relationship between the analyst and
the patient, equates experiences of this imaginal world with
"visions". The owl was my "vision", momentary, fleeting, and
unexpected; it was out of my control, "I" was not responsible, yet I
felt a sense of connection both "beautiful and unbearable" (*ibid.*,
p. 166). Moments such as this have occurred in my therapeutic
work, and my research.

Working with a profoundly deaf client, I had a dream of her
inside a bottle floating on an expanse of water, which I felt was not
my dream but Elaine's. When I tentatively shared this, as an image,
she exclaimed, "That's me in there." It is hard to explain to someone who has not experienced this, but we were both moved in a

way that I had not anticipated and I felt a strong connection, both tense and exciting. It was fleeting, but powerful none the less. The experience "moved" us in more ways than one, because the insights gained changed the direction of the therapy. Later Elaine explained, "I looked at it in two ways, at the time I was drinking and that was me in there, also because of my life at the time I was still stuck in there. It was about me being trapped, trapped in the bottle." (Boyd, 2007, p. 97) The Jungian understanding, as exemplified by Schwartz-Salant (1988) and Field (1991), would see the dream image as arising out of the *mundus imaginalis*, the space between two people, where unconscious communication is carried out.

> The meeting of two people is like mixing two different chemical substances: if there is any combination at all, both are transformed You can exert no influence if you are not susceptible to influence. [Jung, 1964b, par. 163]

In the words of Bion, "learning about" needs to yield to "becoming" (Tresan, 1995, p. 432). This process of becoming requires change or transformation and, although not about "cure", one of the aims of psychotherapy is to bring about change. Transformation is a multi-dimensional concept, and my work and my research are concerned with change, both personal and professional. The goal of transformation is not the same as achievement; it is an ongoing interactive process, not an end product. Ultimately, transformations are seen as part of a process of development towards wholeness, through an integration of the unconscious and the conscious. Jung calls this process individuation. Transformation does not exclude, it incorporates. "A transformed personality feels both new and old, enlarged and yet deeply familiar" (Stein, 1995, p. 46).

Mezirow's theory of transformative learning is based upon critical reflection and uses the work of Habermas and his three distinctive kinds of knowledge: technical, practical, and emancipatory. Critical reflection upon the first two leads to greater self-knowledge, growth, and freedom. This critical reflexivity is seen as the key (Mezirow, 1991, p. 41) and transformative or emancipatory learning occurs through reflection and "the accretion of new layers of meaning as we seek to be understood and to understand others in dialogue" (*ibid.*, p. 215). Cranton and Roy, drawing on the work of Boyd (1991), link transformation with the Jungian concept of individuation challenging the cognitive, rational approaches to include imagination and a soulful perspective, what West (2004) would call "soul attending".

When we participate consciously and imaginatively, we develop a deepened sense of self, an expansion of consciousness and an engendering of soul (Cranton & Roy, 2003, pp. 90–92).

Transformation is, I believe, inevitable: the client and therapist are both changed by the work together, as are researcher and researched, each being a catalyst for change in the other. You, the reader, will be changed by your dialogue with this text, just as I am changing now, even as I write. Transformative learning, however, relies upon consciously participating in the journey of individuation. The process of "transformation implies a consciousness-raising that enhances thinking processes" (Wade, 1998, p. 714). Soul and spirit do not carry as much ontological weight as the ego but, by considering these aspects, which compensate for attitudes of Western culture, ego consciousness becomes more supple. The idea of transformation presupposes an ego that is strong enough to contain and to be transformed, but for this to happen it must not be rigid (Mathers, 2006).

I stood at a threshold, feeling apart from the owl, yet also a part, *in a liminal space* and *feeling the tension of separation and connection*; a place that is perhaps familiar to the practitioner–researcher, who may feel the tension inherent in dual roles. The researcher, too, stands at the threshold. For some, to cross that threshold is to accept the rules: at many sacred sites, for example, the visitor is requested to take off her shoes, or cover her head. Does the entrance to research require compliance to other rules? Will there be a welcome for someone who does not accept those rules, who will not take off her shoes? Although Jung was struggling to establish the credibility of his psychology within the scientific milieu of the day, he did not conform to the "rules" and was quite scathing in his criticisms.

> For a certain type of intellectual mediocrity characterised by enlightened rationalism, a scientific theory that simplifies matters is a very good means of defence because of the tremendous faith modern man has in anything that bears the label "scientific". [Jung, 1958b, par. 81]

He classified himself as an empiricist who adheres to the phenomenological standpoint, but saw imagination and intuition as vital to our understanding, valued by poets and artists, but equally valuable in the "higher grades of science, where they play an increasingly important role supplementing rational intellect" (Jung, 1964a, p. 92). As seen in the discussion of the *mundus imaginalis,* imagination can be a linking factor between therapist and client and between the researcher and the researched. I would also suggest that the use of the imagination has direct application to data analysis and, as a result, new vistas on the data are opened up (Boyd, 2005, p. 197) that can facilitate the presentation of data in a more readily accessible manner, rather than it petrifying into intellectual theory.

From the uncertain to the not-known . . .

I have tried to explain how Jungian theory impacts on my own research and contributes to my knowledge and practice development. To help clarify my thoughts, my academic supervisor simply asked what drew me to Jung. I recorded my response.

> Essentially his phenomenological approach, with a respect for the creative and the spiritual/numinous aspects of experience. His work with the unconscious is positive but retains a healthy regard for the ego. His psychology aims to establish a dialogue between, and integrate [with], the conscious self (ego) and the larger personal Self of the unconscious. Imagination and creativity are vital. He acknowledges subjectivity and contextual influences, valuing critical reflection and transparency. The extension of his ideas to include that of the collective unconscious is problematic and challenging yet it moves my soul! [In addition I note that he is] human and fallible, contradictory and not systematic in his writings: his work does not form a coherent whole. [diary entry, 25 May 2005]

Jung's tolerance of uncertainty and paradox gives me the confidence to tentatively share my thoughts. Above all, I find his teleological approach more satisfying than a causal–reductive approach that seems to focus on the past. As a result, I see my research as intensely personal–individual *and* also collaborative–collective, emergent, fresh, *and* rooted in past research traditions, both liberating *and* restricted by a greater responsibility. It is unique *and* ordinary, foolish *and* wise, temporary *and* lasting in its transformatory effect (Boyd, 2006, p. 73).

I believe my Jungian approach adds value to my work, but the question remains: does it have a value for the practice of others? My understanding of Jungian theory has informed my research but it cannot provide a meta-narrative. My work has no more *intrinsic* worth (and no less) than other research, including RCTs, but, as Rolfe points out, it is the decision taken by those in authority (in my case the NHS) to authorize its value, to validate or denigrate my efforts in their hierarchy of evidence (Rolfe, 2005, pp. 154–155). Like Jung, I do not profess a methodology shaped to academic taste, or seek explanations that have no bearing on life. I seek a practical method, which helps us to explain things in a way that is justified by the outcome for the client (Jung, 2001, p. 192).

> He who seeks finds, and he who *always* seeks, always finds. Because of this I am happy that I see conclusiveness nowhere, but much rather a dark expanse, full of mysteries and adventure. [Jung, 1933, p. 106]

. . . and so the whirl owl flies.

Note

1. Although Jung is reputed to have said "I do not want anybody to be a Jungian. I want people, above all, to be themselves" (van der Post, 1976), I use the term Jungian because, in being myself, I am influenced by the way Jung thought, practised, and taught, as well as by the thoughts and writings of those Samuels (1985) has named "Post-Jungians".

References

Avis, M., & Freshwater, D. (2006). Evidence for practice, epistemology, and critical reflection. *Nursing Philosophy*, 7: 216–224.

Bachelard, G. (1964). *The Poetics of Space*. Boston, MA: Beacon.

Beebe, J. (2004). Can there be a science of the symbolic? *Journal of Analytical Psychology*, 49: 177–191.

Boyd, J. (2003). Pregnant: the sculpture of Anish Kapoor from a Jungian perspective. Cambridge: *Cambridge Jungian Circle*.

Boyd, J. (2005). Where two worlds meet: an exploration of the client's experience of dream-work in time limited therapy. *Psychodynamic Practice*, 11: 189–204.

Boyd, J. (2006). Disillusionment, dreams and indestructible life: choosing the right research methodology. *Journal of Critical Psychology, Counselling and Psychotherapy*, 6: 70–75.

Boyd, J. (2007). Counselling with a profoundly deaf client and the impact of a therapist's dream: a case study. *Counselling and Psychotherapy Research*, 7: 92–99.

Boyd, R. (1991). *Personal Transformations in Small Groups*. London: Routledge and Kegan Paul.

Braud, W., & Anderson, R. (1998). *Transpersonal Research Methods for the Social Sciences: Honoring Human Experience*. Thousand Oaks, CA: Sage.

Clulee, N. (1980). Paracelsus. *Macmillan Encyclopaedia*. London: Macmillan.

Coppin, J., & Nelson, E. (2005). *The Art of Inquiry: A Depth Psychological Perspective*. Putnam, Spring.

Corbin, H. (1972). *Mundus Imaginalis: Or the Imaginary and the Imaginal*. Woodstock, Spring.

Coward, N. (1930). *Private Lives*. Kila: Kessinger.

Cranton, P., & Roy, M. (2003). When the bottom falls out of the bucket: toward a holistic perspective on transformative learning. *Journal of Transformative Education*, 1: 86–97.

Damasio, A. R. (2000). *The Feeling of What Happens*. London: Vintage.

Dehing, J. (1990). Jung and knowledge: from gnosis to praxis. *Journal of Analytical Psychology*, 35: 377–396.

Elliot, A. (2004). *Harvie Krumpet*. Melodramatic Pictures in association with Australian Film Commission.

Etherington, K. (2004). Heuristic research as a vehicle for personal and professional development. *Counselling and Psychotherapy Research*, 4(2): 49–63.

Field, N. (1991). Projective identification: mechanism or mystery? *Journal of Analytical Psychology*, 36: 93–109.

Freshwater, D. (2005). Writing, rigour and reflexivity in nursing research. *Journal of Research in Nursing*, 10: 311–315.

Freshwater, D., & Rolfe, G. (2004). *Deconstructing Evidence-based Practice*. London: Routledge.

Freshwater, D., & Stickley, T. (2004). The heart of the art: emotional intelligence in nurse education. *Nursing Inquiry, 11*: 91–98.

Goleman, D. (1996). *Emotional Intelligence: Why It Can Matter More than IQ*. London: Bloomsbury.

Hauke, C. (2000). *Jung and the Postmodern: The Interpretation of Realities*. London: Routledge.

Hauke, C. (2006). The unconscious: personal and collective. In: R. K. Papadopoulos (Ed.), *The Handbook of Jungian Psychology* (pp. 64–73). London: Routledge.

Hopcke, R. H. (1997). *There Are No Accidents: Synchronicity and the Stories of our Lives*. London: Macmillan.

Jung, C. G. (1933). On psychology. *Neuer Schweizer Rundschau, 2*, p. 106.

Jung, C. G. (1953a)[1916]. The personal and the collective (or trans-personal) unconscious. *C.W., 7, Two Essays on Analytical Psychology*, R. F. C. Hull (Trans.) (pp. 63–78). London: Routledge & Kegan Paul.

Jung, C. G. (1953b)[1916]. The synthetic or constructive method. *C.W., 7, Two Essays on Analytical Psychology*, R. F. C. Hull (Trans.) (pp. 79–87). London: Routledge & Kegan Paul.

Jung, C. G. (1953c)[1916]. New paths in psychology. *C.W., 7, Two Essays on Analytical Psychology*, R. F. C. Hull (Trans.) (pp. 243–262). London: Routledge & Kegan Paul.

Jung, C. G. (1953d)[1916]. The structure of the unconscious. *C.W., 7, Two Essays on Analytical Psychology*, R. F. C. Hull (Trans.) (pp. 263–294). London: Routledge & Kegan Paul.

Jung, C. G. (1954a)[1926]. Analytical psychology and education. *C.W., 17, The Development of Personality*, R. F. C. Hull (Trans.) (pp. 65–107). London: Routledge & Kegan Paul.

Jung, C. G. (1954)[1929]. Problems of psychotherapy. *C.W., 16, The Practice of Psychotherapy*, R. F. C. Hull (Trans.) (pp. 53–75). London: Routledge & Kegan Paul.

Jung, C. G. (1956)[1924]. Two kinds of thinking. *C.W., 5, Symbols of Transformation*, R. F. C. Hull (Trans.) (pp. 7–33). London: Routledge & Kegan Paul.

Jung, C. G. (1958a)[1938]. The autonomy of the unconscious. *C.W., 11, Psychology and Religion: West and East*, R. F. C. Hull (Trans.) (pp. 5–33). London: Routledge & Kegan Paul.

Jung, C. G. (1958b)[1938]. Dogma and natural symbols. *C.W., 11, Psychology and Religion: West and East*, R. F. C. Hull (Trans.) (pp. 34–63). London: Routledge & Kegan Paul.

Jung, C. G. (1959)[1936]. Concerning the archetype with special reference to the anima concept. *C.W., 9(i), Aion,* R. F. C. Hull (Trans.) (pp. 54–72). London: Routledge & Kegan Paul.

Jung, C. G. (1960)[1928]. The structure of the psyche. *C.W., 8, The Structure and Dynamics of the Psyche,* R. F. C. Hull (Trans.) (pp. 139–158). London: Routledge & Kegan Paul.

Jung, C. G. (1961)[1929]. Freud and Jung: Contrasts. *C.W., 4, Freud and Psychoanalysis,* R. F. C. Hull (Trans.) (pp. 333–340). London: Routledge & Kegan Paul.

Jung, C. G. (1964a). *A Man and his Symbols.* London: Aldus.

Jung, C. G. (1964b)[1957]. The undiscovered self (present and future). *C.W., 10, Civilisation in Transition,* R. F. C. Hull (Trans.) (pp. 247–305). London: Routledge & Kegan Paul.

Jung, C. G. (1964c)[1934]. A rejoinder to Dr. Bally. *C.W., 10, Civilisation in Transition,* R. F. C. Hull (Trans.) (pp. 535–544). London: Routledge & Kegan Paul.

Jung, C. G. (1966)[1930]. Psychology and literature. *C.W., 15, The Spirit in Man, Art and Literature,* R. F. C. Hull (Trans.) (pp. 84–105). London: Routledge & Kegan Paul.

Jung, C. G. (1968). *The Collected Works: 16.* London: Routledge & Kegan Paul.

Jung, C. G. (1971a)[1921]. The type problem in psychopathology. *C.W., 6, Psychological Types,* R. F. C. Hull (Trans.) (pp. 272–288). London: Routledge & Kegan Paul.

Jung, C. G. (1971b)[1921]. The type problem in modern philosophy. *C.W., 6, Psychological Types,* R. F. C. Hull (Trans.) (pp. 300–321). London: Routledge & Kegan Paul.

Jung, C. G. (1977)[1936]. The Tavistock Lectures. Lecture IV (Discussion). *C.W., 18,* R. F. C. Hull (Trans.) (pp. 124–134). London: Routledge & Kegan Paul.

Jung, C. G. (2001)[1933]. *Modern Man in Search of a Soul.* London: Routledge.

Lees, J. (2001). Reflexive action research: developing knowledge through practice. *Counselling and Psychotherapy Research, 1*(2): 132–138.

Lees, J. (2003). Developing therapist self-understanding through research. *Counselling and Psychotherapy Research, 3*(2): 147–153.

Mantzoukas, S. (2005). The inclusion of bias in reflective and reflexive research: a necessary prerequisite for securing validity. *Journal of Research in Nursing, 10*: 279–295.

Mathers, D. (2006). The purpose of meaning and the meaning of purpose. *Independent Group of Analytical Psychology Seminars.* London.

McLeod, J. (2001). *Qualitative Research in Counselling and Psychotherapy.* London: Sage.

Mezirow, J. (1991). *Transformative Dimensions of Adult Learning.* San Francisco, CA: Jossey Bass.

Okri, B. (1998). *A Way of Being Free.* London: Phoenix House.

Papadopoulos, R. K. (2006). Jung's epistemology and methodology. In: R. K. Papadopoulos (Ed.), *The Handbook of Jungian Psychology* (pp. 7–53). London: Routledge.

Peat, F. D. (1995). Alchemical transformation: consciousness and matter, form and information. A talk given in Padova October 1995 to the Club of Budapest. Retrieved 28 May, 2008, from http://www.fdavidpeat.com/ideas/ideas.htm.

Polanyi, M. (1958). *Personal Knowledge: Towards a Post Critical Philosophy.* London: Routledge.

Rolfe, G. (2005). Where is John Paley when you need him? *Nursing Philosophy, 6:* 153–155.

Samuels, A. (1985). *Jung and the Post-Jungians.* London: Routledge.

Samuels, A. (1989). *The Plural Psyche: Personality, Morality and the Father.* London: Routledge.

Samuels, A., Shorter, B., & Plaut, F. (1986). *A Critical Dictionary of Jungian Analysis.* London: Routledge.

Schwartz-Salant, N. (1988). Archetypal foundations of projective identification. *Journal of Analytical Psychology, 33:* 1–36.

Schwartz-Salant, N. (1998). *The Mystery of Human Relationship: Alchemy and the Transformation of the Self.* London: Routledge.

Shamdasani, S. (2003). *Jung and the Making of Modern Psychology: The Dream of Science.* Cambridge: Cambridge University Press.

Shamdasani, S. (2006). Psychologies as ontology-making practices. In: A. Casement & D. Tacey (Eds.), *The Idea of the Numinous: Contemporary Jungian and Psychoanalytic Perspectives* (pp. 1–19). London: Routledge.

Stein, M. (1995). *Jungian Analysis* (2nd edn). Chicago, IL: Open Court.

Tresan, D. I. (1995). Training. In: M. Stein (Ed.), *Jungian Analysis* (pp. 419–436). Chicago, IL: Open Court.

van der Post, L. (1976). *Jung and the Story of Our Time.* London: Penguin.

Wade, G. (1998). A concept analysis of personal transformation. *Journal of Advanced Nursing, 28,* 713–719.

West, W. (2004). *Spiritual Issues in Therapy: Relating Experience to Practice.* Basingstoke: Palgrave Macmillan.

Westwood, T. (2005). Academics' dynamics: re-writing referencing. *Psychodynamic Practice, 11*: 165–176.

CHAPTER SIX

Exploring the meaning of hope and despair in the therapeutic relationship

Christine Crosbie

"To love and bear; to hope till hope creates
From its own wreck the thing it contemplates"

(Shelley, "Prometheus Unbound")

T he genesis of this research project lies in a critical incident (Moustakas, 1990, p. 17) that took place in December 2004. It came at a time when I was grappling with a research proposal on the inevitability of abuse in the therapeutic relationship—a topic which emerged from my anxiety about this possibility as a practising counsellor and was connected with my experience as a client in an intensive and lengthy period of psychoanalytic psychotherapy that had ended some ten years previously.

I read widely around the issue of therapist abuse. I found that other therapy "patients" had had similar experiences to mine, particularly in relation to feeling totally disempowered, which had felt abusive (House, 2003), and I discovered that there was a strong and developing critique of psychotherapy because of the sometimes abusive nature of the relationship (House, 2003; Masson, 1993).

Doing this reading took me down some dark internal paths. I found the discussion around therapy as either seduction or rape (Forrester, 1990) particularly difficult, as it awakened the suffocating fear and intense anxiety that I had often felt at being invaded and deconstructed during my own psychotherapy. It was a relationship in which I had felt completely exposed and utterly trapped, sucked into a dependency from which the only escape was, paradoxically, more exposure and further dependence until I had worked through the transference and the therapist would let me go.

Entering into this frame of mind again, my spirits sank very low. In this state of despair I realized that my confusion and disappointment about the process and outcomes of my own therapy was having a profound effect on my counselling practice. I could see no way out of the pit of abusiveness that seemed to me to lurk within the therapeutic relationship. I saw my own counselling practice as abusive, and myself as abuser. I could not see how I was to carry on as a counsellor in this state of mind.

Over the ensuing months, my anxiety lessened as my research focus shifted to the need for *hope* in the therapeutic relationship and I read widely on this subject. However, I found much of the literature to be contradictory. First, there is little consensus on a definition of the concept. For instance, Snyder (1995), from a cognitive–behavioural perspective, defines hope as "the overall perception that goals can be met" and consists in "an interaction of two factors: agency (goal directed energy) and pathways (planning to meet goals)", while Farran, Herth, and Popovich (1995) describe hope as having four processes: experiential, spiritual or transcendent, rational, and relational. In a similar, holistic vein, Lynch (1965, p. 31) sees hope as coming "close to being the very heart and center of a human being . . .", and, as such, perhaps indefinable.

Opinions also vary on the usefulness of hope as a therapeutic tool. Yalom, for instance, from the existential perspective, equates hope with the client's "high expectation of help before therapy" and suggests that this is "significantly correlated with positive therapy outcome" (Yalom, 1985, p. 6), while Bergin and Walsh (2005, p. 9) cite a range of literature which claims that "hope holds the potential to shackle clients to a fantasy about the way life should be or should have been . . .", and is, therefore, damaging.

However challenging, it was reading the literature on the character of hope that gave me the strength to believe that I could tackle the despair inherent in the notion of therapeutic abuse by revisiting and deconstructing my experience of psychoanalytic psychotherapy. This, then, became the purpose of my research.

The research methodology emerged gradually. The personal nature of the research ensured that my approach was necessarily subjective, and I used a method of critical self-reflexivity to gather data (see, for instance, Etherington, 2004; Freshwater & Rolfe, 2001; Maxey, 1999). This postmodern understanding of reality as personally and socially constructed led me to consider hermeneutics as a means of analysing the data.

The purpose of hermeneutical interpretation is to seek out hidden meanings in a text: to find what is not immediately obvious. This seemed particularly appropriate to my research, since I had felt that my "material", when brought to my psychoanalytic therapist, had been very thoroughly analysed, and yet I had still felt misunderstood. Perhaps I could find a new understanding through a different, more radical sort of interpretation "whose results challenge many of the prevailing notions of the therapy profession" (McLeod, 2001, p. 24).

Hermeneutic interpretation is characterized by a circle or spiral, and involves determining the meaning of the separate parts in the light of the text as a whole, with further exploration producing new meaning from the parts, which changes the meaning of the whole, and so on. This process is endless, changing as I change, but an ending can be made when "the meanings of the different themes make sensible patterns and enter into a coherent unity" (Kvale, 1996, p. 48).

Another advantage of hermeneutic analysis is that it can be seen as going beyond the contextual limitations of most other postmodern approaches, indicating the possibility of a transcendent reality that fits with my own understanding of the spiritual basis for human being (and also fits with Lynch's philosophical basis for research [Lynch, 1996, p. 146]). George Steiner, for instance, sees the act of hermeneutic engagement as having a moral aspect that presupposes the existence of the transcendent (1989, p. 8), and contends that we can only engage in this way with works of art or literature because of a belief that we will encounter the divine within them. Generating my "text" for analysis and working with it hermeneutically, taking a "wager on the meaning of meaning" (*ibid.*, p. 4), enabled me to see how the divine and transcendent can be embodied in the personal and specific.

I present my results in the form of a narrative analysis of my process. I wanted to tell a story that, by compelling the attention of the reader, would convey the "truth" of my experience and open up new meanings in the reader's own story. As described by Polkinghorne (1995, p. 16), the creation of a narrative plot has strong links with the hermeneutic process: "The emerging plot informs the researcher about which items from the gathered data should be included in the final storied account". This narrative can be evaluated by the reader in terms of its coherence, "resonance" (Braud, 1998, p. 225), and "its capacity to provide the reader with insight and understanding" (Polkinghorne, 1995, p. 20). To test the success of my account in these terms, I involved four counselling colleagues to participate in the research as readers and commentators on the emerging analysis.

*   *   *

My research journey

The fact of possessing imagination means that everything can be redreamed. Each reality can have its alternative possibilities. Human beings are blessed with the necessity of transformation. [Okri, 1997, p. 49]

I came to the truth through engaging imaginatively with the stories and texts of others. It was as though I could not turn my face to the possible trauma that I might find in reconnecting with my psychotherapeutic experience, and so I approached it obliquely, in disguise. From the first, my research journey was transfigured by story and myth, and then transformed by a more hopeful encounter with theory. Vande Kemp (1984, p. 31), writes, "Fantasy permits a 'seeing through' and beyond the problem, which is exactly what hope permits us to do", and Lynch also connects "the life of hope with the life of the imagination", seeing this combination as potentially therapeutic because it takes place in relation to another person: it is "an act of collaboration or mutuality. Hope not only imagines; it *imagines with*" (1965, p. 23).

When it came to analysing my research data, I found that it fell into three distinct phases, which could be seen as a parallel process to the beginning, middle, and closing stages of my therapy.

Phase 1: down to the roots of despair

There is a Canadian First Nations' story about the need to dwell in the roots of the tree in order to reach the free air of its branches. Another story, by the Japanese novelist Murakami (2003), tells of a man who, when fearful of being overwhelmed by powerful emotions of loss and anger, finds a dried-up well in a deserted garden near his house and climbs down into it. There, he has strange "illusions" and enters a kind of alternate reality. Eventually, he has an "illusion" of release and resolution and wakes to find the well filling with water.

These images helped to convince me that I must go down to the roots of my despair, the bottom of the well, in order to find sustenance and move upwards. As Thorne (1998, p. 105) says,

> Authentic hope always lies through and beyond despair and is seldom discovered without moving into the darkness and risking the loss of the few remaining reference points that seem to make some sense of the bewildering landscape.

The roots of my journey start with my birth into a family already struggling to come to terms with the multiple disabilities of my sister. Two years older than me, my sister was born with a brain malformation that left her with severe epilepsy, barely controlled by a heavy weight of drugs, global learning delay, and a strange growth pattern that resulted in short stature and curvature of the spine.

It has taken my lifetime to reach an understanding of the impact of my sister's disabilities on me. I now think that one effect of living with someone in such physical and psychical distress was the gradual extinguishing of hope within me—as an escape, perhaps, from the *"pain* of hope" (Farran, Herth, & Popovich, 1995).

For me, as a child, the strongest emotion was guilt. It seemed that all my "successes" were tarnished by the awareness of my sister's "failures". One interpretation is that I gradually came to believe that for me to "have" anything meant depriving her further. I developed a habit of self-deprivation that persisted into my adult life, affecting my approach to relationships and work. No action of mine could appease the guilt I felt. Despairing of ever making amends to my sister for the sin of being well when she was not, I sought to make amends to the world through one job after another. My trauma may have been rooted in the relationship with my sister, but it was compounded by my relationship with my mother and her difficulties in "containing" (as described by Winnicott) my distress as a baby while also responding to the often greater distress of my sister.

When I was aged thirty-seven, a crisis in a personal relationship sent me to seek therapy. Ignorant of the different therapeutic approaches, I was put in touch with a psychoanalytic psychotherapist who said that her orientation was along the lines of Freud, Klein, Winnicott, and Bowlby. With the exception of Freud, I had heard of none of these, but I was desperate and went ahead anyway. Therapy was to take place with me lying on a couch; I was to see her for three sessions a week with no proposed limit to the length of the therapeutic relationship. I was given no choice.

As I started therapy I had a profound belief that my therapist was going to make me well; that, as a result of the therapy, I would be "sorted out" and released into a life of plenty. I would have no more pain. I would be like the phoenix, a mythic bird who "characteristically arose live from the ashes of its own funeral pyre" (Babits, 2001, p. 342).

I recall vividly the first dream I related to my therapist (which, unusually, she did not interpret):

> It is dark and I am walking down a deserted road. I pass by a car, parked on the other side of the road. Looking at it closer, I realize that although it is identifiably my car, a red Polo VW, it has no number plates. I am puzzled about what it is doing there.

For a long time I have thought that this dream signified my lack of identity (or "self", or "ego-strength", depending on therapeutic approach) as I went into therapy. Now, as I start the research process, I think it might have indicated something else: that I am going into therapy blind; I am a car stalled by the wayside, and I do not know what I am doing or where I am going.

A book on the history of myth by Karen Armstrong (2005) comes along to give me a sense of direction, having great resonance with my therapeutic journey, and I write an account comparing the two. The first myths depict the "Sky God" as a remote creator, and the "Great Goddess" as "implacable, vengeful and demanding" (*ibid.*, p. 38), and "the cause of death and sorrow . . ." (*ibid.*, p. 49). I realize that at the start of therapy I saw my therapist as the Great Goddess—of whom I am envious and wish to destroy (or so she interprets). I have high hopes, but they are distant, like a Sky God. I begin to bond with Mother Goddess (my therapist) and am increasingly dependent upon her.

The realization of the connection between mythic journeys and my therapeutic journey produces a shift in perception. I have, it seems, connected with the archetype of the Great Mother, as articulated in Jungian theory. Gordon (1993) describes how archetypal processes can "enrich our inner world, enliven it, activate imagination and restore to us a sense of the wondrous, the awesome, the mysterious, the poetic" (p. 111). The danger with archetypes, however, is that we become over-identified with them. Now I wonder whether it was the therapist or myself who was the Great Mother. I am reminded of my therapist's comment, at an early stage in the therapy, that I was both the abused and the abuser in my relationships with my mother and sister, or "sometimes . . . the goddess, sometimes the witch" (*ibid.*, p. 120).

Now, in revisiting these times, I am released from the trap of the archetype by contemplating its effects. I am able to go beyond what felt like the limiting interpretations of my therapist at the time, which indicated a "cause-and-effect approach to explaining psychic reality" (Hall, 1993, p. 75), inevitably leading to "a deterministic conception of the person with its associated traits of blaming and victimhood" (*ibid.*). I had felt as though my past were being mined for examples to fit a theory: I had felt *determined* by my past, and *fixed* within it.

Suddenly this mode of thinking has changed, and I am released to think about it differently. In my research diary I write, "This liberates me into realizing that you *could* view people differently and also into realizing how trapped I am in my relationships with my clients by my own view that people are so defined/confined . . . trapped!" (23 January 2006).

This trap was mirrored in the early stages of my therapy. After a while I had stopped thinking that a magical cure was possible, but had retained the belief that the therapist *knew* what was wrong with me and could put it right if she chose to do so. Much as I might rage against my helplessness, I felt that I was being deconstructed, hollowed out, with nothing to put in its place. I no longer did anything for myself: I dreamed for the therapist; I thought for the therapist; I talked about my therapist as others might talk of their lovers; I delivered what I thought she wanted. And when she interpreted this as my need to feed her, I knew that she was right, and that I was helpless to do any other.

Helpless and hopeless. As Moltmann (2002, p. 9) says: "The despairing surrender of hope does not even need to have a desperate appearance. It can also be the mere tacit absence of meaning, prospects, future and purpose".

Phase 2: from despair to hope

One of the issues that had come up during the early stages of my therapy was my relationship with my mother (who has since died). Now, in the second phase of the research, I encountered this issue again, and again I was able to approach it anew through a work of the imagination: a novel by Sue Monk Kidd (2001). This tells the story of the struggle of a fourteen-year-old girl, Lily, to come to terms with the trauma of accidentally shooting her mother dead when she was aged four. At a significant moment in her journey, Lily seeks a sign from her dead mother that she loves her. No sign arrives until, a while later, she is given a photo of herself as a little girl with her mother gazing at her. She is moved to the roots of her being, and is able to set aside her enormous anger about what has happened to her, and move on. I finish reading the book during the day; that night I have a dream.

> It is dark and I am not sure where I am, but there are other people around. I am given or come across a photo to put in place of one of my mother that I already have. The photo I replace is of my mother looking sad, and the one I put in its place is of my mother with her dog, a

scrawny mongrel. In the dream I am puzzled as to why my mother wants me to have this photo of herself.

"Following this dream, I experience a real shift in my feelings towards my mother, a realization that I don't need her to send me signs, because I always knew she loved me, even though I found her difficult in many ways. And so forgiveness, which as the novel says is often very difficult to do, came easily. And even, writing this, I don't know what I have to forgive. My mother was herself, and did her best, what more could she do? This links, I think, to my rejection of the long-standing victim archetype in which my mother was to blame" (Research Diary, 22 February 2006).

I have reached, perhaps, what Farran, Herth, and Popvich (1995, p. 6) refer to as "the *heart* of hope". As a result I have a real sense of becoming myself, of growing into myself; even a readiness to contemplate new parts of myself that I may find difficult, and to re-engage with my therapeutic journey through my research.

When I do so, I find that my attitude towards my therapy has changed—from the anger and rage towards my therapist that I felt in the first phase of the research to something more modulated and adult. This seems to reflect the changes that occurred during the middle stages of my therapeutic journey. Although I remained deeply envious of my therapist's power, and too often wallowed in guilt, I began to take my share of the responsibility for my life. This was not an easy process and I often felt something like a Greek tragic hero, "enmeshed in pain and perplexity" (Armstrong, 2005, p. 100). Steeped in the reasoning and insights provided by the "way" (Freudian and Kleinian), my life story had been reinterpreted in the light of the Freudian myth and the old myths no longer worked. I had given up the hope that all my problems would be resolved by this process, and came to accept the muddy complexity of being.

In the research process new understanding emerges. I revisit the dream I had at the start of therapy and see it differently. Where before I had seen a car with no identity, now I see a car in search of itself; that the possibilities of identity are many; that I was, and am, in the process of becoming.

Phase 3: hope and despair—a necessary polarity

At the start of this final phase of collecting research data, I find my mood of hope is suddenly and inexplicably shattered. I become seriously self-critical. I read the completed research projects of others and am filled with dismay. The fullness of their accounts of their process seems likely to elude me. I am particularly envious of the research report of one colleague who had gained so much from her (psychodynamic) therapy. I feel in retrospect that I did not make enough of my therapy, that if it failed it was my fault.

Reading others' research also brings to the fore anxieties about my relationship with my research supervisor, and I reflect in my research diary on my desire to please him and my fear of letting him down (13 March 2006). I am suddenly thrown from hope into despair. I do not want to face the difficulties inherent in this relationship; I decide, momentarily, that the only answer is to give up the research, and to give up counselling. This brings me full circle to the feelings I had at the start of the research. Have I gained nothing?

Then I realize that I am apparently in a parallel process with the ending of my therapy. Karen Armstrong writes of the final phase in the history of myth (*ca.* 1500–2000) as the death knell of mythology. As people gained new optimism, there was also numbing despair as the meaning that myth had given life crumbled.

Similarly, as my therapeutic journey comes towards an end, my hope is tinged with despair as the myths that have given meaning to my life have crumbled, and I feel that little has been put in their place. I have realized my lack of importance in the eyes of the world, and struggle to find a balance between feelings of insignificance and grandiosity. Although still sometimes assailed by unspeakable rage towards myself and the therapist, nevertheless I have reached something like Klein's "depressive position" (see Steiner, 1993, p. 11). Psychotherapy held out much hope for transformation, and some of this has been disappointed. I leave therapy dissatisfied, without needs fully met, and without much acknowledgement by the therapist of the distance I have travelled.

Now, through this research, I have had the opportunity to engage with these feelings of disappointment and despair in new ways. Where my experience of therapy was narrow and limiting, "my project is to do the reverse: by searching for meaning (of hope/despair), finding limitless meanings. The process is one of liberation, opening up and then to see what limits are self-imposed, to claim back, to identify my own constraints" (research diary, 15 March 2006).

With this in mind, I begin to look at other perspectives through which to view my "text", starting with humanistic approaches, the optimism of which, as identified by Rowan (1988, p. 12) contrasts with the pessimism he sees as inherent in the backward-looking approach of psychoanalysis. This was not a perception that was new to me. What was new was my reaction. In the past I would have flipped from one side of the coin (or polarity) to the other: psychoanalysis "bad", so humanistic "good". This time I do not do so. Instead, for the first time, I see the two theories as necessarily held in tension if one is to learn from the other and I am to move on. As Moltmann says,

> Hope's statements of promise . . . must stand in contradiction to the reality which can at present be experienced. They do not result from experiences, but are the condition for the possibility of new experiences. [2002, p. 4]

The French philosopher, Derrida, puts this in a wider context, suggesting that in ordinary usage one end of a polarity, or binary opposite, is always favoured over the other in order to support the dominant discourse in society (see Freshwater & Rolfe, 2004, p. 155). This perception helps me to reinterpret my data and realize that it does not show a triumph of hope over despair, or even a triumph in holding the two in balance. What it shows is that I often feel despair, and often feel hope, and that it is impossible to describe my world and relationships without viewing both emotions as essentially interdependent.

I am becoming more like Ged, Earthsea Wizard (in Le Guin, 1993, pp. 164–166) at the end of his journey.

> Ged reached out his hands, dropping his staff, and took hold of his shadow, of the black self that reached out to him. Light and darkness met, and joined, and were one . . .

> ". . . It is over". He laughed. "The wound is healed," he said, "I am whole. I am free." Then he bent over and hid his face in his arms, weeping like a boy . . .

Discussion

Transforming the self

Before starting this research I was in a difficult position as a practitioner. I understood counselling theory, I had taken on board some techniques, I was fairly self-aware. But, when it came to relating to clients at a deep level, I found I was often inarticulate and frozen, immobilized by fear. I now realize that my experience of therapy had been so disempowering that I had no belief in its healing potential. Above all, I feared using my power as a counsellor in case it damaged my clients.

Doing this research has liberated me from this fear and transformed my counselling practice. I have been able to look at my experience of psychotherapy anew, and have come up with an understanding of myself less constrained by the theories or views of others, and more able to be an actor in the world. How has this happened?

First, and paradoxically, I was able to break free from my therapeutic experience only as a result of that experience and the insights it gave me. I knew I had gained something from that relationship, but was still too wrapped in its snares to appreciate how much I had gained. Doing this research helped me to see that one of its gifts was a belief in the essentially benign character of my inner world. I did not feel threatened by my dreams and imaginings; I was able to use them and work through them to the gold they might contain. Spending hours on the couch exploring the links between images and emotions meant I fell easily into the same mode of exploration when engaged in the research. Moreover, I was predisposed to self-analysis (as described by Horney, 1962) both because I had the means and I "knew from experience that in analysis nothing short of ruthless honesty with oneself is helpful" (ibid., pp. 27–28).

Second, the research led me down previously unexplored avenues. I was drawn to understand more about the importance of myth in the unfolding story of human being, and through this to the significance of Jung's work on archetypes. I realized I had been caught in the Great Mother archetype in the relationships with my mother and, through transference, my therapist. Recognizing the role of that archetype in my life has helped me to break free of its grip. Here, the method of my data analysis was particularly helpful.

I was drawn instinctively to hermeneutics without really under-standing why. Now I can see that it was the capacity of this method to supply an "other", in the form of my text, with which to engage in dialogue that was most useful. Jung writes that the archetypes

> cannot be integrated simply by rational means, but require a dialec-tical procedure, a real coming to terms with them, often conducted by the patient in dialogue form, so that, without knowing it, he puts into effect the alchemical definition of the *mediatatio*: "an inner colloquy with one's good angel". [2003, p. 4]

Third, the research liberated me to a new understanding of the role of polarities in human thought and feeling. Before embarking on the research, I was in touch mostly with the despair inherent in the idea of therapeutic abuse; I wanted to focus on hope in the ther-apeutic relationship in order to escape from the despair. Through the research, I have been able to see the essentially interdependent nature of polarities, "the paired opposites, where the One is never separated from the Other, its antithesis" (*ibid.*, p. 45). Perhaps the power of my research lay in this resolution of polarities, for, accord-ing to Jung, this is "a field of personal experience which leads directly to the experience of individuation, the attainment of the self" (*ibid.*).

Transforming the relationship

This research has led me to new understandings of the ways in which the relationship between counsellor and client can be trans-formed. This has been a process which involved first examining the role that *power* plays in the relationship, and the *violence* implicit in the imbalance of power; and second, reaching some conclusions about ways to be as a therapist that *acknowledge and use* unequal power relations to the client's good.

The nature of power in therapy

Derrida talks of the violence inherent in silencing difference (see Bernstein, 1991, p. 184). Similarly, in the therapeutic relationship there can be violence in the use of words and in the way things are put by the therapist that do not allow for engagement and discussion, but only for acceptance, willing or otherwise. All the work that I have had to do since my therapy finished, including this research, witnesses to the fact that my voice was partially silenced in the therapeutic relationship: I was not allowed to take a full part in my own unfolding story and do enough of the work myself at the time. This prevented my individuation and kept me in the role of powerless victim, always blaming the other. As Judith (2004) points out,

> Lack of autonomy is often characterized by *blaming* ... Blaming places both will and responsibility outside ourselves. If we are grounded in our autonomy, then we are the cause of our lives and we are able to take appropriate responsibility and power. [*ibid.*, pp. 174–175]

I recently re-read parts of Forrester (1990), which was a precipitating factor in doing this research, and was puzzled about my initial reaction. What was he saying that brought on such overwhelmingly dark feelings? And then I realized. It was not the text but the title that resonated with my therapeutic experience. For me, as a client at that time, it did not matter whether the therapist was engaged in an act of rape or seduction, for both felt invasive. There were times when I did indeed feel "raped" by her interpretations, entered by force and violated, but more pervasive was the feeling of being seduced, of being taken somewhere by the enchantment of the other, of being manipulated into continuing the relationship by my growing dependence on her. Seduction is a much more subtle use of power than rape, and likewise more difficult to detect when you are in its grip.

For House (2003), it is therapy's "regime of truth" (p. 29ff) that is responsible for the therapist's abuse of power. What is at issue here is how we use therapy as "power over" the client. This presents us with a problem. If avoiding the abuse of therapeutic power is so important, does this mean that we should aim for a therapeutic relationship that is powerless? According to Maxey (1999), this is not even possible, for "... power is performed in all we do" (p. 202): it is inescapable. Moreover, owning one's own power is beneficial, for "power is the ability to make change and exists for one reason only—transformation" (Judith, 2004, p. 182).

This dilemma is faced head on by Larner (1999) in his unravelling of the implications of Derrida's deconstruction of power for a "deconstructing" form of psychotherapy. Larner sees that the problem lies in how to give power to the client without using the power of the therapist in so doing. Clearly, an impossibility. He suggests that, for Derrida, "Deconstruction is a double 'both/and' reading which thinks opposites—for example, meaning/non-meaning, power and non-power—*together*" (ibid., p. 45). We do not *avoid* the use of power in the therapeutic relationship, we acknowledge it and share it. This leads to

> a therapy which teaches therapists to say to the client: "I would like to learn to live, I am with you, no better. I struggle with my demons too." This is the power of non-power, humility and poesis where therapy becomes a narrative lived out in the session. [*ibid.*, p. 46]

Parker (1999, p. 2) describes this as "deconstructing therapy", something which is "always *in process* rather than something fixed, a movement of reflexive critique rather than a stable set of techniques".

Creative uses of power in therapy

But how to put "deconstructing therapy" into practice? My research has indicated some ways forward for my practice and that of others.

First, my deconstructive research process has only been possible because I have opened up the space that had felt closed down in my therapy. There, only certain aspects of what I said gained attention. Here, in the research, I could look at anything—it all had meaning.

Now I want, in my practice, to focus on the psychic space available to the client and on how my words and presence can open up or close down that space.

Second, my choice of hermeneutics as a methodology for this research has led me to a growing appreciation of its role in counselling practice. In the same way that my culture, class, race, and prejudices influenced my relationship with my text when analysing my data, so do these factors influence me and a client when we meet in the counselling space. We can acknowledge and work with these differences through dialogue. As Anderson and Goolishan (1992, p. 29) comment, dialogue helps us to co-develop "new meanings, new realities and new narratives . . . In this hermeneutic view, change in therapy is represented by the dialogical creation of new narrative".

Third, the research has led me to reflect on the nature of healing in the therapeutic relationship. For a long time I equated healing with the notion of therapeutic "cure", which is linked to the cause and effect thinking of logical positivism. Now I see that healing is not cure, but more a binding of the psychic wound that may come apart and need further healing as life circumstances change. Additionally, the research has challenged me to think laterally about "causes", linking them, for instance, to a concept in physics of "reverse causation" (see, for instance, LaFee, 2006), which is based on an understanding of time as non-linear. In this way we could be influenced as much by the future as by the past. This is an idea which has much in common with Jungian "synchronicity" (Jung, 2003, p. 48) and also for the way that Heidegger, and later Lacan, work with language, where ". . . the future is not simply the yet-to-come, rather it comes towards us, met in the decisions we make" (Pound, 2007, p. 193). The hermeneutic circle could be seen, in this analysis, to be a description of the nature of time and our relationship to it. And so, I have now completed the research *because I have found a fit* between the influence of the past and the call of the future, between despair and hope; the ends of the circle have met, the *gestalt* is complete, the trauma has healed.

Fourth, I have been able to develop a new understanding of how to build an essentially ethical relationship with the client, and the vital importance of so doing. This came out of my use of hermeneutics in creating a text in which I could see myself as "other" and relate to myself differently as a result, enabling new insights. As Larner (1999) says: "An ethical relation to the other is one that maximises the difference that makes a difference, and this is the activity of writing, conversation, and the development of the person's narrative" (p. 46).

In similar vein, Warren (2005) explores the links between hermeneutics and the ethical concerns of Levinas and proposes a movement towards an "ethical-hermeneutics".

> So, while the Other is initially understood through our own preju-
> dices . . . the trace of the Other is still present . . . The trace of
> otherness calls out to me and the understanding of this Other

transcends my already formed conceptions of her, causing breach and reinterpretation. [p. 26]

This enables me to view the other not through the prism of theory, but as "strangely other" (Larner, 1999, p. 48), seeing the therapeutic encounter "as sacred and as "wonder'" (*ibid.*, p. 46). It is this approach that ensures that the relationship is non-violative, and that the therapist is "powerful and non-powerful simultaneously, powerful against violence in the ethical relationship, yet nonpowerful so as to allow the other to speak" (*ibid.*).

Finally, I am left with a powerful sense of the justice inherent in this approach and the links that this makes with social justice and political action in the world. In this perspective, both Hitler's treatment of the Jews in the twentieth century and present day Western hostility towards Muslims can be seen to emerge from a lack of respect for the "other", and result in actions of considerable violence and injustice. A therapeutic relationship where the therapist maintains their "power over" the client is essentially violent and can do nothing to change the wider culture of violence. A "deconstructing" therapy, however, could be just such a challenge to injustice in society. Is it too much to hope that the therapeutic relationship can become a crucible for a new way of relating to others and, as such, become a force for changing the way humans relate in the outside world?

References

Anderson, H., & Goolishan, H. (1992). The client is the expert: a notknowing approach to therapy. In: S. McNamee & K. J. Gergen (Eds.), *Therapy as Social Construction* (pp. 25–39). London: Sage.

Armstrong, K. (2005). *A Short History of Myth*. Edinburgh: Canongate.

Babits, M. (2001). The phoenix juncture: exploring the dimension of hope in psychotherapy. *Clinical Social Work Journal, 29*(4): 341–350.

Bergin, L., & Walsh, S. (2005). The role of hope in psychotherapy with older adults. *Aging and Mental Health, 9*(1): 7–15.

Bernstein, R. J. (1991). *The New Constellation*. Cambridge: Polity.

Braud, W. (1998). An expanded view of validity. In: W. Braud & R. Anderson (Eds.), *Transpersonal Research Methods for the Social Sciences* (pp. 213–237). Thousand Oaks, CA: Sage.

Etherington, K. (2004). Research methods: reflexivities—roots, meanings, dilemmas. *Counselling and Psychotherapy Research*, 4(2): 46–47.

Farran, C. J., Herth, K. A., & Popovich, J. M. (1995). *Hope and Hopelessness: Critical Clinical Constructs*. Thousand Oaks, CA: Sage.

Forrester, J. (1990). *The Seductions of Psychoanalysis: Freud, Lacan and Derrida*. Cambridge: Cambridge University Press.

Freshwater, D., & Rolfe, G. (2001). Critical reflexivity: a politically and ethically engaged research method for nursing. *NT Research*, 6(1): 526–537.

Freshwater, D., & Rolfe, G. (2004). *Deconstructing Evidence-based Practice*. Abingdon: Routledge.

Gordon, R. (1993). Archetypes on the couch. In: R. Gordon (Ed.), *Bridges* (pp. 104–127). London: Karnac.

Hall, J. (1993). *The Reluctant Adult*. Bridport: Prism.

Horney, K. (1962). *Self-Analysis*. London: Routledge & Kegan Paul.

House, R. (2003). *Therapy Beyond Modernity*. London: Karnac.

Judith, A. (2004). *Eastern Body, Western Mind*. Berkeley, CA: Celestial Arts.

Jung, C. G. (2003). *Four Archetypes*. London: Routledge.

Kvale, S. (1996). *InterViews: An Introduction to Qualitative Research Interviewing*. Thousand Oaks, CA: Sage.

LaFee, S. (2006). *Cause and Defect*. www.signonsandiego.com/news/science

Larner, G. (1999). Derrida and the deconstruction of power. In: I. Parker (Ed.), *Deconstructing Psychotherapy* (pp. 39–53). London: Sage.

Le Guin, U. (1993). *The Earthsea Quartet*. London: Penguin.

Lynch, G. (1996). What is truth? A philosophical introduction to counselling research. *Counselling*, 7(2): 144–149.

Lynch, W. F. (1965). *Images of Hope: Imagination as Healer of the Hopeless*. Baltimore, MD: Helicon.

Masson, J. (1993). *Against Therapy* (2nd edn). London: HarperCollins.

Maxey, I. (1999). Beyond boundaries? Activism, academia, reflexivity and research. *Area*, 31(3): 199–208.

McLeod, J. (2001). *Qualitative Research in Counselling and Psychotherapy*. London: Sage.

Moltmann, J. (2002). *Theology of Hope* (2nd edn). London: SCM.

Monk Kidd, S. (2001). *The Secret Life of Bees*. London: Headline.

Moustakas, C. (1990). *Heuristic Research*. Newbury Park, CA: Sage.

Murakami, H. (2003). *The Wind-up Bird Chronicle*. London: Vintage.

Okri, B. (1997). *A Way of Being Free*. London: Phoenix House.

Parker, I. (1999). *Deconstructing Psychotherapy*. London: Sage.

Polkinghorne, D. E. (1995). Narrative configuration in qualitative analysis. In: J. A. Hatch & R. Wisiewski (Eds.), *Life History and Narrative* (pp. 5–23). London: Falmer.

Pound, M. (2007). Eucharist and trauma. *New Blackfriars, 88*(1014): 187–194.

Rowan, J. (1988). *Ordinary Ecstasy* (2nd edn). London: Routledge.

Snyder, C. R. (1995). Conceptualizing, measuring, and nurturing hope. *Counseling and Development, 73*(3): 355–360.

Steiner, G. (1989). *Real Presences*. London: Faber and Faber.

Steiner, J. (1993). *Psychic Retreats*. London: Routledge.

Thorne, B. (1998). *Person-Centred Counselling and Christian Spirituality*. London: Whurr.

Vande Kemp, H. (1984). Hope in psychotherapy. *Journal of Psychology and Christianity, 3*(1): 27–35.

Warren, J. (2005). Towards an ethical-hermeneutics. *European Journal of Psychotherapy, Counselling and Health, 7*(1–2): 17–28.

Yalom, I. (1985). *The Theory and Practice of Group Psychotherapy* (2nd edn). New York: Basic Books.

CHAPTER SEVEN

Ethics and reflexivity in practitioner enquiry: three detectives and other stories

Sabi Redwood

> "Ethics makes safe. It throws a net of safety under the judge-
> ments we are forced to make, the daily, hourly decisions that
> make up the texture of our lives. Ethics lays the foundation
> for principles that force people to be good; it clarifies
> concepts, secures judgements, provides firm guardrails
> along the slippery slopes of factical life. It provides princi-
> ples and criteria and adjudicates hard cases. Ethics is alto-
> gether wholesome, constructive work, which is why it enjoys
> a good name"
>
> (Caputo, 1993, p. 4)

E thics enjoys a good name, as the philosopher John Caputo
points out. When we meet it on our way, we doff our
metaphorical cap as if to a kindly but distant dignitary, and
exchange brightly polite greetings before walking by. At times we
hurry on, relieved at not having been stopped and involved in
earnest conversation; at others the memory of a trespass briefly
nudges our conscience, but usually we do not question our reverence to the goodness of ethics' wholesome character. In this chapter,

I do not put on my best face and walk quickly past, but stop and talk to ethics, inquiring after its goodness and questioning its rights to stand above critique. I make no excuses for my impertinence as I refuse to listen to its lecturing and ask it to speak in particularities, not generalities. I turn down its offer of a map and certain directions and watch it unravel before my eyes, like this metaphor, which struggles to connect with you, the reader. You have probably already unmasked me as a fraudster and are aware of my use of the word "we". Notice how much work this tiny word does: as a rhetorical device it sets you up as being part of something both you and I belong to and creates an illusion that we share a common understanding. Resist this trick of trying to recruit you into my project; beware of my attempts to talk to you directly. It is a trick. It is my attempt to fix you in my mind, pin you down, and make you the same as me. But, seriously now, who would pick a fight with ethics? Who would, on a sunny day, risk incurring the wrath of ethics by turning away and walking on the other side of the street? I, for one, am not that brave. On the other hand, if we were, just for a moment, to think "against ethics" as Caputo (1993) does, would all hell break loose? Would ethics discharge its wrath against us in some cataclysmic thunderstorm? Maybe such thinking would be no more than a small, albeit terrifying, realization that we are really much more on our own with our decisions in our practice and in our research than ethics would have us believe; that ethics' careful spelling out of our responsibility and obligation fails to guide us in the rampant uncertainty of life; and that we are condemned to the perpetual anxiety that we have not done enough for those with whom we work and research.

In this chapter, I explore the genesis of the concept of research ethics and trace the discourses that have shaped practice relating to enquiry and research. I work with metaphors, but I offer no solutions, no simple prescriptions for practice. In other words, I provide none of the comforts that follow when we settle for one explanation and shut off our thinking to other possibilities. In producing this text, I have not set out to fix the system or put things right, and so I announce my failure right here. I will necessarily disappoint and thwart expectations if you are hoping to find answers. Moreover, I may be accused of obscuring a familiar problem instead of producing some clarity to help solve it. However, rather than help formulate answers to address problematic issues in the ethical review and conduct of qualitative research carried out by practitioner–researchers, I wish to breach the borders surrounding the territories of traditional scientific research and the ethics that govern its practice. Narratives have been produced in relation to these territories and practices which are presented as "natural", as necessary, inevitable, and self-evident; in other words, they have closed and sealed themselves off against an outside of the non-scientific, the anecdotal, the frivolous, the political, and the tainted. In this enclosure, the field of research ethics unfolds in a kind of lofty space beyond the reach of power and exists unaffected by its relation to the messy world of practice. The borders of this enclosure are becoming increasingly tightly drawn as regulatory policies prescribe language and put words into the pens and mouths of researchers and ethics committee reviewers. These narratives are also taken for granted to such an extent that they have become invisible and have ceased to be the subject of critical analysis. This has diminished the vocabulary with which to speak about research ethics and has congealed researchers' imagination to think otherwise. I wish to trouble the move that brought about the "taken-for-grantedness" of certain interpretations of ethics and science, and the production of the reality effect through which these dominant interpretations attempt to place themselves beyond challenge and negotiation. What I am trying to do in this text is to resist the temptation of closure, of settling for one final interpretation. Or, to use Foucault's words, I am resisting the temptation "to tame the wild profusion of existing things" (Foucault, 1970, p. xvi).

From Nuremberg to Helsinki

Practitioners in the human service professions are familiar with the ethics of the everyday. (I refer to human service professions instead of listing professional groups such as workers in health and social care, nurses, occupational therapists, physiotherapists, social workers, educators, etc.) They are obliged professionally to respond to the need of the "other" who appeals to them for help; for example, a person who is unable to wash and dress independently, or requests counselling for emotional distress, or who is recovering after surgery and asks for pain relief. These are more or less predictable obligations that have been domesticated by various systems created to cope with the demands of human need and suffering. Although the practitioner's conduct is not prescribed, there are, none the less, certain scripts and discourses that have been shaped by professional ethics and guidelines for behaving and acting in relation to the other who calls for assistance. Ethical behaviour is, to a large extent, defined through regulation and codes for practice. In the case of human service practitioners' research with, on, or for patients/service users, ethics demand that they are, at the very least, protected from harm. Despite moves away from paternalism in the human service professions, many service users/patients, as well as participants in research, tend to be construed as vulnerable and in need of protection. They are seen as vulnerable to exploitation and as limited in their ability to give or to refuse their consent. But who is it that is being given shelter by ethics? Patients/service users and research participants, or practitioner–researchers? Ostensibly, the answer is simple. It is the patient/service user and research participant, construed as defenceless and vulnerable, who requires protection, and this need for protection provides the justification for regulatory practices to contain and prevent the risk of harm to the vulnerable. The logic works by positioning the practitioner–researcher in contrast to the defenceless patient/research participant; in other words, practitioner–researchers carry with them the potential for being unscrupulous and exploitative even if they have never exhibited this character flaw (Halse & Honey, 2005), and to become the metaphorical "bad apples" in the barrel of human service practice and research. There is a logic at work here which is embedded in the familiar narrative of the World Medical Association's Declaration of Helsinki on the Ethical Principles for Medical Research Involving Human Subjects (1964), based on the Nuremberg Code, which in turn is routinely cited as a watershed in the history of research with human subjects (Hazelgrove, 2002).

At the end of the Second World War, the Allied forces, under the leadership of the USA, conducted a series of trials for the prosecution of members of the Nazi regime in the town of Nuremberg in the American zone of occupation. The "Doctors' Trial", as it became known, was the first of twelve trials of individuals accused of war crimes and crimes against humanity. Doctors and medical scientists were tried for the horrific experimentation on internees of the Nazi concentration camps in the name of science and the war effort. The Nuremberg Code, as it became known, was a set of ten principles against which the Nuremberg judges measured the culpability of the accused. Its central tenet is that of consent, which must be informed and voluntarily given by a person who is competent to do so—not children, the mentally sick, captive populations, or those deemed vulnerable to coercion. The trial lasted nine months and concluded in August 1947. It revealed the tortuous murder and mutilation of thousands of human beings in the name of medical science and in the service of public health, soldiers, and the civilian population.

I suggest that this focus on the Nazi regime in the genesis of research ethics' regulation reinforces two particular explanations that have become so fossilized that they are stifling critical debate about ethical responsibility in research. One is the notion that the circumstances that led to the atrocities in the name of science in the criminal and totalitarian regime of Nazi Germany were unique, and are therefore unlikely to be repeated in modern Western liberal democracies. The other is the image of the type of doctor and scientist on trial at Nuremberg as the deranged Nazi pseudo-scientist engaged in lethal experiments in the seclusion of the death camps (Hanauske-Abel, 1996). Yet, neither the Nazi regime nor the medical or scientific establishment (many of whom were never prosecuted for their crimes) appear to have been isolated by the international community. Indeed, Hanauske-Abel (1996) and Geidermann (2002a,b) present evidence of the active involvement of the medical professional and academic elite, with international connections and financial support, in a wide range of activities carried out by the Nazi regime. In her research, Hazelgrove (2002) brings to the surface further evidence of this complicity, which, in the sanitized version of medical research that took place in the USA and the UK, has been concealed: the involvement of the Allies in Nazi medicine and their interest in the scientific potential of the experiments, as well as the use of the experimental data recovered from the Nazi doctors. Of course, their condemnation of the atrocities would have sounded less sincere had they shown their willingness to benefit from their results. Hanauske-Abel (1996) identifies a pattern of convergence of otherwise separate political, scientific, and economic forces in the emergence of the Nazi regime, a pattern that he also detects in the conditions that gave rise to the Tuskegee syphilis study and the human radiation experiments in the USA which clearly contravened the Nuremberg code, yet carried on over many years despite their similarities to the human experimentation carried out in Nazi Germany. There is an inclination to dismiss the atrocities exposed at the trials at Nuremberg as a unique set of circumstances with a cast of uniquely evil individuals. However, the notion that Nazi Germany was an evil regime that was shunned by other nations and whose medical professionals and scientists were deranged and morally bankrupt individuals and in its clutches, that this "sheer madness" that would never again be repeated (Jones, 1981, in Hanauske-Abel 1996, p. 1460), and it is nothing more than a "a grim cautionary tale" (Leaning, 1996, p. 1414), may be misleading and dangerous and has probably already been proved wrong many times over.

In the Western liberal democracies, regulatory structures proliferate in an attempt to apply a universally relevant solution that will protect us all from all evil-doers by producing binding principles for conduct in research. Indeed, these universal standards and principles are also exported into other cultures and colonize research carried out in those very different contexts. Research ethics are closely related to bioethics, a conceptual framework that is underpinned by the idea of individualism, finding expression in calls for autonomy, individual rights, self-determination and privacy and rejecting any interference which limits personal freedom (Fox 1990). Bioethics, as a term, came into use in the 1960s in connection with concerns relating to the scientific and technological advances in the field of medicine (Fox, 1990). The development of the term has run in parallel with the increasing opening up to public scrutiny and debate of medical ethics described by Rothman (1991), and the participation of powerful groups such as government, the church, the law, and the media in these debates. Growing professional and public concern about the moral conditions under which human experimentation could be carried out played a major role in triggering its inception. In more recent years, bioethics as a field of inquiry and debate has moved towards questions relating to the beginning and end of life, for example, *in vitro* fertilization, genetic engineering, organ transplantation, and euthanasia. Another theme in the evolution of bioethics has been the growing costs of, and demands on, healthcare, including issues of economics and rationing. The moral philosophers Beauchamp and Childress (2001) make the connection with the idea of personal autonomy as

> an extension of political self-rule to self-governance by the individual: personal rule of the self while remaining free from both controlling interferences by others and personal limitations such as inadequate understanding, that prevent meaningful choice. [p. 68]

Thus the idea of giving "consent" to participate in research becomes a crucial building block in the construction of research ethics from a biomedical perspective. This perspective, which values autonomy of the individual self as the highest moral good and speaks in the language of "rights" in favour of "responsibility", has structured relationships with others in particular ways. The notion of contract is important here, understood as an agreement between rational, autonomous, and independent people. In relation to research ethics, the concept of "written consent", which is given voluntarily and by a person who is "competent" to understand its implications, probably derived from the importance attached to such contractual agreements. Similarly, veracity and truth-telling, which are crucial to the field of bioethics, are evoked in guidelines to ensure that participants be informed of risks.

The foundation of all the bioethically-inspired codes of research ethics in operation in the liberal democracies is the conflation of the ethical with the reason of the Western tradition. Bioethics has been shaped by Greco-Roman thinking, which has privileged rationality and theory (Christians, 2003, 2005; Kearney, 2003), separated facts and values (Brinkman 2004; Brinkman & Kvale, 2005; Giorgi, 2006), and differentiated between descriptive ethics (what is) and normative ethics (what ought to be) (Hedgecoe, 2004). Bioethics construes the individual as a universal subject, an abstract entity transcending context and the specificity of experience. The individual is portrayed as some disembodied unit of free-floating reason. Codes of ethics institutionalize the "top-down" model of ethical decision-making which applies the formal logic of mathematics by starting with an abstract and universal principle and deriving from it judgements for particular situations (Homan, 1991). Bioethicists such as

Beauchamp and Childress (2001, p. 385) claim that "this model is simple and conforms to the way virtually all persons learn to think morally". Interestingly, they do not offer an empirical basis to this statement. Thus, the particular is subsumed under an abstract ethical rule (Mattingly, 2005). Ethical problems are presumed to have correct solutions that can be deduced from general principles, independent of the person, and social and cultural factors that are relegated as irrelevant. Any "local meanings" in relation to ethical issues are dismissed as ethical relativism, a grave accusation in the dominant bureaucratic structures that regulate research in Western liberal democracies (Hedgecoe, 2004).

The principle of autonomy has triumphed over others, such as beneficence and justice, which, although still important in ethical reasoning, tend to be subsumed by the dominance of the idea that the autonomous individual can make choices as to whether or not to participate in research provided they are free from coercion and have been given adequate information (Corrigan, 2003). In this way, the relationship between researcher and researched is presumed to be a contractual arrangement between two rational, autonomous individuals guided by universal, context-free, ethical rules which, if they are applied in a reasonable manner, will ensure that the researched are treated ethically. Grounded in the assumptions of ethical deduction and "relationship-as-contract", the discourse of research ethics has become a confident, hermetic narrative that holds out the promise that the adoption of an ethical standpoint will solve any particular dilemma.

Closely related to the principle of autonomy is the concept of informed consent. It is commonly described as the cornerstone of research ethics' policy. It is based on the assumption that what will happen in a research study can be fully known and transformed into full and accurate information that can be presented to autonomous participants who are able to make informed choices about the consequences of their decisions. The protocol for obtaining informed consent from individuals usually involves giving potential participants an information letter, which states in clear and unambiguous language the purpose of the research, the reason why the individual has been selected, and what participation in the research will entail, including any demands, disadvantages, risks, benefits, pain, discomfort, or inconvenience that might be involved.

Assurances about the participant's right to withdraw from the study without justifying their decision and to have their confidentiality and privacy protected are usually also given. The discourse of the protection and safeguarding the welfare of participants is augmented when research seeks to include children, the mentally ill, the learning disabled, as well as the critically and terminally ill, who are seen as vulnerable and particularly at risk because of their "mental incompetence". Critics of universalist standards for research ethics question whether it is the participant who is being protected, or whether it is the researcher who uses the principle and procedures of informed consent as a professional safeguard. Homan (1991) suggests

> [w]e have now reached a point where researchers are operating the principles of informed consent not to protect their subjects but to protect themselves and to guard against the possibility that subjects will claim their rights through litigation. [p. 73]

Thus, the question of who is being given shelter by ethics is more problematic than the conventional narrative of the Nuremberg Code and the Declaration of Helsinki would suggest. Yet, its discourse has assumed an authority that has shaped thinking and decision-making in research, even in disciplines which have little in common with bioethics:

> The positivist medical model of research ethics has had exceptional discursive power and has been taken up and imposed on disciplines such as the social sciences and humanities, even when these disciplines employ radically different epistemic frames and forms of data collection and analysis. The widespread infiltration of the positivist model of research ethics has worked to visibly and invisibly inscribe the management, surveillance, and control of research ethics in ways that appear natural, benign and eminently reasonable to "any rational subject". Most researchers accept the requirement (if not the desirability) of ethics review before research commences. Yet the biomedical model also casts research ethics in a shroud of scientific neutrality and universal certainty that crafts an illusion that ethics approval means ethical research, begetting a compliance approach to research ethics and to the ways that researchers think through ethical questions. [Halse & Honey, 2005, p. 2153]

However, it is interesting that there are dissenting voices, which critique principle-driven regulation of biomedical research because international consensus on universalist ethical norms as "lowest common denominator" (Plomer, 2005, p. 23) appears to be failing subjects in biomedical research and leaves them vulnerable. Poor communities in developing countries and regions of political and military unrest have been targeted by pharmaceutical companies for trials that would not have cleared the regulatory hurdles in the USA or the EU, for example. Plomer (2005) also suggests that

> increasing globalisation of medical research is heightening the tension between the aspiration to universality of ethics driven regulation and the emerging reality of the diversity of moral cultures in democratic societies and the need to respect plurality and ethical diversity. [p. 1]

Yet the power of this universal model of ethics has emerged despite, or maybe because of, an increasing diversification of research methods in health care (Daly & McDonald, 1996). The previously exclusive focus on tissues, organs, and clinical treatments has widened to include seeing people in their social context, which, in turn, has led to an increasing involvement of non-medical disciplines such as sociology, psychology, and anthropology (*ibid.*). With ethics committees facing difficulties in coming to informed decisions about the ethical implications of proposals submitted for review, there has been a move to develop guidelines for what is to count as both ethical and scientific research (Ashcroft, 2003; Beauchamp & Childress, 2001; Faden & Beauchamp, 1986; Rothman, 1991). Underlying this move are two assumptions: first, an assumption that it is indeed possible to generate guidelines that apply traditional criteria of bioethics—as well as notions of reliability and validity—to research that does not adopt this traditional, realist approach. Thus has emerged a meta-narrative (Lyotard, 1984) of research ethics that has led to a reduction of methodological possibilities in research using non-traditional approaches. The effects of this methodological narrowing have been described by qualitative researchers and can broadly be summarized as a narrative in which the dominant discourse favours deductive and hypothesis-driven research to the disadvantage of qualitative approaches (see, for example, Redwood, 2005; van den Hoonaard, 2001; Whittaker 2005). The second assumption underlying biomedical conceptions of research ethics is that moral decisions do not take place before principles are applied. As Hoffmaster (1994), for example, points out, "considerable moral work gets done in deciding how a situation is to be characterised, and that moral work can determine how issues are resolved" (p. 1157). The decision to focus on patient autonomy and informed consent in medical research ignores other factors that may also be important to patients, who may feel abandoned to make difficult choices (Corrigan, 2003). Furthermore, the seemingly straightforward classification of individuals as "children", or as belonging to a "vulnerable group" such as the mentally ill, or those close to death, has a serious effect on what ethical questions can be asked. The classification occurs prior to the application of any ethical theory of principle. Similarly, the construction of theoretical categories matching those in social reality or lived experience also has profound intellectual and ethical implications (Halse & Honey, 2005). Yet, such concerns are entirely ignored within the biomedical model of research ethics.

So, if research ethics cannot be reduced to a set of principles and guidelines that can be applied to a research protocol and followed in the event of a decision being required, what does it mean to practise research "ethically"? If the values that are claimed to underpin these principles cannot just be expressed as simple rules for conduct, how do we communicate with others on issues of ethics, especially in reflexive research carried out by practitioner–researchers? What happens if we, as I suggested at the beginning of this chapter, think without and against ethics?

Three detectives

I like using metaphors as a means to keep open various possibilities for interpretation. Rather than imposing an order by categorizing and using language to construct literal meanings, metaphors work through association, implied relationships, and resemblances. The reader is invited to understand one thing in the terms of another, and to explore points of similarities and differences in the relationship that the author sets up by using a metaphor (Sharpe, 2005; St Pierre, 1997). Thus, the metaphor does not stand for something else that is "real", but works in tension with a word borrowed from another context. It may enable you to engage imaginatively with this juxtaposition of terms and their conventionally attributed meanings, and transfer their interpretations of those meanings from one context to another, making possible surprising, funny, discomfiting, or simply absurd connections. The metaphor offers a possibility of multiple interpretations and may work to keep open the "wild profusion of existing things".

In the methodological literature, the researcher as detective has been a popular and powerful metaphor (Moring, 2001). Here, the problem-solving activity of the detective is transposed to that of the researcher. Another feature the researcher shares with the detective is a positioning as "outsider". Detectives move in various worlds, the middle-class, police, and criminal worlds, yet they themselves belong to none. As such, they are liminal figures; in other words, they inhabit the "in-between" of different worlds. I will follow in the footsteps of Moring (2001), who explores three detective genres in her deconstruction of the metaphor: Arthur Conan Doyle's Sherlock Holmes, the character of the criminal psychologist or profiler (by way of example I will use the character of "Fitz" in the UK television series *Cracker*), and Daniel Quinn from Paul Auster's novel *City of Glass*.

Holmes is, perhaps, the most famous fictional detective, and is renowned for his expertise at using careful observation and deductive logic to solve complex cases. He works in the area of scientific reason in terms of strict causal determinism of human behaviour, excluding everything but rational intelligence (Moring, 2001). He advocates the hypothetico–deductive model of reasoning for understanding the world and the "other" of the criminal mind and motivation. The psychological profiler, such as Fitz, on the other hand, is more concerned with understanding the complex world of lived experience from the point of view of the individual. His process of detection attends to the situated and relational aspects of the experience and places more emphasis on emotional and psychological truths than on correct police procedure. This often brings him into conflict with colleagues. He has foibles and weaknesses that, rather than producing distractions, help illuminate aspects of the case which further his understanding of both the case and, importantly, himself as detective. His practical reasoning relates to the application of a moral judgement in the situations that arise among those involved in the case. Whereas Holmes is a paragon of virtue and social correctness, Fitz is an archetypal anti-hero: overweight, an alcoholic and heavy smoker, he is unfaithful to his wife and is addicted to gambling. He frequently swears and puts down his colleagues with devastatingly acid sarcasm. Yet, he is, like Holmes, an expert in his field. Although there are some superficial differences, Holmes and Fitz share much common ground: first, a belief in the existence of a reality. Of course, Holmes is more likely to see an objective and neutral one, whereas Fitz tends to see it as socially constructed. Second, they share a belief in causality, although Fitz is less inclined to believe in the linearity of it. Finally, they share a conventional assessment of validity; in other words, the case is solved, and the criminal is convicted and incarcerated (or hanged). It may be seductive to think of Fitz as radical and disruptive of social orders in opposition to Holmes' conservatism. However, as metaphorical figures of the detective, both return to a reassuringly stable present. The evil monster is contained, the violation of the existing moral order has been explained and punished, and normality is restored so that the good citizens can carry on their usual lives.

Contrasting the stability and continuity of Holmes and Fitz, Moring (2001) introduces another figure, that of Daniel Quinn, whom she presents as "a dystopic figure of societal transformation" (p. 364). Following Latour (1993), she continues, "the projects of modernity and postmodernity share the same features, except for the hope". Here, the internal and the external world are intertwined in such a way that we cannot separate the author, the narrative, and the experience presented in the novel as a whole. The following excerpts are paragraphs from *City of Glass* (the first is the opening paragraph) in which reality, space, time, and identity are juxtaposed in a disorientating, almost threatening way:

It was a wrong number that started it, the telephone ringing three times in the dead of night, and the voice on the other end asking for someone he was not. Much later, when he was able to think about the things that happened to him, he would conclude that nothing was real except chance. But that was much later. In the beginning there was simply the event and its consequences.

> Whether it might have turned out differently, or whether it was all predetermined with the first word that came from the stranger's mouth, is not the question. The question is the story itself, and whether or not it means something is not for the story to tell. [p. 3]

And later, towards the end of the story,

> Quinn was nowhere now. He had nothing, he knew nothing, he knew that he knew nothing. Not only had he been sent back to the beginning, he was now before the beginning, and so far before the beginning that it was worse than any end he could imagine. [p. 104]

While the classic detective arrives at a solution to a crime, the more recent metaphysical sleuth "finds himself confronting the insoluble mysteries of his own interpretation and his own identity" (Merivale & Sweeney, 1999, p. 2). Daniel Quinn is a writer of detective fiction, to which he is drawn because it presents the detective as capable of locating the truth beneath the surface of confusing and contradictory clues through decoding and logic, so making sense of them, and thus he believes reality is revealed to him. Both the identity and the logic of a detective that he takes on serve as his anchor and prove to him (albeit temporarily) that he has a place in the world (Swope, 1998). Unfortunately, unlike the cases Quinn writes, the case he becomes involved in and lives through in Auster's novel fails to produce the tidy conclusion his own sense of self as detective depends on. Furthermore, this failure also points him towards the instability of the world, as well as to the failure of language to be transparent. Meanwhile, the reader witnesses how his sense of himself disintegrates, fragments, and dissolves. The figure of Daniel Quinn is very different to those of Holmes and Fitz. In terms of continuity, one could argue that the latter two operate within the continuity of the reassuringly stable and modernist world, whereas Quinn inhabits a discontinuous, "homeless", and alienating postmodern landscape that offers no comfort, no shelter. There are no maps to guide him and no guard-rails to hold on to. He never finds for himself a space in the world that is his own. As such, he is a deeply troubled and troubling figure.

You may well be able to recognize researchers, or your students and colleagues, in the figures of Holmes and Fitz. Or you may find them in the texts in academic journals and books. They are connected to the world through material relationships; they find real clues and they make judgements with consequences that lead them to further clues; they deduce and come to correct conclusions; they create meaning in the confusion and make the invisible visible to those less clever than them. They are self-assured, confident, competent, smug even. They are who they are because they are good at their job of detection. Yet, do we recognize those others in Quinn? Or are we more likely to recognize ourselves in his agonizing search for truth and resolution beneath the cacophony of surface noises that our "data" might produce? Do we recognize ourselves in the anxiety that we will not find the vital clue that will lead us out of the maze; in the panic that what we produce will not be acceptable and that we will be found out to be an impostor? In those dark nights of the soul, do we find ourselves asking ourselves whether, in fact, we have no business here at all, no right to ask all these questions after all?

I was tempted to finish this chapter here and leave you in the bleak and disturbing world of Daniel Quinn. But, as it is such a cheerless place, devoid of hope and optimism, it is not a good place to end. But maybe it is a good place to start talking about ethics in qualitative research. It is hardly ideal, but possibly more fruitful a beginning than professional codes of ethics and absolutist principles to guide all research.

Reflexivities and emotion

I refer to reflexivity in the plural as it is surrounded by much debate in the social sciences and human service professions. Numerous typologies have been suggested (for example, Finlay, 2003; Gough, 2003; Lynch, 2000; Macbeth, 2001; Marcus, 1994; Wilkinson, 1988). A useful way of conceptualizing reflexivity in research may be through the heuristic device of the continuum: at one end point is reflexivity as accounting for the person of the researcher, an explication of her or his horizon in order to amplify the "other", or, more specifically in the research context, the participant. Here, reflexivity is understood as critical self-awareness, where researchers actively engage their pre-understandings in the interpretive process in order to help them appreciate precisely that which is different (Grodin,

1994). At this end of the continuum, it is used as a means to ensure methodological rigour and to render the research account more transparent. Both aims are contiguous with traditional notions of validity and reliability. As Macbeth (2001) notes, "there is a promise of methodological advantage and even newly minted knowledge to be gained by the disciplined move to the reflexive space" (p. 48). Here, reflexivity is about the researchers' accountability *vis-à-vis* their audience. At the other end of the continuum, the concern is for the complex relationship between the researcher, the researched, the role of language, data, analysis, representation, and knowledge. Whereas the positivist approach prescribes a one-sided relationship in which the "researched" are identified as the passive subjects whose only responsibility is to provide data in a manner that has been predetermined by the researcher (Carter & Delamont, 1996), working from a feminist and poststructuralist perspective, Lather (1986) stresses how meaning is negotiated and co-constituted in a reciprocal relationship.

Feminists have challenged the conceptualization of the universal, autonomous subject and the separation of self and others, proposing instead an ethic of care and responsibility in which concrete circumstances and relationships shape ethical decision-making. Rather than being grounded in general principles and their applications, an ethic of care is primarily concerned with human relationships and their inherent responsibilities, as well as with compassion, empathy, and nurturance. It also involves attention to the concrete particularities of the specific situation and their connectedness to other particularities. Concepts like receptivity, relatedness, and responsiveness become more important than rights, norms, rules, and ideals. Rather than assuming that we can think more clearly about others when we think of them as distant and essentially *like us*, the feminist ethical model stresses that we have to make moral decisions from *within* relationships, valuing care, closeness, and the individual difference of the other. According to Noddings (1984), the basis for caring is the engrossment with others, empathy and social action on behalf of the other. Researchers working within an ethic of care respect the dignity of their participants, communicating their voices and providing an interpretive analysis explicitly aimed to benefit them (Gunzenhauser, 2006). Thus, researchers do not ground their knowledge claims in their own ethical positioning, but work with participants to understand their perspective and interest in order to learn how to care for them.

As a moral epistemolgy, feminst ethics attempt to represent the relational and emotional aspects of the other's experience through an immersion in the lives of the participants, displacing their own motivations and developing a caring relationship with participants. Yet, to make knowledge claims on the basis of caring relationships calls for a different approach to knowledge that is not disinterested or impersonal on the one hand, or culturally imperialistic or foundationalist on the other (Code, 1995). She writes,

> A moral–political epistemology critically engaged with issues of context, location, and respect cannot easily be derived from an alignment of care with femininity that would establish a set of principles centred around connection and commitment to displace the objectivist theories of autonomous man. . . . Its requirements are better served pluralistically, in case-by-case analyses of places where objectivist, epistemological–moral presuppositions are actively subverted in innovative practices. Because such analyses work from the "inside" out—from specific locations and practices towards theoretical articulation—they lack the foundations that epistemologists expect from projects of constructing a theory of knowledge. Yet my contention is that those foundations have never offered the security they have promised. [p. 111]

There is a growing body of literature to suggest that researchers, especially those working with participants using interpretive approaches, need to balance their needs for information with their obligation towards and care for those who participate in their studies (Etherington, 2007). Key to achieving this balance is the creation of a transparent and dialogic relationship through adopting a reflexive stance. Ellis argues for a relational ethics (2007) that acknowledges the interpersonal connectedness between researcher and research participants, and between researchers and the communities within which they live and work. As Frank (2004) observes, this connectedness does not become static at the point at which ethical review takes place, because research relationships change over time as the research project moves through its various stages:

We do not act on principles that hold for all times. We act as best we can at a particular time, guided by certain stories that speak to that time, and other people's dialogical affirmation that we have chosen the right stories . . . The best any of us can do is to tell one another our stories of how we have made choices and set priorities. By remaining open to other people's responses, to our moral maturity and emotional honesty . . . we engage in the unfinalized dialogue of seeking the good. [*ibid.*, pp. 192–193]

This narrative turn, which recognizes the extent to which perceptions are embedded in their telling and how people rely on story-telling to understand their relationships with others (Charon & Montello, 2002), has inspired researchers to investigate particular ethical issues within their studies.

Similarly, Guillemin and Gillam (2004) call for a reflexive model of research ethics that works to continually examine ethical concerns as they arise in research relationships, rather than working from the premise that research that has been approved by a formal review process will not, as it unfolds, pose unexpected or unintended concerns. They use the term "microethics" (borrowed from Komesaroff, 1996) to describe the everyday and ordinary situations that arise in research practice and that require the researcher to respond. They also include the notion of sensitivity to "ethically important moments" in order to develop a language to articulate, validate and understand ethics-in-practice. They propose a new perspective on reflexivity as "a sensitizing notion that can enable ethical practice to occur in the complexity and richness of social research" (Guillemin & Gillam, 2004, p. 278).

Emotions in research continue to be constructed in opposition to rationality and professionalism, and have therefore been marginalized and avoided in research accounts with the effect that novice researchers are unprepared for the level of emotional engagement that qualitative research requires (Wincup, 2001). The work done in rendering private lives and personal experience open in such a way that they can become public knowledge, as one aim of qualitative research, necessarily requires emotional engagement with participants and self, as Jaggar (1996), Ribbens and Edwards (1998), Usher (2000), Gilbert (2001), Wincup (2001) and Rager (2005) have argued. Pickering (2001) draws attention to emotionality as playing a central part in the research process, but considers that it has been relegated through researchers' self-censorship and confessionals. As such, these marginal accounts seem to apologize for the researcher's emotionality, its unpredictability and disorder, rather than locate it as an important source for knowledge production and decision-making. To illustrate this point and develop it further, I draw on a study I undertook with a number of doctoral students who were carrying out research projects in National Health Service settings and who were using qualitative approaches in their own work. "Emotion work", as part of their research process, featured strongly. This work was predominantly practical and had to do with, for example, arranging an interview or an episode of non-participant observation. It involved establishing a productive rapport with different actors in the research field, which was a function of a number of factors, but the emotion work was a matter of developing trust between the doctoral students and their participants, and, in some instances, with the social environment in which the study took place. This trust was based on their participants being confident in the students' sensitivity and rigour, that "professional rules" of confidentiality would be followed, and that, at worst, the information they provided would not be used against them and at best, would bring benefit to them or others. Some of the students stressed in their conversations with me that establishing this trust was not related to the formal process of obtaining informed consent, but that it was something that happened in social contact preceding the actual data collection. In order to present the face of a trustworthy professional, the researcher–participants managed relationships in the field "back-stage", as it were, from gaining access to the research site by working with senior managers to gauging interpersonal tensions among staff in hospital ward areas resulting from heavy workloads, crisis situations, or disagreements. Being insiders, or ex-insiders, the students were mindful of these contingencies, which established their credibility as people who, while not doing their participants' jobs, had a good idea of what their day-to-day working life might be like. Yet, at times, they were taken by surprise and required to make decisions about what "emotional identity" to present, not only with regard to the participants, but also to people indirectly involved in their research. Insider or outsider? Practitioner or researcher? Supervisor or researcher? Tutor or researcher? Familiar guest or uninvited stranger? Dealing with participants' emotional distress during interviews was a contingency a number of students faced. In fact, it was anticipated as one of the risks of interview-based research, which students routinely addressed in their applications to the ethics committees. This was usually expressed as providing contact details of a counsellor if the student assessed the interviewee as particularly vulnerable at the end of an interview. This aspect of the students' performance was part of the discourse of emotional vulnerability that construes people as unable to cope with the consequences of emotional distress, and which thereby not only medicalizes human experience, but also manages contemporary subjectivity (Furedi, 2004). Furedi critiques what he calls "therapy culture", which offers a vocabulary through which people make sense of the individual's relationship to society from an assumption of an emotional deficit, a lack of coping skills, and a consciousness of poor self-esteem. He argues that contemporary representations of the vulnerable self, which cannot be expected to cope in adversity, function to disempower people, and undermine subjectivity and agency. Such constructions of the vulnerable self bear a family resemblance to discourse of emotional intelligence, which was also invoked by the students to describe an ability to respond sensitively and productively to the sort of research situations I described above. Proponents of the doctrine of emotional intelligence, for example Goleman (1996), consider that a lack of self-awareness and an unwillingness to acknowledge one's true feelings are responsible for both individual distress and the problems facing society in general. Their argument construes emotionally illiterate people as potentially destructive personalities who bear responsibility for many of the ills facing society (Furedi, 2004). A side-effect of such a discourse is the transformation of social and cultural problems into psychological ones, which pathologizes individuals, thus moving responsibility from social structures to the psychological make-up of individuals.

In our conversations, talk about reflexivity was related to the discourse of emotionality as a kind of self-monitoring process, a move towards greater accountability and towards the production of an, if not sanitized account of the research (as was the case for some of the students, particularly those who undertook their doctorate at faculties of healthcare and medicine), one that legitimizes emotion as part of the research process. Thus, reflexivity was talked about and used as an imaginary "cure" for the researcher's processes of meaning-making and as a device for better knowing, as if it were possible to cancel out the researcher's subjectivity. Indeed, in the face of ethics committees' methodological suspicion, and sometimes outright censure of projects that use qualitative approaches, and other alternative frameworks for knowing and knowledge, reflexivity was evoked as a prescription against undue bias, a methodological move to make qualitative research more like its biomedical, statistical cousin. Burman (2006) suggests that reflexivity as research practice functions performatively as an invitation to confess within a discourse of methodological improvement. The effect of this discourse of reflexivity and emotional intelligence is that structural issues are reduced to personal ones. Burman stresses that this is not a necessary product of reflexivity, but "an expression of what happens when an ethical–political commitment becomes transformed into a technocratic intervention" (p. 325); in other words, a technique for self-surveillance, which manages emotions and normalizes some subjective accounts while pathologizing or marginalizing others. These discourses are dangerous in so far as they seem to "reinstate the rational unitary subject" (*ibid.*) through a process that decontextualizes and abstracts emotions to such an extent that they become an adjunct to cognition. I do not mean to suggest that emotions are not involved in the sensitive perception of situations, in ethical decision-making, and in the representation of self in research accounts. Instead, I wish to resist the discourse that constructs reflexivity first as another technology of the self, and second, as an internalized tool for surveillance that sanitizes emotions.

Thinking about ethics should not be limited to the stage of data collection, where the relationship between researcher and researched is closest. It spans the process from the questions we ask about our practice and those we seek to serve, our assumptions about how knowledge can be produced and which methods are most suitable, to the analysis of data and the language and style we use when producing the final research text, be it a journal paper, a dissertation, or a formal report. The process of revealing the complex relationship between language, data, researcher, and researched may be seen as an aspect of reflexivity that foregrounds the struggles and complexities of doing engaged research (Pillow, 2003). Pillow (*ibid.*, p. 175) terms this reflexivity "uncomfortable" because it pushes towards the unfamiliar and the confounding. Put another way, a reflexive text is crafted to disrupt the comforts of familiar knowledge representations and to account for the struggles of those who participated in the research process, including the researcher. Yet, it is a challenge to create such a text, a text which seeks to open up possible patterns and possible explanations, inviting the reader to enter into a dialogue with the text, rather than to provide an authoritative version of the "truth" based on evidence, in a culture that expects research texts to conform to traditional notions of science, reliability and validity, quality, and academic language. If, according to Hertz (1997), the purpose of reflexivity is to produce research texts that challenge their own interpretations and lay open the process of knowledge production, how can researcher–practitioners reflect their responsibility in their writing? One answer is abandoning the shelter of third person writing, detachment, and objectivity, whereby we exclude ourselves from the research lest our subjectivity contaminate the data, the analysis, and research text. Instead, the practice of reflexivity means writing ourselves into the research process and text in order to convey something about how understanding was constructed, and may be being actively constructed by the reader.

Here, I finish this chapter for a second time. This may be a more hopeful space, furnished with ideas and references, but it is really only another beginning; a beginning only slightly different to the one in which I suggested that we are really much more on our own, like Daniel Quinn perhaps, than ethics would have us believe. I take my leave with the words of Bauman (1998):

> And so we come to the greatest paradox of the strategy of moral life ... the greater the moral responsibility, the dimmer is the hope of its normative regulation. The more we need to act, the less we know what we ought to be doing. The more pressing the demand, the deeper the silence about what it demands us to do. The larger the responsibility to be taken, the less we are sure of what taking up that responsibility would need to consist of. It is easy to spell to out the guidelines, even the norms, for small and insignificant, trite and inconsequential responsibilities. It is much more difficult, nay impossible, to do the same for responsibility truly immense,

consummate and seminal. The more it counts what we do, the less
certain it is what it is we ought to be doing. [p. 20]

References

Ashcroft, R. (2003). The ethics and governance of medical research:
what does regulation have to do with morality? *New Review of
Bioethics, 1*(1): 41–58.

Bauman, Z. (1998). What prospects of morality in times of uncertainty?
Theory, Culture and Society, 15(1): 11–22.

Beauchamp, T. L., & Childress, J. F. (2001). *Principles of Biomedical Ethics*
(5th edn). Oxford: Oxford University Press.

Brinkman, S. (2004). The topography of moral ecology. *Theory &
Psychology, 14*(1): 57–80.

Brinkmann, S., & Kvale, S. (2005). Confronting the ethics of qualitative
research. *Journal of Constructivist Psychology, 18*: 157–181.

Burman, E. (2006). Emotions and reflexivity in feminised education
action research. *Educational Action Research, 14*(3): 315–332.

Caputo, J. D. (1993). *Against Ethics*. Bloomington, IN: Indiana University Press.

Carter, K., & Delamont, S. (1996). Qualitative research: the emotional
dimension. Cardiff papers in a qualitative research. Avebury,
Aldershot, Hants.

Charon, R., & Montello, M. (2002). Memory and anticipation: the practice of narrative ethics: introduction. In: R. Charon & M. Montello
(Eds.), *Stories Matter: The Role of Narrative in Medical Ethics* (pp.
ix–xii). London: Routledge.

Christians, C. G. (2003). Ethics and politics in qualitative research. In: N.
Denzin & Y. S. Lincoln (Eds.), *The Landscape of Qualitative Research:
Theories and Issues* (pp. 208–244). Thousand Oaks, CA: Sage.

Christians, C. G. (2005). Ethical theory in communications research.
Journalism Studies, 6(1): 3–14.

Code, L. (1995). *Rhetorical Spaces: Essays on Gendered Locations*. New
York: Routledge.

Corrigan, O. (2003). Empty ethics: the problem with informed consent.
Sociology of Health & Illness, 25(7): 768–792.

Daly, J., & McDonald, I. (1996). Introduction: ethics, responsibility and
health research. In: J. Daly & I. McDonald (Eds.), *Ethical Intersections: Health Research, Methods, and Researcher Responsibility*
(pp. 5–17). St Leonards, Australia: Allen and Unwin.

Ellis, C. (2007). Telling secrets, revealing lives: relational ethics in research with intimate others. *Qualitative Inquiry*, *13*(1): 3–29.

Etherington, K. (2007). Ethical research in reflexive relationships. *Qualitative Inquiry*, *13*(5): 599–616.

Faden, R., & Beauchamp, T. L. (1986). *A History and Theory of Informed Consent*. New York: Oxford University Press.

Finlay, L. (2003). The reflexive journey: mapping multiple routes. In: L. Finlay & B. Gough (Eds.), *Reflexivity: A Practical Guide for Researchers in Health and Social Sciences* (pp. 3–20). Oxford: Blackwell Science.

Foucault, M. (1970/2002). *The Order of Things: Archaeology of the Human Sciences*. Abingdon: Routledge.

Fox, R. (1990). The evolution of American bioethics: a sociological perspective. In: G. Weisz (Ed.), *Social Science Perspectives on Medical Ethics* (pp. 201–217). Dordrecht/Boston/London.

Frank, A. (2004). Moral non-fiction: life writing and children's disabilities. In: P. J. Eakin (Ed.), *The Ethics of Life Writing* (pp. 174–194). Ithaca, NY: Cornell University Press.

Furedi, F. (2004). *Therapy Culture: Cultivating Vulnerability in an Uncertain Age*. London: Routledge.

Geiderman, J. M. (2002a). Ethics seminars: physician complicity in the Holocaust: historical review and reflections on emergency medicine in the 21st century, Part I. *Academic Emergency Medicine*, *9*: 223–231.

Geiderman, J. M. (2002b). Ethics seminars: physician complicity in the Holocaust: historical review and reflections on emergency medicine in the 21st century, Part II. *Academic Emergency Medicine*, *9*: 232–240.

Gilbert, K. R. (2001). Introduction: why are we interested in emotions? In: K. R. Gilbert (Ed.), *The Emotional Nature of Qualitative Research* (pp. 3–15). Boca Raton, FL: CRC Press.

Giorgi, A. (2006). Facts, values and the psychology of the human person. *The Indo-Pacific Journal of Phenomenology*, *6*: Special Edition. Accessed at www.ipjp.org/SEmethod/Special_Edition_Method-01_Giorgi. pdf on 30 May 2008.

Goleman, D. (1996). *Emotional Intelligence: Why It Can Matter More than IQ*. London: Bloomsbury.

Gough, B. (2003). Deconstructing reflexivity. In: L. Finlay & B. Gough (Eds.), *Reflexivity: A Practical Guide for Researchers in Health and Social Sciences* (pp. 21–35). Oxford: Blackwell Science, Oxford.

Grodin, J. (1994). *Introduction to Philosophical Hermeneutics*. New Haven, CT: Yale University Press.

Guillemin, M., & Gillam, L. (2004). Ethics, reflexivity, and "ethically important moments" in research. *Qualitative Inquiry*, *10*(2): 261–280.

Gunzenhauser, M. G. (2006). A moral epistemology of knowing subjects: theorizing a relational turn for qualitative research. *Qualitative Inquiry, 12*(3): 621–647.

Halse, C., & Honey, A. (2005). Unravelling ethics: illuminating the moral dilemmas of research ethics. *Signs, 30*(4): 2141–2162.

Halse, C., & Honey, A. (2007). Rethinking ethics review as institutional discourse. *Qualitative Inquiry, 13*(3): 336–352.

Hanauske-Abel, H. M. (1996). Not a slippery slope or sudden subversion: German medicine and National Socialism in 1933. *British Medical Journal, 313*: 1453–1463.

Hazelgrove, J. (2002). The old faith and the new science: The Nuremberg Code and human experimentation ethics in Britain. *Social History of Medicine, 15*(1): 109–135.

Hedgecoe, A. M. (2004). Critical bioethics: beyond the social science critique of applied ethics. *Bioethics, 18*(2): 120–143.

Hertz, R. (1997). *Reflexivity and Voice*. Thousand Oaks, CA: Sage.

Hoffmaster, B. (1994). The forms and limits of medical ethics. *Social Science and Medicine, 39*(9): 1155–1164.

Homan, R. (1991). *The Ethics of Social Research*. Harlow: Longman.

Jaggar, A. M. (1996). Love and knowledge: emotion in feminist epistemology. In: A. Garry & M. Pearsall (Eds.), *Women, Knowledge and Reality: Explorations in Feminist Philosophy* (pp. 166–190). New York: Routledge.

Kearney, R. (2003). *Strangers, Gods and Monsters*. London: Routledge.

Komesaroff, P. (1996). Medicine and the ethical conditions of modernity In: J. Daly & I. McDonald (Eds.), *Ethical Intersections: Health Research, Methods, and Researcher Responsibility* (pp. 34–48). St Leonards, Australia: Allen and Unwin.

Lather, P. (1986). Issues in validity in openly ideological research: between a rock and a soft place. *Interchange, 17*(4): 63–84.

Latour, B. (1993). *We Have Never Been Modern*. Cambridge, MA: Harvard University Press.

Leaning, J. (1996). War crimes and medical science. *British Medical Journal, 313*: 1413–1415.

Lynch, M. (2000). Against reflexivity as an academic virtue and source of privileged knowledge. *Theory, Culture and Society, 17*(3): 26–54.

Lyotard, J. F. (1984). *The Postmodern Condition: A Report on Knowledge*. Minneapolis, MN: University of Minnesota Press.

Macbeth, D. (2001). On reflexivity in qualitative research: two readings and a third. *Qualitative Inquiry, 7*(1): 35–68.

Marcus, G. E. (1994). What comes just after "post"?: the case of ethnography. In: N. K. Denzin, & Y. S. Lincoln (Eds.), *Handbook of Qualitative Research* (pp. 563–574). Newbury Park, CA: Sage.

Mattingly, C. (2005). Toward a vulnerable ethics of research practice. *Health: An Interdisciplinary Journal for the Social Study of Health, Illness and Medicine, 9*(4): 453–471.

Merivale, P., & Sweeney, S. E. (1999). *Detecting Texts: The Metaphysical Detective Story from Poe to Postmodernism.* Philadelphia, PA: University of Pennsylvania Press.

Moring, I. (2001). Detecting the fictional problem solvers in time and space: metaphors guiding qualitative analysis and interpretation. *Qualitative Inquiry, 7*(3): 346–369.

Noddings, N. (1984). *Caring: A Feminine Approach to Ethics and Moral Education.* Berkeley, CA: University of California Press.

Pickering, S. (2001). Undermining the sanitized account: violence and emotionality in the field in Northern Ireland. *British Journal of Criminology, 41*: 485–501.

Pillow, W. S. (2003). Confession, catharsis or cure: rethinking the uses of reflexivity as methodological power in qualitative research. *International Journal of Qualitative Studies in Education, 16*(2): 175–196.

Plomer, A. (2005). *The Law and Ethics of Medical Research: International Bioethics and Human Rights.* London: Cavendish.

Rager, K. (2005). Compassion stress and the qualitative researcher. *Qualitative Health Research, 15*(3): 423–430.

Redwood, S. (2005). Colliding discourses: deconstructing the process of seeking ethical approval for a participatory evaluation project. *Journal of Research in Nursing, 10*(2): 217–230.

Ribbens, J., & Edwards, R. (Eds.) (1998). *Feminist Dilemmas in Qualitative Research: Public Knowledge and Private Lives.* London: Sage.

Rothman, D. J. (1991). *Strangers at the Bedside.* New York: Basic Books.

Sharpe, R. (2005). Metaphor. In: *The Oxford Companion to Philosophy.* Oxford: Oxford University Press.

St Pierre, E. A. (1997). Methodology in the fold and the irruption of transgressive data. *International Journal of Qualitative Studies in Education, 10*(2): 175–189.

Swope, R. (1998). Approaching the threshold(s) in postmodern detective fiction: Hawthorne's "Wakefield" and other missing persons. *Critique, 39*(3): 207–227.

Usher, P. (2000). Feminist approaches to a situated ethics. In: H. Simons & R. Usher (Eds.), *Situated Ethics in Educational Research* (pp. 22–38). London: Routledge Falmer.

van den Hoonaard, W. C. (2001). Is research ethics review a moral panic? *Canadian Review in Social Anthropology*, *38*(1): 19–36.

Whittaker, E. (2005). Adjudicating entitlements: the emerging discourses of research ethics boards. *Health: An Interdisciplinary Journal for the Social Study of Health, Illness and Medicine*, *9*(4): 513–535.

Wilkinson, S. (1988). The role of reflexivity in feminist psychology. *Women's Studies International Forum*, *11*: 493–502.

Wincup, E. (2001). Feminist research with women awaiting trial: the effects on participants in the qualitative research process. In: K. R. Gilbert (Ed.), *The Emotional Nature of Qualitative Research* (pp. 17–35). Boca Raton, FL: CRC Press.

World Medical Association (1964). Declaration of Helsinki on the ethical principles for medical research involving human subjects. World Medical Association General Assembly, Edinburgh.

CHAPTER EIGHT

Epiphany

Roddy McKenzie

Introduction

This book takes its inspiration in part from the political theorist Antonio Gramsci. This and other chapters will implicitly or explicitly embody his ideas and concepts, which manifest most obviously in the determination to present and promote practitioner based research. For my part, I will refer explicitly to Gramsci in that his work will provide both the cohesion and the context in which my own research comes to life and finds its purpose. My aim is to provide an example of practitioner based research that is a critique, a challenge, and a feasible alternative to the dominant contemporary discourse on the spiritual dimension of nursing care.

Traditional intellectuals and the politics of evidence

Antonio Gramsci (1971) makes a distinction between what he calls "organic intellectuals" and "traditional intellectuals." In the first instance, it is necessary to elaborate further on his notion of the traditional intellectual. According to Gramsci, while at one time they had a close (organic) relationship with a particular social group, a key characteristic of traditional intellectuals is that they have become distant and withdrawn from the messy complexity of social life. In addition, they have in common a belief that they are disinterestedly autonomous of political considerations, and this applies to knowledge professionals—in our case nursing researchers and academics.

This manifests in nursing in two ways. The first and most visible aspect is referred to as the theory–practice gap. There is widespread acceptance that a theory–practice gap exists in nursing, and it is a subject that has continually demanded the attention of a variety of sources with general consensus of its salient features (see, for example, Carr, 1996; Hewison & Wildman, 1996, Higginson, 2004; Landers, 2000; Rolfe, 1996, 1998). Second, there has been a closely connected (indeed sometimes overlapping) parallel debate about the reluctance of practising nurses and healthcare professionals to transfer the results of research into practice. Despite a variety of strategies over several decades to resolve this (for example, Briggs, 1972, Department of Health, 1993), healthcare practitioners continue to resist. Again, this is a contemporary issue that continues to demand attention (see, for example, Freshwater 2007; Holloway & Freshwater, 2007). To sum up, Vaughan (1987) maintained that while practice and theory remained separate in nursing, then nurses would experience a disparity between theory and practice. This, in essence, summarizes the theory–practice gap and, by extension, the research dilemma; educators, academics, and researchers (traditional intellectuals), despite the volume of written work referred to above, are seldom found in the environment (social life) of practising nurses and other related disciplines. Indeed, it has been argued that we now have two distinct professions co-existing; one text-based (academe) and the other practice-based (McKenzie, 2007).

Second is the emergence of evidence-based practice. This is an expression that originated in the field of medicine but has since gone on to colonize health care in general. In essence, it demands that health care practitioners base their practice on sound evidence. The nursing profession has generally wholeheartedly embraced evidence-based practice (Walker, 2003). While what counts as evidence is contested, nurses and other healthcare professionals have accepted (uncritically and naïvely) that it is in their best interests, as academics have set about establishing an evidence base (as if none existed). However, the term "evidence-based practice" is in danger of becoming (if not already realized) doubly inscribed, i.e., a term that stands for a particular type of academic and scientific discourse but, more subtly and insidiously, a cultural alibi for the introduction of a particular political ideology.

In academic discourse, the hermeneutic imperative rests with the reader, but this is negated when importing evidence into policy. When a policy "cites" a source in evoking an evidence base in support of its claims, etc., it does not do so within the established norms of scholarly academic discourse. The authors (usually multiple, sometimes anonymous) do not cite the reference with a view to the reader subjecting it to some scholarly scrutiny in order possibly to enter into dialogue over methods, validity, or apparent "truth claims"—rather, they cite it as a fact, an actual as opposed to a relative truth. It is this textual twist that renders academic discourse into political ideology. Traditional intellectuals can no longer claim to be politically autonomous or neutral, while, in the meantime, evidence-based practice seems to be building on, and, with some vigour, adding to, an already well-established theory–practice gap.

The spiritual dimension of nursing care: the dominant discourse

Currently, practising nurses work in an ever more complex and mediated world. Situated in organizations operating an essentially economic model, text-based imperatives proliferate in various guises such as guidelines, policies, procedures, and protocols, all explicitly or implicitly claiming the common ancestry of "evidence", if not assuming the status of evidence by virtue of being text. This is the fertile soil of the politics of evidence as discussed above. Government reports make increasing use of the term and terminology associated with evidence-based practice and, as alluded to above, seek to encourage health-care professionals to base their practice on evidence (see, for example, Department of Health, 1996, 1997, 1998; Scottish Office, 1997, 1998).

The spiritual dimension of nursing care and the surrounding discourse is no stranger to all of the dynamics already discussed in respect of traditional intellectuals—text-based imperatives, the politics of evidence, and the theory and research gaps. In the first instance, Ross (2006) draws our attention to the fact that the provision of spiritual care is *a professional expectation* of nurses, and this is reflected in national and international nursing codes of ethics, educational guidelines, and policies. Second, those writing about spirituality are nurse academics, educationalists, and researchers (hereafter referred to as traditional intellectuals), and it is they who produce the "orientating generalizations" within the discourse. Orientating generalizations are the already-agreed-upon background knowledge that scholars in specific fields take to be true as they debate the issues on which they differ; a debate that, as Swinton (2006) observes, has become saturated and static. And so, I think it is safe to conclude, we have an unholy alliance (no pun intended) between traditional intellectuals and policy makers. Nurses' (and indeed other healthcare practitioners) and patients' personal views and experiences differ from the dominant view, and nurses are caught in another theory–practice gap while being compelled by policy makers to provide spiritual care based on the evidence produced by the academy.

There has been a massive increase, particularly over the past ten years or so, on the subject in question, and clearly a full analysis or critique is out of the question within the confines of this chapter. Therefore, to illustrate the disparity and tension between the dominant discourse and the reality of practice, I will offer what I call significant paradoxes.

Paradox 1

There is an oft repeated mantra that historically nursing has attempted to provide the spiritual/religious needs of patients (Clark, Cross, Deane, & Lowry, 1991; Pullen, Tuck, & Mix, 1996; Swinton, 2006). Perhaps the most striking feature of the writing from the traditional intellectuals is their determination to establish spirituality as something entirely distinct from religion, particularly the Judeo-Christian tradition. Critical debate around this point is, however, absent, and a rather superficial discussion exists as expressed by, for example, Narayanasamy's (1999) concern that developing spiritual care based upon the Judeo-Christian roots of nursing would limit spiritual care to Christian patients only. More recently, Ross (2006) undertook an overview of the research to date in respect of spiritual care in nursing. In her discussion she cautioned that studies from a Judeo-Christian stance were, in her opinion, "biased", the inference being that the validity of those studies in respect of the subject was questionable and presumably should not be included in the evolving evidence base. However, in seeking to "erase" the Judeo-Christian perspective, they expunge their own claims of historically-based ownership of spiritual care, because, for certain, that historically-based spirituality would have been exclusively Judeo-Christian (Bradshaw, 1996a).

Paradox 2

In contrast to the views of the traditional intellectuals, research (their own!) reveals that practitioners equate spirituality with faith and belief, *with* religion (Ross, 1994). The traditional intellectuals have been dogged in their response, producing courses designed to teach nurses about spiritual care and, as Swinton (2006) observes,

> the education of nurses for spiritual care can actually function as a subtle (or not so subtle!) mode of indoctrination wherein narrowly defined understandings of spirituality worked out by academics with their own particular agenda are put forward as *the only* understandings of spirituality that can have utility for nurses. [p. 21]

Paradox 3

While few, if any, practising nurses are writing about spirituality, one aspect that is considered vital by those who are writing about it is that spirituality needs to be part of the worldview of the nurse (Oldnall, 1996; Ross, 1994). However, with the notable exception of writers who write from a declared position (for example, Ann Bradshaw writes from a Judeo-Christian perspective), they are utterly silent on their own spirituality. Those writing about spirituality have adopted an objective, disengaged position in relation to their subject and their "target" audience, which seems disingenuous given the subject matter. Meanwhile, they have, through language, particularly saturated definitions, constructed a reality that makes it difficult to think of the world outside of their categories and frames of reference. Whose worldview is it?

Paradox 4

At present, it is rare that health-care consumers are consulted as to what research questions are worth asking, and/or when a question should be framed differently (Bradburn, Maher, Adewuyi-Dalton, & Grunfeld, 1995). According to Chalmers (1998), the public wishes care to be based on the best scientific and technological evidence available. Part of the problem of implementing so called "best-prac- tice" is that citizens' contributions have seldom been incorporated into the evaluation of treatments; thus, evaluation is not based on an appropriate balance and range of knowledge and experience. In this respect, Ann Bradshaw (1996b) questions whether patients would recognize the concept of "spirituality" as healthcare writers now generally and overwhelmingly describe it. What these writers assume to be "spiritual care" might not, in fact, correspond to patient need or understanding. Bradshaw cites Bowman (1995), who found that professional staff thought that patients' religious needs were met, while patients themselves found this area to be one of the most neglected in the context of their care.

Paradox 5

By necessity, I need to include an orientating note about disciplines and methods. Nursing is considered to be an emerging profession, and has never had a unique, unified, disciplinary vision; there has never been universal agreement on what the proper focus of nursing is or should be. In the drive towards professional status and, there- fore, its own unique body of knowledge, nursing has borrowed the language, theories, and methods of other established disciplines, including, anthropology, sociology, psychology, and medicine. This is intriguing, given the subject matter, for you would think that the natural disciplinary ally with regard to spirituality would be theology. On the contrary, theology is almost entirely absent in the nursing literature. This is amplified when one considers the aim of providing universal spiritual care in a multi-cultural healthcare environment. Other cultures have adopted our modes of science, but by no means our theological models or paradigms. However universal our sciences may be, our ontological and theological paradigms, basic for theological models, are vastly different. On these grounds, it is not possible to assume that a common theological or even philosophical paradigm or viewpoint that encompassed all religious traditions was feasible. This raises one other paradox within the paradox: why have those writing about spiritual care singled out the Judeo-Christian tradition in their determination to separate spirituality from religion? They make no reference to any other established religion.

I could go on, but my ultimate aim was to illustrate the contradictions inherent in the dominant discourse. The challenge now is to develop a counter-discourse that will challenge the culturally accepted norms of the dominant discourse.

Organic intellectuals and the politics of peer communities

In contrast to the traditional intellectual the organic intellectual is one who is engaged in the messy complexity of social life, one who actively participates in that social life. In this instance, that social life is the arena of nursing practice. According to Hall (1996), it is the job of the organic intellectual to know *more* than the traditional intellectuals; really know, not just pretend to know, but to know deeply and profoundly. Gramsci argues that organic intellectuals must be able to elaborate their specialist knowledge into political knowledge. The issue is also one of political representation: who is entitled to speak on behalf of a particular group—a constituency if you like?

From the perspective of the organic intellectual, legitimacy originates from involvement—participation must be open first of all and in principle to those who are *directly* affected by a problem. If it is accepted that a basic tenet of good research is dependent on the formulation of a good research question, then it is *who* is asking the question that becomes a key issue. The focus of the organic intellectual is then more about facilitating "insider research". They become part of an extended peer community. The challenge is to illuminate, articulate, and politicize what Gramsci (1971) would call the "common sense" of the people, the worldview of those health-care professionals and patients whose experience, as part of a peer community, differs from the worldview of the dominant discourse. Bringing this worldview to life is crucial, for, as Hundley (1999) argues, in the absence of evidence that not only has utility but that also resonates with practitioners, practice is based on consensus and experience: in other words, common sense. The means by which we can both illuminate this practice-based evidence and bring it to bear is via a discipline and its methods not usually asso-ciated with healthcare or nursing, and that discipline is folklore. While most traditional intellectuals view folklore as "picturesque" and old-fashioned, Gramsci treats it as a living "conception of the world and life", which stands in implicit opposition to "official" conceptions of the world (Gramsci, 1985, p. 189). Gramsci contends that folklore is a key form in which people's worldviews are stored and transmitted. As a living "conception of the world and life", folklore overlaps significantly with common sense.

The method of ordinariness: self-reflexivity

For my part, I am exploring an aspect of spirituality that lays out the discourse of spirituality in nursing, but that has something significant to contribute to the debate. It is about the spiritual prac-tice of individuals who partake in a ritual that is pre-Christian, but that now accommodates individual expression of personal spiritu-ality which includes all faiths and none and that, crucially, is concerned with healing. It lies within the domain of folklore. My method of inquiry, consistent with folklore investigation, is ethnog-raphy. I have been critical of writers in the dominant discourse not declaring their own spiritual experiences, positions, or worldviews, so, before I share my research in any detail, I will first of all, in the interests of transparency, reciprocity, and declaring my own personal theories, share my own spiritual experiences and beliefs in a manner that is both process and product. To put this in to some context, Walker (2003) argues that researchers are obliged not to let their voice dominate "for fear of controlling" the text, thereby undermining the dialogical and participatory nature of the research. Indeed, the researcher must indulge a certain self-reflexivity and humility when it comes to positioning him or herself in the text alongside the other informants. The increasing emphasis being placed on reflexivity has challenged researchers to write themselves in to the research story (Scott, 1996). Beyond this, it has been established elsewhere that it is desirable, even necessary, for the ethnographer to undergo the experience he/she is attempting to understand. The ethnographer's own experiences should be treated as data (Turner, 2002). So, while eliciting stories—narratives—from informants has always been a core feature of folklore and ethnography, the personal narrative of the researcher as part of the research is becoming increasingly vital. And this, in itself, belongs to a separate emerging discipline, autoethnography. While I am incorporating an autoethnography in my research, it is a legitimate research activity in its own right.

Autoethnography stands at the intersection of three genres of writing that are becoming increasingly visible: (i) native anthropology; (ii) ethnic autobiography; and (iii) autobiographical ethnography. The word "autoethnography" has been used for at least two decades by literary critics as well as by anthropologists and sociologists, and can have multiple meanings (Reed-Danahay, 1997). Like many other terms used by social scientists, the meanings and applications of autoethnography have evolved in a manner that makes precise definition and application difficult. The scope and variety of practices that come under the broad rubric of autoethnography is vast (see Ellis & Bochner, 2000 for a comprehensive account).

Autoethnography is grounded in personal life. Usually written in first person voice, it pays attention to physical feelings, thoughts, and emotions and is profoundly introspective. Honest autoethnography generates a lot of fears, doubts, and emotional pain. There is, of course, vulnerability in revealing yourself, particularly in not being able to take back what you have written or in having any control in how readers interpret your work (Ellis & Bochner, 2000). However, you do come to understand yourself in deeper ways, and with understanding of self comes understanding of others.

Having thus set the scene in terms of defending and explaining my approach, I will not make references to literature in support of the following personal narrative; that is for others to do. But I will simply state that, with regard to my own and others' narratives, the point must not be missed that applying these methods to the study of religious phenomena represents a neutral, non-religious approach. Establishing the nature of religious experience *prior* to any interpretation or definition is an important principle.

Random acts of worship: a personal narrative

I was christened Presbyterian, Church of Scotland. I attended church regularly with my family; my father in particular had strong Christian beliefs. I have good memories of a happy childhood, blissfully ignorant of those facts of life that inevitably unfold for all but differ depending on your environment and social circumstances. My home town, Port Glasgow, was rife with the sectarian divide that permeates Scotland's central belt. I stopped going to church in my early teens (to the quiet dismay of my father), partly because of the hypocrisy of church-going Christian sectarian bigots, and partly because there was nothing about church and the Christian message (as received) that resonated with me in any way

For years, it seemed, I had stared across the River Clyde at the Argyll hills, a place that had been during my childhood both America and where the Second World War had been fought. I guess that pretty well summed up my worldview: Port Glasgow was the centre of the universe. It seemed almost inevitable that I would eventually take to those hills, although what the final catalyst was for doing so remains a mystery to me. A friend and colleague, John Mitchell, and I started to walk and climb in Scotland's mountains in the early 1980s.

Taking to the mountains was one of the major transitional episodes of my life, if not *the* one, which, to this day, I find difficult to articulate. It amounts to an ache around the heart. You see, my reality had become a small town rife with unemployment, sectarianism, violence, and alcohol. It wasn't for me, but it was not until I started to climb that I became fully aware of this, or of the options open to me. My relationship with my home town had become unbearable. It was not a place I had any desire to be associated with, with all the stereotypical images of a Portonian. Certainly, I had strong bonds with family and friends, and, as mentioned, a happy childhood complete with places of childhood safety, but to live in a place that has to be endured or ignored rather than enjoyed is to be diminished as a human being. In short, what happened was that I climbed out (literally, metaphorically, and metaphysically) of my man-made, man-defined reality into something else, something other, something completely natural. Man might have invented the term "wilderness", but it exists despite, and not because of, this, and to truly comprehend wilderness one must experience it.

I discovered that to spend time in such a place had many benefits, apart from the exercise, freshness, and stunning natural beauty, a beauty by which I now judge all beauty. It freed my mind to explore all the possibilities that my life held and allowed me to rub out everything I ever believed or felt, and draw it back in again. I also discovered that, accompanied by a trusted friend (John) and in such a neutral, value-free environment, I could walk and talk through any difficulties that might occur in my life. That it should draw me closer to developing a deeper and more compassionate bond to other human beings was a surprising but welcome side effect; it seems that through detachment grows profound engagement

Mountain walking and climbing introduced me to more than a few immeasurable elements in my life: mortality, impermanence, time and timelessness, sacred space and place. Places are not abstractions or concepts, but are directly experienced phenomena of the lived world, and hence are full of meanings, with real objects and with ongoing activities. They are important sources of individual and communal identity and can be profound centres of human existence to which people have deep emotional and psychological ties. Our relationship with places is just as necessary, varied, and sometimes perhaps just as unpleasant, as our relationship with people. It would seem common-place that almost everyone is born with the need for identification with their surroundings, a relationship with those surroundings, and a need to be in a recognizable place. So, a sense of place is not some fine-art extra, it is something that we cannot afford to be without. To be attached to places and to have profound ties with them is an important human need. In essence, I was tuning out of my man-made and man-defined environment and tuning into something other, something closer to what I believe are the essential facets of human existence: the earth, the sky, the gods, and men.

The sense of timelessness in the mountains is awesome, but it did not speak to me of the futility of our very short time alive. Rather, it spoke of the beauty and potential of life. Mountains introduced me to the need and desire to live as fully and as authentically as possible. At times in the mountains, owing to a combination of the elements (the weather) and the terrain of the mountain, the mountain itself loses all trace of what you might call its humanity. It is not superhuman, it is "ahuman". It does not reject man, it ignores him, but I definitely had a sense of something greater, something far more powerful than most can comprehend.

There is another, perhaps even more abstract, notion that I find even more difficult to articulate, but it is the case that some places (not just in the mountains) have very special feelings or atmospheres about them. Most of us no longer live in a world inhabited by spirits or their symbols, or even where there are any significant holy places. The problem of "special places" is that the modern world simply has no vocabulary in which to voice the palpable "music" of sacred places, one of those places where ordinary, rational people sense the presence of an unknown power. To be human is to live in a world that is full of significant places: to be human is to have and to know your place. I have a very real sense of knowing my place in the world and of my essential "humanness".

Any time that I have had any sense of the numinous, the presence of God, or something "other", has been in wilderness, in silence. It is impossible to express the feeling with any real clarity, but I feel expansive and tiny, timeless and mortal, very, very connected to life and all that is precious to me, and it is a feeling that bursts out rather than floods in. I have a heightened sense of awareness, and on my climbs to summit tops I will see a pebble and think of someone, or think of someone and pick up a pebble. These hills, and their summit cairns, have become important places where I leave pebbles and prayers dedicated to others. Several times I have had strong urges to contact the individual that these small pebbles represent, and every time I have found that individual to be in a time of need. They have always appreciated my contact.

When my father was dying, he requested that I scatter some of his ashes on a mountaintop. He said, "I have always wanted to climb, never got round to it." Nature was a special part of his life; he loved walking. But in that moment he was telling me about his own Christian beliefs. He believed that after he died, he would be on that mountaintop with me, that he would have life after death. More recently, I have, with some friends, started a men's group with the loose idea that we would share and explore our spiritual beliefs and experiences. A diverse group of Christians, Buddhists, Taoists, atheists, and others uncertain or yet to decide. Now, along with my wilderness walks, I engage in what I call RAW—random acts of worship. This includes prayer, meditation, contemplation, silence, talk, and this, writing. But, perhaps more importantly, I feel part of a faith community, a church, as diverse as you are likely to find. At this time in my life, this has become important to me. Who knows where next?

Research

My own research is titled "An ethnography of Scottish healing wells, their contemporary use, and the implications for health care". In 1571, the Scottish Parliament passed an act, forbidding people from making pilgrimages to healing wells. In 2005, it was estimated that there were in excess of 50,000 rags at three surviving wells in the Highlands of Scotland, and this in an area with the full range of health services and a deep respect for organized religion in the form of the Christian faith. These sites are considered to be pre-Christian and, given the dramatic social changes across the centuries, they clearly have remarkable durability. My fieldwork has involved eliciting stories from people who have visited the wells and who have been willing to share their experiences and stories with me. These narratives have revealed that embedded in everyday "secular" talk lies an often hidden memorate; that is, talk concerned with belief that frequently describes a relationship with the numinous. In this case, this might be the Christian God, a source of energy defined as Love, or the Earth itself. My challenge within the context of this chapter is to offer a brief example, by way of vignettes, of my fieldwork before offering, as promised, an interpretation within a framework that both honours the personal narratives (my own included) and challenges the dominant discourse. But first a word about narrative, or, if you prefer, stories.

I have declared that narrative is a key method in giving expression to the experience of individuals—researchers and patients alike. This is captured in the brief introduction to autoethnography I have written above. Although narrative and narratives (whether as narrative analysis or the analysis of narratives) are not new, there has been increasing interest in narrative inquiry among qualitative researchers. Of course, once identified as a method, its use and application evolve rapidly, and indeed this has escalated during the past ten years (Holloway & Freshwater, 2007). Research by Hatch and Wisneiwski (1995) found that narrative inquiry was represented

in many academic disciplines (including those mentioned in relation to nursing in Paradox 5, above), but, as with nursing theory, not
theology. This increasing significance accorded to narrative is generally referred to as the "narrative turn", and is said to be born of postmodern scepticism towards abstract, propositional truth claims.
That depends on your own philosophical and disciplinary insula-
tion, because narrative as I intend to use it is not postmodern but
pre-modern.

As Linda Degh writes,

> From the time "narrative research" established itself as a special
> field of knowledge, narration was reported everywhere and on all
> sorts of occasions, festive and everyday, intentional and accidental.
> In an historic overview, stories were found to be at home in at
> African tribal gatherings; the campfires of Indian big-game hunters;
> Middle-Eastern coffee houses and courts of law; the households of
> European royalty and nobility; the dining halls of monasteries; the
> hostels of itinerant artisans; roadside gatherings of merchants,
> beggars and other travellers; children's nurseries; the camps of
> migrant harvesters; funeral wakes and marriage ceremonies; the
> firesides of farmers; the pubs and general stores; the path to the
> market; the pilgrimage to the shrine of a worshipped saint. [1995,
> p. 49]

So, when I am referring to narrative, it is in this pre-modern sense,
this uniquely human aspect; that is, prior to the "methodologist's
opportunism" that has seen its rise in qualitative research (Clandinin & Connelly, 2000, p. 18), because this is the sense in which it
is least refined and most representative of experience and least
likely to fall foul of disciplinary colonization by those disciplines
already mentioned. This also signals where it sits most comfortably;
that is, within a pre-modern, interpretive frame of reference, one
that brings into the equation the missing discipline, theology.

Kate

> Kate visited the well when her mother was diagnosed with cancer and
> the prognosis seemed poor. Kate described the Clooty Well as "an
> ancient healing well draped in years of other people's hopes and
> wishes". She said, "I had not consciously thought about the Clooty

Well as an 'answer', but this time I stopped and stood and took in the mass of cloth, shoes, baby boots and scarves in front of me, and I thought, why not?"

Kate selected an old jacket that had been a favourite of her mum's. She "... snipped a small strip of cloth from the neckline of the jacket and tucked it into my pocket. I drove round to the Clooty Well and stood for a moment. I wanted peace and quiet to make my wish, so I let the passing cars go. I found a branch over the running water and carefully tied on the strip of material. I held it tight and closed my eyes and asked the power that is life, or love or Energy to help my Mum, to keep her safe and stop her tumours progressing, or even reduce them."

Kate says she is not a religious person in terms of an organized faith, but she says, "When something as devastating as cancer affects your family you are forced to think about death, and in turn life and what it is all about." With regard to the numinous, Kate says, "I'm not sure any of us know, but something inside me feels that there must be an Energy or Source of Love which is nothing to do with our physical being, but is our Soul. The Healing Well was somewhere for me to try to access this source, despite not being sure if I was a complete idiot or not."

Jenny

Jenny, visited the well because her husband was very unwell and close to death. With regard to her visits, she was careful to select a piece of cloth and also waited until she was alone at the site. She described a visualization process, as opposed to a prayer, within which she saw her husband as a young man in his prime, and hoped for some of that strength and vitality to assist him in his situation now and that it would also help her to cope with his deteriorated state. Jenny is a Christian who attends church regularly but saw no conflict between the well and its pagan associations and her religious beliefs and practices. She was clear that her visualization was "a wish or prayer to God" and that this was "through an intermediary that has sufficed for generations of people". She concurred with the received view that the wells were pre-Christian and had been Christianized by the early saints, and in this case St Boniface in particular. She concluded that "holy water is holy water". She was also clear that praying at the well was quite different from praying in church and, in particular, that you were free from the organized direction and routine of the church ceremony.

Towards an interpretive framework

What I am proposing is a tripartite interpretive framework based on the Christian concepts of revelation and salvation and a third concerned with suffering and redemption, with particular reference to the systematic theology of Paul Tillich. I will now provide definitions of these terms and examples of this interpretive framework in action, making obvious the connections to my, Kate's, and Jenny's stories where appropriate, and, of course, to healing and recovery.

Revelation

Revelation (removing the veil) has been used traditionally to mean the manifestation of something hidden that cannot be approached through ordinary ways of gaining knowledge. The mediums of revelation taken from nature are as innumerable as natural objects. Ocean and stars, plants and animals, human bodies and souls, are all natural mediums of revelation. Equally numerous are natural events that can enter a constellation of revelatory character: the movements of the sky, the change of day and night, growth and decay, birth and death, natural catastrophes, psychosomatic experiences such as maturing, illness, sex, danger (Tillich, 1968, p. 132).

My own revelatory experience is often referred to as a "peak experience", and these are frequently reported in trips into wilderness areas (Tacy, 2004). Jenny's and Kate's experiences are more in line with what Grant (1999) refers to as "trauma spirituality", when the fundamental beliefs and concepts upon which people have built their lives crumble and fall apart, in this instance due to illness, death, and dying. The experience may vary, but the collective name that has been suggested is *a journey of intensification*. The phrase *a journey of intensification* conjures up what is found again and again in Christian thought about salvation. Salvation is ultimately about confronting and making sense of multiple overwhelmings—by God, life, death, sin, evil, goodness, people, responsibilities, and more (Ford, 1999, p. 110).

Salvation

It is a striking fact about Christianity that, in its mainstream forms, it has never officially defined one doctrine of salvation. It has lived with a diversity of approaches. Tillich, however, writes explicitly about salvation and health. Salvation is, essentially, healing, the re-establishment of a whole that was broken, disrupted, disintegrated. This is the function of reconciliation, to make whole the man who struggles against himself. It reaches the centre of personality, and unites man not only with his god and with himself, but also with other men and nature (Tillich, 1981). Indeed, the root meaning of the word salvation is health. That has an appropriate range of refer-ence since health can be physical, social, political, economic, envi-ronmental, mental, spiritual, and moral. None of those dimensions is irrelevant to what the major religious traditions understand as salvation. They are concerned with the whole of life in its largest context and, within that, with human flourishing in particular. Most traditions teach that really understanding salvation requires under-going personal transformation (Ford, 1999, p. 103), and in this context that emerges from the journey of intensification, the revela-tory moment.

My experience in nature led to many things: a profound attach-ment to all human beings, a sense of place and of being rooted, a sense of belonging and of my place in the world, and the urge to live life fully and authentically—to name a few. This is a radical holism in which I perceived that everything, and I mean every-thing, right down to the rocks and stones, is connected. For Kate, a sense of community and hope "an ancient healing well draped in years of other people's hopes and wishes", and a universal feeling of love, an energy circling the Earth. For Jenny, "a wish or prayer to God", and that this was "through an intermediary that has sufficed for generations of people".

Suffering and redemption

Having experienced our revelatory moment and salvation, the third and final stage concerns not only the making sense of suffering, but attempting to alleviate that suffering. To do this, however, we must take cognizance of the elements discussed thus far and pay partic-ular attention to the fact that when I am discussing suffering, it is not in the sense of pain from a restricted biomedical/body--physical perspective, although it can certainly include this. Patients and their friends and families do not make a distinction between physical and non-physical sources of suffering in the same way as, for example, doctors do. What I am alluding to is that, in this moment, we have met and come to terms with the fragility of life, with our mortality, and in turn had an experience of and/or with the numinous that has brought us into deep and authentic contact with our very being, our relationship with ourselves and others, and onwards to include a cosmic perspective. This is a heightened state of awareness, a transcendent moment, and a meeting with what Tillich would call the ground of our being, those aspects of our reality that had previously been located in our deep unconscious, now made manifest. This is also a moment in which temporal parameters are stretched and fluid; my father saw himself as having life beyond death, Jenny and Kate connected with a "community" via the well that was ancient: it included past, current, and future generations. The task in this moment is to have the courage to live fully in the knowledge of our mortality and to resolve any dislocation at the levels of self, community, and cosmos. This is essential to alleviating suffering.

With regard to suffering, the work of Cassel (1982) is particularly important. Just as health (within the context of salvation) has many dimensions, so also does suffering, for suffering can occur in relation to any aspect of the person, whether it is in the realm of social roles, group identification, the relation with self, body, or family, or the relation with a transcendent, transpersonal source of meaning. Suffering occurs when an impending destruction of the person is perceived; it continues until the threat of disintegration has passed or until the integrity of the person can be restored in some other manner. Most generally, suffering can be defined as the state of severe distress associated with events that threaten the intactness of the person.

People suffer from what they have lost of themselves in relation to the world of objects, events, and relationships. Meaning and transcendence offer two traditional ways by which suffering associated with destruction of a part of personhood is ameliorated.

Transcendence is probably the most powerful way in which one is restored to wholeness after an injury to personhood. As mentioned above, when experienced, transcendence locates the person in a far larger landscape. The sufferer is not isolated by pain, but is brought closer to a transpersonal source of meaning and to the human community that shares those meanings. Such an experience need not involve religion in any formal sense; however, in its transpersonal sense it is deeply spiritual (Cassel, 1982).

Redemption, in this instance, refers to the ways in which we passively facilitate or actively assist in the relief of suffering. Again, the means by which we approach this are not modern or postmodern, they do not belong to the counselling technologies or to some psychological construct and intervention, rather, they are again premodern. For example, the ways in which we create meaning. For Jenny and Kate it was within the performance of a ritual that involved silence, praying, wishing, privacy (or secrecy), and visualization: all in the pursuit of psychic calm and meaning-making. Johnson (1999) suggests that what palliative care workers call spiritual pain is more accurately labelled "biographical pain": the sense that my life has not added up in the way I would have wanted, and impending mortality means that this is now too late to change.

Thus, we return to stories and narrative, because, for certain, one way of creating meaning is through telling our own stories. Much of my argument here has been made above, but, in addition to that, it has been asserted that it is the impulse to narrate that makes us uniquely human (Kearney, 2002). We work with the meaning of experience when we tell stories. When we partake of life we create meaning, the purpose of life is meaning-making (Reason, 1988, p. 80). Arthur Frank (1991) believes that telling our story is not only essential for our own meaning-making and healing, but he goes further in suggesting that there is a moral imperative in making our stories of illness and healing known to others to help aid their recovery: "storytelling is *for* an other just as much as it is for oneself. In the reciprocity that is storytelling, the teller offers himself as guide to the other's self-formation" (*ibid.*, p. 18). I have shared my story and Kate and Jenny theirs, although in a text that is hard to read (the healing well) but no less understood by those who visit. All of these elements (and more) can and should be brought to bear in caring for others. This is spiritual care.

Cast adrift: a personal response and concluding discussion

What the dominant discourse has in common with mine, then, is the search for meaning, transcendence, and purpose. They also suggest that coming to know and develop the self is important. But this is not solely the domain of psychology, for the search for the essential self is both religious and universal, and those practices already mentioned, prayer, meditation, contemplation, ritual, story-making, etc., are all alternatives to the therapeutic counselling technologies. According to Armstrong (2006), about 900 to 200 BCE, the Axial Age produced spiritual insights that have never been surpassed. In times of spiritual and social crisis, men and women have constantly turned back to this period for guidance. All the traditions that were developed during the Axial Age (Taoism, Confucianism, Monotheism, Hinduism, Buddhism, and Philosophical Rationalism) pushed forward the frontiers of human consciousness and discovered a transcendent dimension at the core of their being. What mattered was not what you believed, but how you behaved. Axial faiths share an ideal of sympathy, respect, and universal concern. What they (the Axial sages) created was a spiritual technology that utilized natural human energies.

The Axial sages put the abandonment of selfishness and the spirituality of compassion at the top of their agenda. If an individual's conviction impels him to act compassionately and to honour the stranger, then he is good, helpful, and sound. This is the test of true religiosity in every single one of the major traditions. Instead of jettisoning religious doctrines, we should look for their spiritual kernel (Armstrong, 2006). In other words, isolate the essence and universalize it. The challenge might then be to find out what it is about the Christian message that is universal, what it shares with the other traditions. I have attempted in a small way to do this. The other point is to appreciate that not only can this universal be taught to non-Christian nurses, but also that Christian nurses can apply the message universally, i.e., not just to Christian patients. It only becomes Christian in the context of the *patient's* experience.

Suffice to say, I can find no models, theories, or concepts in the dominant discourse that would accommodate my own spiritual needs if ever I was hospitalized. Some would argue that the trigger words relating to the key features and definitions of the theories and concepts of the dominant discourse are present in my personal narrative (typically "meaning", "purpose", "fulfilment", and "transcendence"), but they would be wrong. The dominant discourse is without theology and I consider this narrative as illustrative of a personal theology, and, given that it contains an experience of the numinous (my own personal god) and particular spiritual practice, then I would go further and say that this is my personal religion.

With regard to the dominant discourse, Wilber (2006) asserts that before you discuss religion you have to be explicit about what religion you mean, and beyond that, what you mean by religion. He insists that there are some two dozen different religions and spiritualities (not including "new age") and not only do you have to be precise about which of the two dozen you mean, but also on what grounds you are excluding the others. The significance here is that not only do they not explain or justify their exclusions, they do not (as I have said) name their spiritual/religious influences. It seems, then, that not only are they attempting to develop a new and unique spiritual framework, but also it is one that is universal and can be "applied" to all. Is this not a religion? Beyond this question, one other: given the products of the Axial Age, just what do they think they are discovering?

The most obvious omission, however, is that there is no mention of, or reference to, the numinous, and this leads to my conclusion that this is a spirituality that is grounded in humanist psychology. Holloway (2001) points out that there is a link between religious/ spiritual experience and psychology in that we are on the human end of any such experience. The crucial point is that there is "something" on the other end, God or the numinous. Pattison (2001) argues that in the dominant discourse, in essence, we have a spirituality that is free floating, not connected to the numinous in any way. The definitions and models of spirituality being pursued in the dominant discourse are humanist and secular, with a far stronger alliance with sympathetic theories from psychology than from any other source. Given all of this, especially the absence of theology, it is clear that we are dealing with psychology dressed in spiritual clothing. As Cottingham (2003) writes,

> Nothing in life is guaranteed, but if the path we follow is integrally linked, as good spiritual paths are, to right action, and self-discovery and respect for others, then we have little to lose, and if the claims of religion are true, then we have everything to gain. For in acting as if life has meaning, we will find, thank God, that it does. [p. 104]

References

Armstrong, K. (2006). *The Great Transformation; The World in the Time of Buddha, Socrates, Confucius and Jeremiah.* London: Atlantic Books.

Bowman, M. (1995). *The Professional Nurse.* London: Chapman & Hall.

Bradburn, J., Maher, J., Adewuyi-Dalton, R., & Grunfeld, E. (1995). Developing clinical trial protocols; the use of patient focus groups. *Psycho-oncology,* 4: 107–12. cited in Stott, R. (2000). *The Ecology of Health.* Totnes: Green Books.

Bradshaw A. (1996a). Lighting the lamp: the covenant as an encompassing framework for the spiritual dimension of nursing care. In: E. Farmer (Ed.), *Exploring the Spiritual Dimension of Care.* Dinton Salisbury: Quay Books.

Bradshaw, A. (1996b). The spiritual dimension of hospice: the secularisation of an ideal. *Social Science and Medicine,* 43(3): 409–419.

Briggs, A. (1972). *Report of the Committee on Nursing.* London: HMSO.

Carr, E. C. J. (1996). *Reflecting on clinical practice: hectoring talk or reality? Journal of Clinical Nursing,* 5: 289–295.

Cassel, E. J. (1982). The nature of suffering and the goals of medicine. *New England Journal of Medicine,* 306(11): 639–645.

Chalmers, I. (1998). Unbiased, relevant, and reliable assessments in health-care. *British Medical Journal,* 317: 1167–1168. Cited in Stott, R. (2000). *The Ecology of Health.* Totnes: Green Books.

Clandinin, J. D., & Connelly, M. F. (2000). *Narrative Inquiry: Experience and Story in Qualitative Research.* San Francisco, CA: Jossey-Bass.

Clark, C.C., Cross, J. R., Deane, D. M., & Lowry, L.W. (1991). Spirituality: integral to quality care. *Holistic Nursing Practice,* 5(3): 67–76.

Cottingham J. (2003). *On: The Meaning of Life.* Oxford: Routledge.

Degh, L. (1995). *Narratives in Society: A Performer-Centred Study of Narration.* Bloomington, IN: Indiana University Press.

Department of Health (DoH) (1993). *Report of the Taskforce on the Strategy for Research in Nursing, Midwifery and Health Visiting.* London: DoH, HMSO.

Department of Health (DoH) (1996). *Research and Development: Towards an Evidence-based Health Service.* London: DoH, HMSO.

Department of Health (DoH) (1997). *The New NHS: Modern, Dependable.* London: DoH, HMSO.

Department of Health (DoH) (1998). *A First Class Service: Quality in the New NHS.* London: DoH, HMSO.

Ellis, C., & Bochner, A. P. (2000). Autoethnography, personal narrative, reflexivity. In: N. Denzin & Y. Lincoln (Eds.), *Handbook of Qualitative Research* (pp. 733–768) (2nd edn). London: Sage.

Ford, D. F. (1999). *Theology: A Very Short Introduction*. Oxford: Oxford University Press.

Frank, A. W. (1991). *At the Will of the Body: Reflections on Illness*. Boston, MA: Houghton Mifflin.

Freshwater, D. (2007). Reading mixed methods research; contexts for criticism. *Journal of Mixed Methods Research*, 1(2): 1–13.

Gramsci, A. (1971). *Selections from the Prison Notebooks*. London: Quartet.

Gramsci, A. (1985). *Selections from the Cultural Writings*. London: Lawrence and Wishart.

Grant, R. (1999). *The Orange County Register*. Santa Ana, CA.

Hall, S. (1996). Gramsci's relevance for the study of race and ethnicity. In: D. Morley, & K. H. Chen (Eds.), *Stuart Hall: Critical Dialogues in Cultural Studies*. London: Routledge.

Hatch, J. A., & Wisneiwski, R. (1995). Life history and narrative: questions, issues and exemplary works. In: J. A. Hatch & R. Wisneiwski (Eds.), *Life History and Narrative* (pp. 00–00). London: Routledge Falmer.

Hewison, A., & Wildman, S. (1996). The theory–practice gap in nursing: a new dimension. *Journal of Advanced Nursing*, 24: 754–761.

Higginson, R. (2004). The theory-practice gap still exists in nursing education. *British Journal of Nursing*, 13(20): 68.

Holloway, I., & Freshwater, D. (2007). *Narrative Research in Nursing*. Oxford: Blackwell.

Holloway, R. (2001). *Doubts and Loves: What is left of Christianity*. Edinburgh: Canongate.

Hundley, V. (1999). What is it? and why does it matter? *Scottish Journal of Healthcare Chaplaincy*, 2(1): 11–14.

Johnson, M. (1999). Biographical pain at the end of life. Paper given to the Department of Sociology, University of Reading, 4 February. Cited in Walter, T. (2002). Spirituality in palliative care: opportunity or burden? *Palliative Medicine*, 16(2): 133–139.

Kearney, R. (2002). *On Stories*. London: Routledge.

Landers, M. G. (2000). The theory-practice gap in nursing: the role of he nurse teacher. *Journal of Advanced Nursing*, 32: 1550–1556.

McKenzie, R. (2007). The personal must be the political: how and why. *Journal of Psychiatric and Mental Health Nursing*, 14(3): 223–225.

Narayanasamy, A. (1999). A review of spirituality as applied to nursing. *International Journal of Nursing Studies*, 36: 117–125.

Oldnall, A. (1996). A critical analysis of nursing: meeting the spiritual needs of patients. *Journal of Advanced Nursing, 23*: 138–144.

Pattison, S. (2001). Dumbing down the spirit. In: H. Orchard (Ed.), *Spirituality in Health Care Contexts* (pp. 33–46). London: Jessica Kingsley.

Pullen, L., Tuck, I., & Mix, K. (1996). Mental health nurses' spiritual perspectives. *Journal of Holistic Nursing, 14*(2): 85–97.

Reason, P. (1988). *Human Inquiry in Action: Developments in New Paradigm Research.* London: Sage.

Reed-Danahay, D. E. (1997). *Auto/Ethnography: Rewriting the Self and the Social.* Oxford: Berg.

Rolfe, G. (1996). *Closing the Theory–Practice Gap: A New Paradigm for Nursing.* Oxford: Butterworth Heinemann.

Rolfe, G. (1998). *Expanding Nursing Knowledge.* Oxford, Butterworth Heinemann.

Ross, L. A. (1994). Spiritual aspects of nursing. *Journal of Advanced Nursing, 19,* 439–447.

Ross, L. (2006). Spiritual care in nursing: an overview of the research to date. *Journal of Clinical Nursing, 15*(7): 852–862.

Scott, D. (1996). The researchers personal responses as a source of insight in the research process. *Nursing Inquiry, 4*: 130–134.

Scottish Office Department of Health (1997). *Designed to Care: Renewing the National Health Service in Scotland.* Edinburgh: The Stationery Office.

Scottish Office Department of Health (1998). *Clinical Governance: Discussion Paper.* Edinburgh: The Scottish Office.

Swinton, J. (2006). Identity and resistance: why spiritual care needs "enemies". *Journal of Clinical Nursing, 15*(7): 918–928.

Tacy, D. (2004). *The Spirituality Revolution. The Emergence of Contemporary Spirituality.* Hove: Brunner-Routledge

Tillich, P. (1968). *Systematic Theology I (Combined Volume).* Welwyn: James Nisbet.

Tillich, P. (1981). *The Meaning of Health.* Richmond, CA: North Atlantic Books

Turner, E. (2002). A visible spirit form in Zambia. In: G. Harvey (Ed.), *Readings in Indigenous Religions* (pp. 149–174). London: Continuum.

Vaughan, B. (1987). Bridging the gap. *Senior Nurse, 6*(5): 30–31

Walker, K. (2003). Why evidence-based practice now? A polemic. *Nursing Inquiry, 10*(3): 145–155.

Wilber, K. (2006). *Integral Spirituality.* Boston, MA: Integral Books.

CHAPTER NINE

Psychological distress and the emancipation of the psychologically oppressed

Jana Helena

Introduction

For many of us there will be times in our lives when we feel as though we can no longer go on living. Traumatic experiences can disrupt our sense of who we are, and our despair and pain may appear so overwhelming that it is difficult to imagine that we would ever survive it. It may feel as though our world has fallen apart and we might fear that we can no longer hold ourselves together. Caught in a space where nothing holds any meaning any more, and where despair and confusion take over, we may be terrified of breaking down. For some people, however, this feeling seems to come from nowhere. There is no obvious trauma to hook it on. It is as though it is a state of mind with no explanation. The distress cannot be thought about.

What follows is the story of my fear of falling apart, the feeling of lacking a sense of togetherness and coherence inside. It is a story about my adolescence, a time in my life that was both frightening and disturbing. However, this piece of work is not only about the personal and subjective. On the contrary, my personal narrative is used as a vehicle for opening up a space between the personal and the social and political. As I researched into my own experiences, important questions about mental health and clinical practice emerged. It is to these that I shall turn in the latter parts of this chapter.

The beginnings: finding a topic at the heart of me

This chapter began its life several months ago. It was developed as part of my dissertation for an MSc in Therapeutic Counselling and has been reworked for this book. Its birth, however, was far from smooth. At times, I experienced such despair that I wanted to rip it all up and give up writing altogether. Even finding a research topic was agonizing. I had so many ideas, but nothing seemed good enough. At times, I entered a state of overwhelming anxiety and panic. I was unable to think, unable to move. In fact, it was as if I was frozen or paralysed. My mind was completely blank.

A visit to a bookshop seemed to break this spell. The image of a bright yellow book on persecutory anxiety stayed with me, and suddenly I knew what I needed to write about. Anxiety had permeated all aspects of my life. It was as if a constant sense of anxiety hovered in the background and stopped me from living life more fully. But it was not the fear of doing particular things, but an underlying anxiety around life and death, and a fear of not being able to cope that underpinned it all. Anxiety, it seemed, was always connected with a threat of fragmentation, a fear of not coping, of not surviving, of falling apart and non-being. An article by Uhlin (2002) seemed to mirror this sentiment.

He believes that without the existential awareness of non-being, "there would be no significance in the particular things we fear" (p. 179), because any fear or phobia is ultimately concerned with the fear of death or non-being.

However, this piece of work is not about the fear of physical death or dying. It is about a fear of psychological death, about the fear of breaking down, of not being able to hold oneself together psychologically. As such, it is concerned with a fear of disintegration of self and identity, the fear of not being able to continue on being.

Einmal lebt ich (Once I lived)

When I began this research journey, I was taken back to my experiences in adolescence. It is then that my anxiety of falling apart was more present than ever. It is also then that my journey of healing began. Struggling to go on being, I had reached a crisis point in life. I felt dead inside. The title of a book by Natascha Wodin (which I bought from the local library) encapsulated exactly how I felt. *Einmal lebt ich* (Once I Lived), but now it was as though I was no longer alive.

It feels strange to reflect on this now. Some memories seem so clear and vivid, and yet others are so remote and distant, blurred and obscured. Time frames are muddled and confused. I cannot even remember who I went to school with. Perhaps this is not surprising. Good autobiographical memory and states of dissociation usually do not go hand in hand. I struggled to feel myself. It was as if I was in a bubble, in a world of my own. I felt separate and disconnected. I was there but I was not there. I existed, but I did not feel alive. I was obsessed with death and dying, and yet my classmates voted me as "the entertainer of the year". People did not know I was unwell, or maybe they did. I became quite good at hiding. And lying. In fact, my whole life felt like a lie.

I grew up in a small village in Germany as the younger of two children, two girls, with less than a year between us. For many years, I believed that life was fine. I did well in school, had many friends and was often reminded by my parents of how good life was. I should count myself lucky, they said, but I didn't feel lucky. I know, they meant well. They worked hard and provided us with the financial stability they never had. As an adolescent, however, it felt as though my whole life was falling apart. No—I was falling apart, or perhaps I no longer could keep up the façade, the false self I had built around myself. Now, in a constant state of anxiety, I was terrified. I was frightened of being around others. Often I was afraid of leaving home. Some days, I did not even manage to get to school. I set my alarm for five o'clock in the morning, but even then I could not get ready. I would stare in the mirror for hours, transfixed by the image I saw, but not being able to recognize myself. It was as if my soul had left my body. My face was looking back at me, but I did not feel part of it. My mind and body seemed completely separate. With every second and every minute going by, my anxiety heightened. I was aware it was time to leave, but I could not. I was panic-stricken. I wanted to scream, but I had no words to express how I was feeling. Sometimes I would bang my fist against the wall or the door. Often, I would collapse on the bathroom floor, now visibly distressed and upset, with tears rolling down my face. I could not deal with things any more. I hated myself—hated being so pathetic and weak. Searching for razor blades and needles, I began to pick and cut my skin. I wanted to get rid of any blemishes or spots. I never cut deeply. It was more like scraping off any impurities or piercing my skin with needles. Usually, the act of doing so was comforting. For a few moments I felt calm and peace. I was grounded and it was as if a crescendo that had built up inside me came to a halt. But the calm didn't last. Now, hiding under the duvet in my room, I was tormented with shame and guilt. The red marks on my skin had to go, HAD TO DISAPPEAR. WHY WAS I UNABLE TO STOP IT???

I was caught in a vicious cycle and did not know how to get out. Life was something that happened to other people, not for me. Sometimes I wished I could fall asleep. I did not want to die, but I wanted somebody to turn the clock forward, because I could tolerate this pain no longer. At the time, I could not understand what had happened. I did not know what I felt and why I felt it. I thought I had a good life until then, a good upbringing and childhood—so why did it all go wrong? Why was I so fragile? So frightened? And why did I feel so out of control?

For years, I was resistant to seeking any help. I wanted to feel better, and yet on some days, I didn't even believe that I had any problems. I was referred to psychotherapists and psychiatrists, but never managed to stay for more than two sessions. I remember one saying to me, "It seems like you are stuck in a very dark hole." I just laughed. Of course, he was right, but I was not ready to acknowledge the depth of the pain I felt. Having internalized parents who struggled to deal with feelings, I was dismissive of my own vulnerability. Emotional pain had to be turned into physical wounds, because they were tangible. I could watch them bleed and heal again. As Lines points out, watching the wounds heal may give the self-harmer "the illusion that the self is healing, that their skin and psyche can hold themselves" (quoted in Strong, 2000, p. 37). This notion has always strongly resonated with me.

Later in life, I came to understand that my difficulties did not all of a sudden appear in adolescence, but had roots in my infancy. I realized that this fear had permeated my life, perhaps even since birth. I recalled recurring childhood dreams of being burnt by a witch, my obsession with death and fear of dead people hiding in my room. At the time I associated the latter with having been exposed to the dead body of the local vicar. My RE teacher took us to see him, lying in a coffin, padded with white cloths. I could not rid myself of this image; he looked pale, life had left his body. However, I now believe that I was so terrified because it resonated with a fear of internal death, disintegration, and fragmentation. My sense of self was fractured and I was terrified of not being able to feel myself any more. Caught in a space where I was neither alive nor dead, I feared both, but was unable to verbalize my distress. In fact, I had no means of communicating with those around me, other than by scarring my "pretty" face. It was a bit like saying "Look, I'm hurting. Things are not the way they seem," while feeling deeply ashamed. Around the same time, I also began to overeat.

Through my personal therapy and training as a counsellor, I have learnt to reflect on my feelings and thoughts and committed myself to a journey of self-discovery. A theoretical exploration of the conscious and unconscious meanings of self-harm on my previous training course provided me with relief and a better understanding of what propelled this behaviour, although—adhering to academic conventions—I never disclosed my personal interest in this topic. Despite this lack of reflexivity in the actual piece of work, I began to construct my own narrative with my relationship with my mother at its core, and began to associate many of my problems with a lack of containment early in life. Constantly busying herself to avoid feelings of emptiness and depression, my mother was unable to recognize our needs as children. As I grew older, I simply felt out of control: I had no internal soothing parent to call upon.

Furthermore, I also understood that the overbearing and smothering quality of my mother's care left little space for me to be or grow. Accustomed to complying with her needs and feelings, I lost touch with my own. Aggressive impulses had to be repressed. If I wanted my mother's love, I had to be what she wanted me to be, and in protecting her, I directed my anger against the self. In fact, it seems as though I have punished myself for wanting anything other than what my mother did, and self-harming became the only way of attacking her, of attacking an internal mother who was overbearing. Even when I was an adolescent, she treated me like a child—preparing breakfast, even buttering the bread. Her love, it felt, was killing me, and the only way I could escape (at least physically) was by moving abroad.

Today I no longer feel enmeshed in our family dynamics, and yet, difficult feelings remain. I recognize my ambivalence towards my mother, who is both caring and yet overbearing. Sometimes it is as if I cannot stand her love and I feel a need to rid myself of her devouring presence. It is like something sticking to my body, and I feel a desperate urge to tear it off. During a trip to Germany in December 2004, in the midst of writing my research proposal for my dissertation, familiar feelings resurfaced. Again I felt choked and smothered. I felt the tranquillity and calm of the village, but also the deathlike stillness of this place. The winters are dark in the valley, burdened by heavy fog. There is no life. And I could feel it deep inside me. It is a feeling of not being able to breathe.

However, I also began to think about my relationship with my father, and a deep sense of sadness emerged. It is as if we never got to know each other. Shying away from any meaningful contact, only light and humorous conversation seemed tolerated. My family, I understood, are unable to deal with feelings. And while my mother is overbearing, my relationship with my father is characterized by its absence. He has never come to see me since I moved abroad, and perhaps he never will.

The role of theory

When I first submitted this as my dissertation, a lengthy exploration of the theoretical understandings of the fear of breakdown followed. Mainly drawing on psychodynamic theories, which link disintegration anxiety to failures in the early mother–infant relationship, I explored Winnicott's theory on ego integration and Bion's concept of containment. I came to believe that clinical fear of breakdown relates to an absence of holding in early childhood, and endorsed Winnicott's position that the fear of breakdown is the fear of a breakdown "already experienced" early in life (Winnicott, 1974,

p. 104). However, drawing on Lacan, I also recognized that this was not only about that which was missing. For him it is "the lack of a lack" (Evans, 1996, p. 12) that produces intolerable anxiety. Disintegration anxiety was, therefore, not only about the absence of the breast, but about "its enveloping presence" (*ibid.*). In this way, I came to believe that my fear of breaking down was primarily about a suffocating presence, about a fear of being smothered and of not being able to exist as a separate person.

But even this understanding was one-sided. It never took any account of my relationship with my father. Immersed in psychoanalytic theory, I had become lost in a world of mothers and babies, where the father was pushed outside, hovering on the periphery. Reading Bacon (2003), I turned my gaze to the role of the father. For him, phobias arise in the absence of the father, in the absence of an outer limit containing the self. Without the father, so Bacon (2003) says, there is no limit. There are no boundaries, and to be boundlessness is one of the "great unconscious terrors" (p.164). In fact, as my story has highlighted, it is this feeling of being utterly out of control and of not having a skin to hold the self that is so terrifying.

In focusing on the lack of containment by my mother, then, I had forgotten about the role of the father. Now, I understood that my problems were not just about the lack of attunement by my mother, but related to the absence of my father, the lack of limits and discipline.

This insight had a profound impact on me, not only on a personal level, but also professionally. As a counsellor, I realized, I not only needed to strive to be a good-enough mother, but I also needed firm boundaries and limits, qualities that are often associated with the father.

As such, theory not only changed my understanding of myself, but it also enabled me to think about clinical practice in a different way. Even though there is no position outside theory, theory itself is always restrictive. It fails to capture the messiness and complexity of life, and, while it grounded me, it also seemed dead and meaningless. In fact, several readers commented on the lifelessness of my theory section in contrast to the aliveness of my personal narrative. Perhaps, I began to wonder, the very structure of my dissertation came to represent something of my struggle between life and death.

Research methodology

In doing this study, I have decided not to send out questionnaires, conduct interviews, or follow a more traditional research format. On the contrary, I have decided to write my own story and follow my own process. My life has become the site of the fieldwork, and in researching into my own experiences I have become therapist, client, and researcher. In what follows I shall say a bit more about some of the central concepts and methodologies used.

Narrative analysis—storytelling and research

Perhaps one of the most important contributions recognizing the richness of storytelling stems from psychologist Jerome Bruner, who has become well known for his work in the fields of social psychology, developmental psychology, and cognitive science (McLeod, 1997). He argues that narrative knowledge "is a legitimate form of reasoned knowing" (Polkinghorne, 1995, p. 9) and not about self-expression alone. According to Bruner (1985), there are two modes of cognitive functioning, which offer two distinctive ways of ordering experience and of constructing reality. He refers to the traditional logical–scientific mode of knowing as paradigmatic cognition, and storied knowledge as narrative cognition (*ibid.*). While the paradigmatic mode has been held as the exclusive mode of functioning for the generation of trustworthy and valid knowledge, Bruner reminds us that narrative discourse also produces worthwhile knowledge. Indeed, as Ricoeur (1986) has pointed out, stories are particularly suited as a linguistic form expressing lived human experience (cited in Bruner, 1987, p. 12).

Drawing on this distinction, Polkinghorne (1995) suggests that there are two ways in which narratives can be used for the purposes of research. While the *analysis of narratives* employs paradigmatic reasoning in locating common themes or concepts among the stories collected as data, *narrative analysis* views life as constructed through the telling and re-telling of stories. It "does not seek to find conceptual themes, but instead tries to capture the messiness, depth and texture of lived experience" (Etherington, 2004b, p. 50). In this way, stories can be seen to

> create the effect of reality, showing characters embedded in the complexities of lived moments of struggle, resisting the intrusions

of chaos, disconnection, fragmentation, marginalization, and incoherence, trying to preserve or restore the continuity and coherence
of life's unity in the face of unexpected blows of fate that call one's
meanings and values into question. [Ellis & Bochner, 2000, p. 744]

As such, I believe that stories offer something fundamentally
different, yet equally valid to our understanding of the world.
While models and theories impose order upon experiences
(McKenzie, 2002), stories provide us with a form, which can communicate the struggles, confusion, and moral dilemmas that we
encounter. In this respect, they can become an essential part of
professional development, enabling us to think of psychic life in its
complexity.

However, needless to say, narrative accounts like this one are
not easy to manage. In writing this, I have often struggled to see
how I could include all my thoughts in a coherent narrative. Often,
I felt impotent and helpless. It was as though I could never quite
capture what I wanted to say, and I questioned the limits of
language itself. And yet, I knew that if I was going to complete this
piece of work, I needed to find ways of managing this instability
and uncertainty. Of course, as counsellors we often have to do the
same.

Reflexivity

In breaching the conventional separation of researcher and subject
(Jackson, 1989), I became both the dynamic subject and object of this
study. In fact, my own subjectivity and conscious experiencing of
myself as researcher and researched became the site of the research.
In this way, reflexivity as the process of reflecting critically on the
self as researcher, the "human as instrument" (Lincoln & Guba,
1981), became the methodological vehicle for this study (Etherington, 2004a).

This, I recognized, not only forces us to come to terms with our
choice of research problem (Lincoln & Guba, 2000), but also with
our constantly developing and changing selves. As Reinhartz (1997)
argues "we not only *bring* the self to the field . . . [we also] *create* the
self in the field" (cited in Lincoln and Guba, 2000, p. 183). The

research field in this sense becomes dynamic, boundaryless, unstable, and in constant process. As Lees (2001) points out,

> It is as though one is continually failing to capture the essence of what one is trying to say: the original experience is continually being lost and overshadowed by new experiences and thoughts, and the complexity is obscured by "high, hard ground" snapshots. [p. 136]

While in quantitative research and in most approaches to qualitative research, the research process is divided into a series of distinct stages—question, literature review, data collection, data analysis, and results (*ibid.*, p. 135), this narrative analysis involved a re-visiting of experience and drawing together of events and happenings into a "temporally organized whole" (Polkinghorne, 1995, p. 5). As such there has been no linear and clearly defined process. The story has continuously evolved as it was written. Indeed as Richardson (2000) argues "writing is also a way of 'knowing'—a method of discovery and analysis. By writing in different ways, we discover new aspects of our topic and our relationship to it' (p. 923).

As I continued to immerse myself in my subject matter, this study shifted from its introspective focus to the outside. My subjectivity, I realized, was not an end in itself, but rather provided a bridge between the personal and social. In exploring my own experiences, I not only understood that "every text has meaning only in relation to other texts" (Derrida, 1976, cited in Freshwater & Rolfe, 2001, p. 531), but that ultimately it is through the exploration of the personal and the subjective that theories are developed and challenged. In this way, the reflexivity used in this piece of writing is not only concerned with a turning back on itself, but is best described by what Freshwater and Rolfe (2001) refer to as reflexivity type II (*ibid.*). Rather than being concerned with introspection alone, the focus of this research is turned outwards towards the social and political world. As such, it touches on the work of critical theorists, who encourage us to challenge non-reflexive affirmation of tradition to seek "human emancipation" in circumstances of domination and oppression. "In order for this to occur," so Holub (n.d.) says, "we must possess the ability to reflect upon and to reject pernicious or regressive aspects of our heritage."

In other words, we can all become intellectuals and philosophers (Holmes, 2002, p. 74). In reflecting on ourselves and the world, we not only develop an increased awareness of our own beliefs and values, but can begin to deconstruct and reconstruct our world. In many respects, this is one of the most important discoveries of this research project.

In the remaining section, I shall explore in more detail how, by connecting with moments of madness in my own life, I began to question the polarity of sanity and madness at the heart of Western psychiatry and to reflect on issues of power and the counselling relationship. In this way, this project has not only enabled me to understand myself better, but changed my clinical practice. It gave me the confidence to trust my own experiences and observations and to become both researcher and practitioner.

Implications for clinical practice

As an adolescent I was taken to see several psychotherapists and psychiatrists. "Clearly something isn't right with you," my mother said. And, in some respects, she was right. My behaviour was strange, and eventually I couldn't face going to school any longer. I dropped out, and began to believe her story—the story of my family. Subsequent years seemed to confirm what they already knew. I was "all over the place"—unlike my sister. My relationships were anything but healthy and I was even scared of switching on a stereo for fear I would break it. As the years went by, however, I began to question this story. Who is mad or sane, I concluded, is far more complicated than often assumed. My experience of working in a crisis unit that offers an alternative to psychiatric hospital for people with often long-standing mental health issues has confirmed this hunch. Perhaps madness, and the process of going mad, is actually comprehensible.

Unfortunately, as workers, we often delude ourselves into thinking that we are sane and somehow exempt from ever experiencing profound mental distress. The client becomes weak, while we assume a position of power and authority. Left with the polarity of the sane and the insane, the healthy and the sick, there is a widening gulf. That which appears strange soon becomes thought disordered, delusional, or, more vaguely, a manifestation of the borderline, a catch-all term whose meaning has clearly become "imprecise, confused, even contradictory" (Widlöcher, 1981, cited in Maleval, 2000, p. 2). And, in zooming in on the pathology of the client, we lose touch with the client's personhood.

Undoubtedly, madness exists. However, what I question is not the existence of madness itself, but the certainty with which some distinguish the so-called healthy or sane from the sick and mentally ill. The boundaries of mental health and mental ill health, I believe, are far more unstable than traditionally assumed. Rosenhan's experiment is a good case in point (described in Freshwater, 2003, p. 166).

In researching the question of whether the sane can be distinguished from the insane, he had eight pseudo patients admitted to psychiatric hospitals by stating that they had been hearing voices. Following admission, they ceased to simulate symptoms, but, despite their display of sane behaviour, the pseudo patients were never discovered. "Indeed in these circumstances their very normality was interpreted as psychiatric symptomatology" (*ibid.*).

However, not only is it difficult to distinguish the healthy from the sane, the reality is that even the so-called sane are not sane all the time (Freshwater, 2003). According to Melanie Klein (1998), there are psychotic parts to us all. As we fail to develop a permanent sense of maturity, psychotic processes and mechanisms are ubiquitous throughout life as we oscillate between paranoid–schizoid functioning and the depressive position. In particular, when stress and anxiety break through our usual defences, more primitive ways of functioning may be revealed (Gomez, 1997).

Furthermore, let us remind ourselves that it is not only individuals who may suffer from psychosis, but whole systems and organizations. While the classificatory system in regard to mental health is set up and represented as truth, who is to say that this is really the case? After all, mental illness is only socially constructed. What is deemed to be normal or abnormal behaviour depends on the particular culture and society in which we live. In some non-Western cultures, for instance, mental illness states are deemed to be enlightened states of mind. Even the traditional Irish view saw the spontaneous visionary state of the schizophrenic as a spiritual crisis, rather than an illness *per se*. And, as Eisenberg (1988) points out, often "the concepts we invent to account for disease come to shape not only the observations we make and the remedies we prescribe, but the very manifestations of disease itself" (p. 1). In other words, what is believed to be true about behaviour or illness also affects the very behaviour and illness it attempts to explain, and our expectations and prognosis of the disease affects its very manifestation.

According to Laing (1969), however, societal expectations and values not only have an impact on the course of somebody's mental illness, but rather they are often the cause of it. He questions the view of mental illness as being located in the individual alone and draws our attention to the fact that

> our "normal" and "adjusted" state is too often the abdication of
> ecstasy, the betrayal of our true potentialities, that many of us are
> only too successful in acquiring a false sense of self to adapt to false
> realities. [ibid., p. 12]

Furthermore, how can we really claim that society is sane whereas the individual isn't when so-called "normal men have killed perhaps 100,000,000 of their fellow men in the last fifty years" (Laing, 1967, p. 30)?

Although we may be inclined to think of a person whose experience is psychotic to be ill in some significant way (Davidson, 1992), he urges us not to make the mistake of assuming that the majority of people is always sane, whereas the so-called mad individual is not. On the contrary, he viewed madness as an extreme but entirely logical reaction to the irreconcilable demands and pressures of someone's family life and society as a whole. Madness in this sense is seen as an expression of immense distress, which is not to be idealized, but nevertheless can be a cathartic and transformative experience. In this way, Laing (1969) believed that the confused speech of people undergoing a psychotic episode were attempts at communicating worries and concerns in situations where this was impossible or not permitted. Madness, far from being un-understandable, thus made sense in the context of somebody's life history.

This, I believe, calls for a new relationship with clients, one that does not pathologize the other but recognizes them in their personhood, in their uniqueness and variety. While the medical model, with its emphasis on concepts such as "biochemical imbalances", "disorder", and "malfunction", may sometimes feel more comfortable and less burdensome, because it does not require us to think about the cause of all the hurt and pain experienced (Davidson, 1992), mental life cannot be viewed as being separate from somebody's life and history. In researching my own experiences, I realized not only how complex life is, but why I have always been sceptical of reductionist approaches to counselling and psychotherapy. Models and theories may bring comfort and often help us bear the unbearable, but clinical practice does not fit into neat boxes. Rather than theorizing and intellectualizing about distress, perhaps

> it is more a mark of one's humanity to be able to just be with someone, no matter what state they are in, without needing to act on them in some way, without attempting to change them to suit one's own book, so to speak, and yet still vibrantly alive to their humanity. [*ibid.*, p. 8]

This, we cannot learn from theory seminars or lectures. Rather, it requires us to be in touch with our own life experiences, with who each of us is as a person. In fact, perhaps it is only through the painful awareness of our own suffering and life experiences that we can begin to relate to others in a more meaningful way and accompany them in their journey of self. Self-awareness thus cannot be an additional aspect to professional training, rather, it needs to be at the heart of it. After all, working therapeutically requires primarily "an ability to be in tune with one's feelings and other aspects of one's own experience in relation to clients" (Davidson, 1997, p. 2).

This kind of research, then, far from being self-indulgent or narcissistic as some critics would have us believe, fosters skills and qualities that are central to clinical work. In fact, I often feel that this project has transformed my personal and professional self. Although painful, it has enabled me to find my voice, as I began to trust my own observations and thoughts. As in the research I no longer needed to bracket my own experience, so in my work with clients I no longer had to leave my "life" outside the door. I was able to meet with the other, not only as a professional, from a position of detachment, but also as a human being. Furthermore, no longer scared of transgressing the rules of my previous training, I was now able to be with clients in a deeper and fuller sense. Leaving my therapist voice and posture outside, I realized I had much more to offer to clients. I allowed myself be affected by clients, to be emotionally touched rather than denying myself permission to have feelings of my own. And in opening myself to myself I not only seemed to open myself to others, but also experienced a new sense of interrelatedness and connection with myself and others.

According to Clarkson (2003), it is through this very interrelatedness between people that change and healing takes place. The therapeutic relationship, and therefore also our ability to work with and be in this multi-faceted relationship, is at the heart of therapeutic work. This, clearly, requires more than just theoretical understanding. It requires us to be human, to be whole as persons, and to see the other in their personhood and not their pathology. While some behaviour may appear strange at first, in the context of somebody's life it loses its madness. Let us take Saeed, for instance (all names are changed to protect his identity). He has suffered multiple losses as a result of war and torture and was admitted to the crisis unit believing that Princess Diana and Michael Jackson will come to visit him and take him home. Of course, Saeed is delusional, but is it really so mad that he started to believe those things?

Madness, far from being mad itself, is an attempt to live with a situation that is unliveable. Certainly, most clients I have worked with are not born mad. Perhaps some of them are more vulnerable than others to becoming disturbed, but often their difficulties seem to relate to rather horrific childhood experiences or some form of other trauma. Unable to accept the reality of their situation, some cling on to omnipotent fantasies and, when they can no longer be sustained, plunge into a deep depression or retreat into a world of their own. But perhaps even our understanding of trauma needs to be revised. As my story has shown, we do not have to have suffered horrific abuse to develop later difficulties in life. Although it has been difficult for me to acknowledge this, perhaps not letting your children grow up and become their own person is also soul killing.

Conclusion

The aim of this study was to explore, to reflect, and question. It began as a journey to self during which I encountered pain and sorrow, despair and anger, but also joy and relief. In exploring my experiences, I not only came to understand myself better, but began to question the polarity of sanity and madness, and realized that self-awareness and our ability to be in relationship is pivotal to the therapeutic task. As it is through the interconnectedness between people that change and healing takes place, we cannot leave our selves outside the door. Who we are as people and what we believe about human nature, about ourselves and others, about what it is to be sane or mad, informs everything that we do in the consulting room. While much is said about holistic approaches, in the mental health field we still often treat others as objects, and in focusing on their pathology, diagnosis, and symptoms, we forget that there is a real person behind with a story to tell. Madness, far from being un-understandable, makes sense in the context of somebody's life and society as a whole, and the question of who is mad is far more complex than often assumed. Perhaps this view stems from my own fear of being pathologized, but I do not think this should discredit my opinion. Certainly, in writing this story, I have left myself vulnerable, but I have also found a voice that has enabled me to be more present with clients and to assert myself in work in a different way.

In many respects, of course, this is just a story. It is the story of my adolescence, my fear of falling apart, and the way I have come to understand myself over the years. However, I no longer regard stories as second best to theoretical analysis. On the contrary, while "models and theories impose order and rationality upon experiences" (McKenzie, 2002, p. 26), it is only through stories that we can begin to understand people as they struggle and deal with the complexities of life. As such, it almost seems absurd that counselling research should exclude this dimension. For, if effective counsellors really utilize their own life experiences in the quest of understanding others, why, we may wonder, do we still struggle to accept the value of autobiographical work?

Academia, sadly, I have to conclude, suffers from its own degree of madness. Obsessed with re-writing that which has already been said, "referencing, etymology and obedience, represent some of the main barriers to our developing a creative and transformational style of reading, writing, thinking, and being" (Westwood, 2005, p. 165). Of course, I, too, have to be accused of that. Fearful of letting my own subjective experience stand alone, I have turned to references to ground, justify, and validate. While theory has enabled me to understand my experience, perhaps in looking to established theories I have simply sought to confirm that which is already known. Reassured that somebody else had felt the same, it alleviated the fear of being alone. When, I wonder though, can we begin to truly value our own experiences and observations and build from them? To have the courage to trust ourselves and our experiences?

In many respects this study, for me, has been a significant step towards that. Its main lack, however, is in the privacy in which it unfolded. Over the past few months, I have written and re-written this piece of work, but have shared only little of this process with others. In fact, perhaps it was only possible for me to write this in a language other than my mother tongue and in the safety of my own space and private thoughts. The challenge, thus, will be to invite others to respond to this story and to overcome my fear of exposing myself. In submitting this as a chapter for this book, perhaps I am taking another step.

Epilogue

The decision to publish this piece of work was not an easy one. For months I was procrastinating. Initially, I felt honoured when I was asked to edit my dissertation as a chapter for this book, but then I found myself unable to return to what I had written then. Things had changed. My life had changed and my story was no longer the same.

I could not reconnect with where I was when I submitted this, and I was frightened of being judged and ridiculed. I had left myself vulnerable and exposed and I was not sure whether I could trust anyone with what I had written. Furthermore, I wondered about my family. How could it ever be right to publish something so personal?

Perhaps, in the end, I reached a compromise. I decided to publish this under a pseudonym, to protect myself, but also others close to me. How I will feel when this is in print, I do not know. For now, I want to acknowledge the struggle but also the value in doing such personal writing. Clearly, at times, it would have been safer to withdraw and crawl back to a place of safety. But part of me does not want to do this any more. I do not want to hide any longer. I want to talk about my experiences, and how, in researching these, I have become more me as a person and practitioner.

References

Bacon, R. (2003). Fathers and phobias: a possibly psychoanalytic point of view. In: S. Morgan, (Ed.), *Phobia*. London: Karnac.

Bruner, J. (1985). *Actual Minds, Possible Worlds*. Cambridge, MA: Harvard University Press.

Bruner, J. (1987). Life as narrative. *Social Research*, 54(1): 11–32.

Clarkson, P. (2003). *The Therapeutic Relationship*. Second Edition. London: Whurr.

Davidson, B. (1992). The Role of the Psychiatric Nurse [Online]. Available: www.bendavidson.co.uk/professional_pages/publications/books/estrife/chapters.htm, [2005, September 30] originally published as "What can be the relevance of psychiatric nurse to the life of a person who is mentally ill?" *Journal of Clinical Nursing*, 1(4): 199–205.

Davidson, B. (1997). The paradox of psychiatric nursing: making a difference by attempting to change nothing [Online]. Available: www.bendavidson.co.uk/professional_pages/publications/books/estrife/chapters.htm, (accessed 30 September 2005), revised version published in *Nursing Times*, 93(25): 52–54.

Derrida, J. (1976). *Of Grammatology*. Baltimore, MD: Johns Hopkins University Press. Cited in Freshwater, D., & Rolfe, G. (2001). Critical reflexivity: a politically and ethical engaged research method for nursing. *NT Research*, 6(1): 526–537.

Eisenberg, L. (1988). The social construction of mental illness. *Psychological Medicine*, 18: 1–9.

Ellis, C. E., & Bochner, A. P. (2000). Autoethnography, personal narrative, reflexivity—researcher as subject. In: N. K. Denzin & Y. S. Lincoln (Eds.), *Handbook of Qualitative Research* (pp. 733–768). London: Sage.

Etherington, K. (2004a). *Becoming a Reflexive Researcher—Using Our Selves in Research*. London: Jessica Kingsley.

Etherington, K. (2004b). Reflexive methods: reflexivities—roots, meanings, dilemmas. *Counselling and Psychotherapy Research*, 4(2): 46–63.

Evans, D. (1996). *An Introductory Dictionary of Lacanian Psychoanalysis.* London: Routledge.

Freshwater, D., & Rolfe, G. (2001). Critical reflexivity: a politically and ethical engaged research method for nursing. *NT Research*, 6(1): 526–537.

Freshwater, D. (2003). Researching mental health: pathology in a post-modern world. *NT Research*, 8(3): 161–172.

Gomez, L. (1997). *An Introduction to Object Relations.* London: Free Association.

Holmes, C. A. (2002). Academics and practitioners: nurses as intellectuals. *Nursing Inquiry*, 9(2): 73–83.

Holub, R. C. (n.d.). Habermas, Jürgen. [Online] Available: www.press.jhu.edu/books.hopkins_guide_to_literary_theory/jürgen_habermas.html (accessed 12 September 2005).

Jackson, M. (1989). *Paths Toward a Clearing: Radical Empiricism and Ethnographic Inquiry.* Bloomington, IN: Indiana University Press.

Klein, M. (1998). *Love, Guilt and Reparation and other Works 1921–1945.* London: Vintage.

Laing, R. D. (1967). *The Politics of Experience.* New York: Ballantine.

Laing, R. D. (1969). *The Divided Self.* Harmondsworth: Penguin.

Lees, J. (2001). Reflexive action research: developing knowledge through practice. *Counselling and Psychotherapy Research*, 1(2): 132–139.

Lincoln, Y. S., & Guba, E. G. (1981). *Effective Evalation: Improving the Usefulnessof Evaluation Results Through Responsive and Naturalistic Approaches.* San Francisco, CA: Jossey–Bass.

Lincoln, Y. S., & Guba, E. G. (2000). Paradigmatic controversies, contradictions, and emerging confluence. In: N. K. Denzin & Y. S. Lincoln (Eds.), *Handbook of Qualitative Research* (pp. 163–188). London: Sage.

Maleval, J. (2000). Why so many "Borderlines"? [Online] Available: www.londonsociety-nls.org.uk/maleval-borderlines.htm (accessed 28 October 2004).

McKenzie, R. (2002). The importance of philosophical congruence for therapeutic use of self. In: D. Freshwater (Ed.), *Therapeutic Nursing* (pp. 22–38). London: Sage.

McLeod, J. (1997). *Narrative and Psychotherapy.* London: Sage.

Polkinghorne, D. (1995). Narrative configuration in qualitative analysis. In: J. A. Hatch & R. Wisiewski (Eds.), *Life History and Narrative* (pp. 5–23). London: Falmer.

Richardson, L. (2000). Writing: a method of inquiry. In: N. K. Denzin & Y. S. Lincoln (Eds.), *Handbook of Qualitative Research* (pp. 923–948). London: Sage.

Ricoeur, P. (1984). *Time and Narrative*. Chicago, IL: University of Chicago Press cited in Bruner (1987). Life as narrative. *Social Research*, 54(1): 11–32.

Strong, M. (2000). *A Bright Red Scream—Self-Mutilation and the Language of Pain*. London: Virago.

Uhlin, B. (2002). Ontological insecurity. Existential anxiety and the roots of schizophrenia. *Existential Analysis, 3*(2): 178–189.

Westwood, T. (2005). Academics'dynamics: re-writing referencing. *Psychodynamic Practice, 11*(2): 165–176.

Widlöcher, D. (1981). Les concepts d'état limite in Actualités de la schizophrénie (sous la direction de P. Pichot) PUF, 55–70 cited in Maleval, J. (2000). Why so many "Borderlines"? [Online] Available: www.londonsociety-nls.org.uk/maleval-borderlines.htm (accessed 28 October 2004).

Winnicott, D. W. (1974). Fear of breakdown. *International Review of Psychoanalysis, 1*: 103–107.

Wodin, N. (1989). *Einmal Lebt Ich*. Frankfurt: Luchterhand Literatur-verlag.

CHAPTER TEN

Searching for a voice

Ashwini Bhalla

"I sometimes feel I have nothing to say and I want to communicate this"

(Damien Hirst, British artist, 1965)

M y starting point for this chapter is a lecture period of a counselling training course that took place in November 2001. The atmosphere was tense, laden with anxiety as students grappled to understand and prepare for the workload. A friend voiced disgruntled feelings about the coursework, joking and laughing about it, somewhat teasing the tutor across the classroom filled with students. On observing this, I noticed my feeling of jealousy. My friend was *relaxed, carefree*, joking with the tutor, whereas I was *stiff, frozen*. I was struck by my *rigid* state and marvelled at the *ease* with which she teased. I realized that such a rigid state has been persistently present throughout my life, passing off as "normal and natural". My jealousy, I later reflected, was due to my desire to also express myself as *easily* as my friend did, without struggling with insecurity or fear. I had been aware of my difficulty to *voice* myself. However, this was the first time I became vividly aware of my rigid state.

This incident provided the starting point of my autoethnographic research project on the course—an MSc in Therapeutic Counselling. In the project, I adopted a critically reflexive approach (Freshwater & Rolfe, 2001) in which I researched into the incident in order to gain self-understanding and the natural confidence of having a free voice as well as to transform my clinical practice. The research process evolved cyclically, through continuous reflection on the incident, in order to make the intricacies of the clouded areas of the experience transparent. Descriptive, dialogic, and critical phases continued throughout the research process, stimulating questions rather than providing answers. In contrast to most research projects, I did not divide my research text into sections according to the different aspects of the research (literature review, data, analysis, results, limitations), but embedded them throughout the process. The research unfolded retrospectively after the incident and developed in an unstable, subjective field. In the following six sections, I provide a thematic analysis of the key aspects of the process that I undertook in the research. I then draw the various themes together in a concluding section.

The research charts my process of searching for a voice. What do I mean by *voice*? It is the ability to *express my opinion freely*, from the knowledge that I have the *right* to (Hawker & Hawkins, 1999).

Why was I overcome by a rigid state?

As I approached the time to write up this research (January 2004), I was unable to focus, repeatedly distracting myself by shopping, cooking, eating, etc. On forcing myself to face the writing, I felt nauseous, a choking sensation, breathless, as if gripped by an anxiety or fear of something: perhaps the discovery of my self-truth, or that the moment to encounter an unconscious awareness of this truth had arrived, or a fear of voicing myself through this writing? Reading Ellis's discussion on research experience brought relief; I was not alone in this.

> The self-questioning autoethnography demands is extremely difficult. So is confronting things about yourself which are less than

flattering. Honest autoethnography generates a lot of fears and doubts and emotional pain. Just when you think you can't stand the pain anymore, that's when the real work is only just starting. [Ellis & Bochner. 2000, p. 738]

I have been increasingly aware of my insecurity about speaking out my thoughts and feelings. I realize now that it is due to the negative reactions I might receive from people, especially authority figures; what they may say or believe of me. Indeed, in writing this, I feel embarrassed by possible reactions I might receive from readers, their views and criticisms. I am struggling to voice myself through this process of writing and self-research; it is hard. Again I share Ellis's reflection:

> . . . The vulnerability of revealing yourself, not being able to take back what you've written, or have any control over how readers interpret it. Feeling your life is critiqued as well as your work. It's humiliating. [*ibid*.].

However, it is easier to write (indirect communication) than to talk face to face (direct communication). Am I shielding myself from their immediate reactions by time and space?

The display of behaviour I observed by the student in the critical incident, forthright in expressing disgruntled feelings in a fun, joking fashion, has been unacceptable, formidable, and forbidden by most authority figures from the early part of my life. I expected an angry response from the tutor (authority figure), which made me panic, a possible transference from the past. The jealous part of me was actually pleased with her bold, confident, and free-standing self, desiring it for myself.

Why do I fear anger?

Reflection on the following note suggests it is perhaps due to the effects of experiencing anger from people: negative criticism, ultimately resulting in feelings of worthlessness, incapability, and stupidity.

> I'm losing my confidence, feel more diffident . . . unsure of myself.
> It's hard to look people in the eye, converse with them. My aunt's

angry words *"is the mother so stupid! . . . is the mother so blind! . . . is the mother so selfish! . . ."* continually ring through me. [personal note, October 2003]

These words were spoken to me regarding the new man in my life, a relationship disapproved of by all the family because of race difference. I felt belittled, unworthy of respect. This experience felt strangely very familiar. I had regressed to feelings of trepidation, insecurity, fear, and worthlessness in the last eight months of being around my aunt, an emotional state I now recalled feeling as a child around the elders in my extended family. I had the following dream at this time (10 October 2003).

> I am imprisoned in a concentration camp. Soldiers are coming to inspect the cells. I look skinny, pale, and bare. My cell is a small cupboard made from mud, a third of a normal sized door. All very bare, apart from an odd, empty tin container. I stand in front of it, waiting for the inspection . . . terrified. They haven't appeared . . . been quite some time, I step forward towards the main entrance to see if they are near. Others in the camp sneak into my cell and savage it! Drawing out my hidden belongings, which I have no idea I possessed! (Hidden and sealed over in excavated holes of the cell walls and floor.) I am amazed to see how quickly they did it . . . within seconds, and more amazed by the belongings, I had forgotten how *absolutely beautiful* these items were . . . shining brightly, like jewels and gold, a wonderful, precious treasure! I can't believe I have such possessions. The terror I had felt vanished at my delight on seeing this.

Upon waking, I recognized my insecurity and fear of being controlled by authority, and hiding my true talents.

The dramaturgical approach to dream analysis, derived from narrative research, embeds the dream in current concerns, desires, and challenges in life (Boothe, 2001). Using this approach to analyse the above dream, I realized that my challenges and concerns at that time centred round my whole life being criticized: work, personal relationships, parenting. I was receiving, therefore fearing, attacks of criticism from my family at large. I was continually, nervously on guard for long periods, could not relax, simply be myself, or enjoy being with and communicating with others. The desire in the dream could be to guard myself from being "ripped apart" (criticized, or emotionally indecently exposed) by other prisoners (family); however, unsuccessfully, as they find *my possessions* (my life, abilities), and expose them for my punishment. The sight of these possessions brings me delight, as I view them for the first time as the very tools I need to help me escape from this imprisonment. Ironically, it is my lack of abilities that is criticized, and which appear as the necessary tools to overcome this critical scrutiny. My dream, therefore, contains a wish-fulfilling element: to overcome the critical scrutiny of my abilities by evoking the utilization of these very abilities, now seen as valuable and precious by myself, to perform excellently in life, showing myself worthy or "fit".

Returning to anger . . .

Lindenfield (1993) suggests that anger affects self-esteem/confidence by the way it is perceived. Many fierce outbursts of anger were expressed by the elders towards each other and the children. Seeing and experiencing their anger was both frightening and infuriating. The Indian culture views the expression of anger as disrespectful, especially a child speaking its mind. This may be why I felt disabled from voicing my anger, remaining quiet, but holding a passive anger, as personal therapy revealed. Lindenfield (1993) explains that the culture we live in and are raised in shapes our response to threats, hurt, or frustration and may even influence whether the trigger is even noticed.

In the event of expressing my anger, regardless of cultural perceptions or family expectations, further angry responses were yielded: "Why should you be so angry?"; "She's mad, shameless, doesn't know anything nor understand anything". It was as if I had no right to feel angry, was dismissed, feeling stupid and unworthy. No explanations or clarifications were given. *Can children not grow to understand? Only to be seen, not heard?* To express my thoughts and anger resulted in experiencing more of their anger, to remain quiet meant being passively angry. I was caught in a vicious cycle. I therefore agree with Lindenfield (1993) that self-esteem is damaged by actually experiencing disapproval and rejection in direct response to the expression of anger.

Many therapists believe that depression is anger turned within. Lindenfield (1993) suggests it is a means of coping with being powerless and very unsafe in original pattern-setting relationships, where feelings of anger and frustration are first experienced. This helps to understand my depressive personality and self-blaming attitude for others' mistakes or inconsiderate ways. My therapist frequently stated, "Anyone can do whatever they want with you." Perhaps I have taken on the helpless part of my mother:

> My parents behave helplessly, refusing to see where they can take control even when advised, hiding behind the justification of customs, traditions, culture. [Personal therapy, 2001–2003]

Confrontation, even now as an adult, is agonizing; I find myself skirting around the topic to avoid the hard truth that might hurt the individual. This presents a serious implication for my counselling practice: *do I avoid confronting clients with the truth?* Lindenfield (1993, p. 81) advises, "learning to express anger assertively is an essential prerequisite for handling other people's anger sensitively and skilfully, and also to help others learn how to manage theirs". Getting my own house in order first through personal self-development (this research project), personal therapy, and continuous self-reflection, is vital.

I dislike this picture of myself; it sounds self-piteous, miserable, like a victim. It adds to the difficulty of voicing myself in this writing, as I find myself hesitating. Again, I find support from Ellis and Bochner (2000, p. 748) ". . . often our accounts of ourselves are unflattering and imperfect, but human and believable . . ."

Over the course of this project, I hesitated to answer inquiries from friends on this research. Feeling insecure and embarrassed by my predicament of "voicelessness", I avoided the question by vaguely responding with, "It's a self-development project." With further questions of interest from them, I ducked and dived with, "It's not the conventional method of research, more exploratory, reflective, cyclical in its process, it actually raises more questions than answers . . . it may not come to any firm conclusion . . ." I feared their view to be "She's really quite pathetic, stupid . . ." The sound of the critical voice, which makes me feel inadequate, tried to control me. I became free by admitting that the subject of my research is my sense of voicelessness. It raised some concern: maybe easier to study someone else, why subject yourself to a self-demolition/interrogation process?

In choosing to research my *self*, the ethical issue of care is towards myself. In hindsight, I see the big step I took in exposing myself to the insecurity of becoming vulnerable. However, it is better to uncover the long-felt silence within myself, to realize and become more conscious of the *stirring* on the other side of my silence.

Further thoughts on anger . . .

Having frequently suffered from migraines since childhood, I was surprised to read that it is one of the dangers of a sustained physiological state of anger (Lindenfield, 1993). While headaches can be a symptom of stress and strain, this theory indicates that perhaps my passive anger may be underlying the cause of my migraines.

I experienced the following while writing (Research journal 21 February 2004–1 March 2004).

> Constant headaches/migraines for about ten days, difficult to write, think it's due to emotional nature of this work.

> Reminds me of an intense migraine attack (February), just before therapy, lasted five days. Reflected on the cultural conflict I was (re)experiencing, becoming more in touch with my anger.

> Perhaps it is not simply the effects of stress and strain. There is certainly a current conflict with my family, of crossing the cultural boundary of engaging with Indians.

This theory is also supported by body psychotherapy, based on the belief that problems become anchored directly within our bodily existence, through symptoms such as stress, emotional suppression, trauma . . . (Totton, 2003).

Trying to voice my beliefs, views, or feelings brings more anger, becoming further excluded from family relationships now. This in turn frustrates me as I am unable to communicate with them and voice myself. It seems I am judged wrong before I have spoken, they know better, are correct, and I am to listen only to them. It has been tormenting and confusing to figure out what is right or wrong. *Am I wrong in all this? Are they actually right in what they say?* Their voices, expressions, words . . . flood my mind, it is hard to find mine through it. I am lost in an anger that consumes me . . . cannot think clearly.

> Out of control, you are at the mercy of your anger . . . you need a new kind of relationship with your emotions, one where you run them instead of them running you. [Maria Arapakis, re-quoted by Lindenfield, 1993, p. 28]

It appears that I have been controlled by my own anger, whether it is at the surface and bursting to explode, or passive where I am completely cut off from a conscious knowledge of it.

How is it possible to reflect and write about these experiences with a calm, objective perspective while this emotional storm is at work within me? I am wary of the charge made to qualitative researchers, of their subjectivity influencing their research; "being unable to avoid mixing personal impressions with descriptive accounts or to expunge their own biases from data collection, analysis, and interpretation" (Borman, LeCompte, & Preissle Goetz, 1986, p. 43). I am guided by Reason (1994, p. 12),

> Critical subjectivity is a quality of awareness in which we do not suppress our primary subjective experience, nor do we allow ourselves to be overwhelmed and swept away by it, rather we raise it to a consciousness and use it as part of the inquiry process.

And Ely, Anzul, Friedman, & Garner (1998, p. 35)

> . . . letting go . . . means the qualitative researcher is more able intensely to "be with" what is happening and to respond to that, instead of worrying about what should or could be happening.

Although my state of freezing is a subtle nuance, I now realize it is felt strongly by myself and the other person. For instance, when strong views were expressed to me by friends or relatives, it seemed like a lecture. "Feelings are intrinsically *interpersonal*: a subtle method for evaluating, reacting to and communicating with other people" (Totton, 2003, p. 9).

Responding to them in the midst of a "lecture" was useless; they did not listen. I then "emotionally freeze". This perhaps is my embodied anger; without outlet, expression, or acknowledgment.

Panksepp (1998) explains that the central role of embodied emotion is in establishing and maintaining a sense of self and self-value; that emotions are the most complex expression of processes by which the body self-regulates, a language by which mind and body speak (cited by Totton, 2003).

In a state of emotional paralysis, when finally asked for my thoughts, I am unable to say anything. My silence yielded further angry statements: *Why don't you say anything? This is typically you, cold!*

Totton (2003, p. 10) suggests that the "social engagement system", which draws together emotional experience and expression, facial gestures, vocal communication, and associated social behaviour, develops when the environment is perceived to be safe. In the event of "unsafety" or trauma, "a compulsive engagement of responses based on fight/flight or freezing, and perhaps a permanent lack of relational capacities", occurs. In the latter response of flight or freezing, "the adult will tend to show a *dissociative continuum*, involving cognitive, emotional and/or physical freezing and numbness". In therapy, the individual "... seems to be not really 'there', not identified with their here-and-now bodily experience".

These findings indicate that my rigid/frozen state may be due to developmental difficulties of unsafety/trauma. Totton's (2003) suggestion of effects of problems on mind and body having an overall affect on self and self-value, raised also by Lindenfield (1993) as anger affecting self-esteem and confidence, would appear to be evident in my case.

When "lectured" in recent years, I have summoned up strength to say, "I will talk to you later." Gathering up thoughts and feelings, having reflected, I have offered them my view. I believe this is the stirring of empowerment; movement from a passive, powerless self, to assertive, more confident action-taker, considering needs of self and others (Johns & Hardy, 1998).

Keiffer (1984) notes that the empowerment process involves "reconstructing and re-orientating deeply engrained personal systems of social relations" (Johns & Hardy, 1998, p. 52). Voicing and asserting myself to my family members seemed a monstrously daunting task. I had insufficient courage initially to state my thoughts, beliefs, or desires in my life. Their reactions felt too great to handle. I now realize that by using the limited strength I could find to voice myself, it made me feel stronger, more able, and in control of myself. I think, more confident. These initial experiences promoting self-confidence inherently carried a momentum, impelling ensuing experiences towards self-confidence to zip in.

A lack of presence . . .

Personal therapy also revealed my not really being "there". I described a photograph I kept envisioning (9 July 2002):

> I'm 4–6 years old, in Africa. My sister is sat [sic] on a chair and I'm on the table next to it. She looks very eager, happy, excited. I look withdrawn, sad, as if I am trying to hold myself up.

On seeing the photograph, I often wondered *what on earth was wrong with this girl*. Compared with the girl beside her, she could be described as "emotionally lifeless, not present".

> I'm struggling to write at this point, feels like re-living those moments in therapy as I recall them to write. Like repeatedly coming up against a pain barrier, just when I thought I was beyond it (Research journal 14 April 2004).

I recall my previous research tutor's words: when you feel the pain barrier while writing your experiences, you are expressing yourself in a different voice (Research Tutorial, 2002).

> Which voice is this? How many are there? Wasn't I searching for a voice?

"Feelings are not a substitute to political or intellectual activity, but they are *embedded* in human thinking" (Whitelaw, 2000, p. 135).

> I am tearful and heavy with guilt, unable to continue. Confiding to a friend, I was reminded of the support and sacrifices from several people, of valuable time sacrificed away from my son. Life seems to be on hold. I feel the burden to get through this, yet too heavy to make it through . . . My partner supports me with his belief that I am nearing a breakthrough.

It is important to examine personal motivations for undertaking the research (Richardson, 1997). The pressure to complete the research and course, to achieve the qualification, gain accreditation, cannot be ignored. The benefit is personal and professional.

Why was I overcome by this moment of angst? "Once the researcher has entered into the field, it is common to have moments of unexpected *angst*" (Friedman 1998, p. 110). I have just arrived at the possible reason for my "rigid state"; that is, early developmental difficulties to do with unsafety or trauma, which also throw light on my lack of felt presence and spontaneity.

> ... feeling can be a precursor to knowledge and the emotional consequences of pursuing/constructing knowledge. . . . in research, as in psychotherapy, feeling *can* be knowing. [Whitelaw, 2000, p. 134]

Could it be that I have now come to the discovery of that which I have always known, but not understood? Professional log (2002):

> Hidden within are things we know about ourselves but cannot put our fingers on ... My mother's words *"you were a good child, there were no difficulties with you"* came flashing back. I wondered about my feeling of being uninteresting; the insecurity to express myself, not wanting to be heard, hoping not to be noticed, wanting to diminish rather than appear.

I realize now that I felt perturbed by these very words I was writing. They were detached from me, from any emotion . . . had I imagined this? I recollected experiences that had left me with these feelings and thoughts. *Are these words sounded by my frozen self? How is it possible for a frozen self to express itself?* By detaching from any feeling, its voice is expressing itself. ". . . the voice is the expression of the self" (Stengel & Straunch, 2000, p. 5).

Perhaps the pain barrier is presented by my detached feelings to prevent the thoughts that are stirred in this writing to connect with my frozen self.

A divided self?

"Bion (1974) asserted that powerful forces operate in order to prevent us knowing what we truly think and feel. Instead we replace our thoughts and feelings with substitutes" (Freshwater, 1998, p. 179).

I now face the truth that I have detracted from facing my own truth with substitutions (eating, headaches, and migraines). I acknowledge the knowledge of the feeling throughout this writing that this is not *exactly* the full truth; I felt myself skirting around the central event. I believe it is a part that scares yet fascinates me. *Could this be the frozen self?* A strange picture I drew in a class exercise comes to mind (lecture December 2002) (Figure 1).

My attention was captured by Kalsched (2001, p. 3) regarding childhood trauma and development;

> ... when trauma strikes the developing psyche of a child, fragmentation of consciousness occurs, the "pieces" organise themselves according to certain archaic patterns, made up of personified "beings". One part of the ego *regresses* to the infantile period, and another part *progresses*, i.e. grows up too fast and becomes precociously adapted to the outer world, often as a "false self" (Winnicott, 1960a). The *progressed part* of the personality then caretakes the *regressed part*.

Figure 1.   The divided self.

It was as if Kalsched's theory was talking to me, touching a remote inner part of myself. Was this a fantasy of my mind? I recalled a nightmare:

> I was being chased by the devil, I felt terrified. I hid my son (aged five) in a box, no longer terrified . . . just afraid (personal log, October 2002).

Kalsched (2001) explains that in dreams, the regressed part of the personality is usually represented as a vulnerable, young, innocent child self who remains shamefully hidden. And the progressed part as a powerful benevolent or malevolent great being, which protects or persecutes its vulnerable partner, appearing as an angel, miraculous animal, or the devil himself.

It seems like a powerful theatrical drama to me. Kalsched (2001, pp. 1–4) describes it as a "second line of defence, the psyche's archetypal self-care system", to prevent the "unthinkable" from being "experienced", crediting this maladaptive form of defence for its miraculous and life-saving sophistication.

Kalsched's theory points to the possibility of an early childhood trauma in my life, as previously indicated. It also suggests a divided self; the child self protected and persecuted by the progressed, powerful self. I would not have believed this in itself, without the following two dreams (therapy notes, 2 July 2002):

> I came to therapy and sat in the chair. His (therapist's) little girl was happily busy, getting the stage ready for him to show me something . . .

I was amazed to hear my therapist informing me that the child was *my inner child*. I didn't really believe it at the time. I discover in the following dream, that I *am* the little girl from my previous dream as, interestingly, I felt myself to be her this time.

> I (little girl in the dream) knew I had to leave but didn't want to. I wanted to play . . . (therapy notes 15 October 2002)

I am now in touch with my inner child through the dream world.

I feel light-headed, giddy, weightless, detached from my body. I want to continue this writing . . . feeling is overcoming, sapping me. Again a resistance, perhaps the self-care system is too powerful, a psychic numbing?

Kalsched (2001, p. 1) uses the word "trauma" to mean "any experience that causes the child unbearable pain or anxiety".

Among the various forms of trauma are the *cumulative traumas* of unmet dependency-needs, including what Winnicott (1963) describes as the "primitive agonies", the experience of which is "unthinkable" (cited by Kalsched, 2001, p. 1).

I recall my surprise when my therapist said, "Your mother was not there for you." Indeed, she was very busy:

> Everybody else has her attention, help, time, consideration. It's hopeless to fight for it, she's overtaken by it. . . . had I simply given up trying to be heard? [Professional log, January 2002]

I now know why I did not question his statement: "Your mother was not there for you." I did not want to believe it.

Perhaps this is where my anger stems from. Miller (1989, p. 135) writes, "The child in the adult is full of narcissistic rage against the mother because she was not available to him . . ."

She was too busy, unavailable. Those that were, were harsh, critical. Needed to obey them, had to do it their way, any other way was wrong, feared being told off, cannot understand why . . . could not be free.

Perhaps it is for me as Kalsched (2001) describes these individuals;

> "divided within themselves, bright, sensitive, suffered acute/cumulative emotional trauma in early life, becoming prematurely self-sufficient, cutting off genuine relations with their parents during their developing years and caretaking themselves, tending to see themselves as victims of others' aggression, unable to mobilise effective self-assertion or defend themselves, or individuate" [pp. 11–12]

What is my true self? Is it the voice of this true self that I am searching?

Discussion

This research approach has been like juggling three balls: writing the research, being open and responsive to the experience of reflexive writing, and managing the emotional reality of a personally difficult topic. I will now look at these aspects from the point of view of writing the research and the research process as a whole.

Writing the research

This was a difficult process for me. I noticed parallels between my sense of "voicelessness" in life and my struggle in writing this research. There were two aspects to this.

I am used to receiving critical reactions in the past from authority figures and so I anticipated the same thing when voicing myself during this writing. However, my awareness of this process enabled a shift from being frozen to continuing the research. I was thus able to use reflection as a means of debriefing my freezing and moving on.

I am generally used to allowing others to voice themselves before myself, due to my insecurity about the reactions that I may receive. But a similar pattern emerged in this writing. There were large pieces of writing in which I relied on various authors whom I saw as having authority. This was noted by my tutor (February 2004). This prompted the following reflection: "I am hiding, distancing, diminishing my voice behind theirs. Perhaps the aged notion I carry 'she doesn't understand, is stupid, incapable' makes me hide" (research journal February 2004). As a result of this, I then tried in my writing to include other authors without losing my voice in the narrative. This resulted in an ongoing struggle to experience my voice in the research text, as Hertz (1996, p. 7) describes: "reflexivity encompasses voice . . . voice is how the author expresses herself within an ethnography". The experience of voicing myself in the research text has enabled the outcome of a more "voice embodied" self.

The research process

The symptoms of freezing, headaches/migraines, and lack of spontaneity in life were a feature of this writing. During the analysis, I thought the headaches and migraines had reappeared due to recalling past experiences of anger. However, Ellenberger (1970) presents yet another side to journeys of self-analysis; the notion of a "creative illness", which succeeds a period of intense preoccupation with an idea/search for a certain truth. The symptoms of the illness are felt as painful/agonizing, with periods of alleviation/worsening, but the searching thread of truth is never lost (Symington, 1986).

My incessant piecing together of card sequences in the game Spider Solitaire during this write-up was an unconscious preoccupation with piecing together the trail of data/experiences. My emotions, mind, and body were in a fierce battle. Livingstone Smith (1991) suggests these symptoms can be indicators of a fear of the emergence of some terrifying memory, phantasy, or desire. Greenson (1967) considers it a force of resistance, opposing the process of analysis; hindering free associations, the attempts to remember, gain, and assimilate insight operating against the client's ego and wish to change (Livingstone Smith, 1991). The symptoms presented during this write-up appear to be *obstructers* to gaining knowledge of self-truth.

My tutor noticed a contradiction in the research aims: the initial aim of using reflexive research to gain a confident free voice altering to a "side effect" (Kvale, 1996). I recollect my insecure feelings at the time; *can I make these changes? It's my aim, will it be the result?* I had made a claim to change without being confident in the undertaking, being "confused, not clear where to go from here, all wrong? too subjective?" (research journal 28 February–3 March 2004). I was then referred to Kvale (1996) for thematic analysis, and I stumbled on the idea of self-interview, "where any changes are a side effect . . ." I felt freed from the burden of my commitment to make personal changes, and settled for the easier aim of achieving self-knowledge. While self-knowledge was one of the original aims of this research, my haste to use this approach was admittedly a form of escape from the aim of personal change. *So why did I resist the change?*

Schafer (1983, p. 12) suggests ". . . unconsciously analysands can only view understanding and changing as dangerous". Change is difficult, painful, frightening, as seen in hindsight; the anguish, confusion, despair, and angst encountered in this work. However, "Kierkegaard (1944) advocated that angst is positive, it is manifested in the individual who is actively engaged in an existential situation, it may be the precursor to profound change" (Freshwater 1998, p. 181). It is at this place of dynamic disequilibrium that learning, or acquiring of personal truth, takes place. The feeling of confusion and mounting tension forms a "creative tension" that leads to an emerging purpose through which consciousness can expand

(Freshwater, 1998). Despite my unconscious effort to overturn my initial aim of "change" to a "side effect", the self-reflexive process appears to have led me through its necessarily painful path to change. *What is the change?*

Freud (1986) viewed analysis as the technique for restoring the ego, to assert control over the id that has been impaired by early repressions, achieved by recognizing the symptoms of the repressions, listening to and interpreting dreams and free associations (Greenwood & Loewenthal, 1998). The pain barriers encountered along this reflexive trail were repressions. Undergoing them was necessary to make contact with my "state of truth": the discovery of an early issue of unsafety or trauma resulting in a false self. Further research would be required to identify the true self and its voice.

Value of this research for my practice

What are the implications of a "voice embodied self" for my counselling practice? Given that counselling is for clients to voice themselves and the counsellor is there to *listen*, not offer views or opinions but aid the client to reach theirs, this research presents a "delicious irony" (Research Tutorial, 05/04). Freud (1915) remarked "the *Ucs.* of one human being can react upon that of another, without passing through *Cs*" (quoted in Livingstone Smith, 1991, p. 61). The unconscious specifically adapts to understanding intersubjective reality; tuning into the most subtle psychological nuances of people's behaviour, and processing their emotional realities (Livingstone Smith, 1991). This is comparable to the process of osmosis: absorption from a greater concentration. Ferenczi (quoted in Symington, 1986, p. 201) also observed how "some patients show a remarkable, almost clairvoyant knowledge about the thoughts and emotions that go on in their analyst's mind". This theory suggests that my voice embodied self would affect the unconscious systems of my clients. *How do we know this?* Further research to observe the impact of these changes on client work is required.

Credibility of reflexive research

Qualitative research is considered not reproducible, its findings not generalizable. However, as Whitelaw (2000, p. 123) points out;

"generalisability is more diffuse and less tangible". It is concerned with communicating to readers. Therefore, in this research, the *felt sense of voicelessness* may resonate in some shape or form with the reader.

The research relies on reflexivity, which has the ability to promote personal growth and self-actualization on the part of the researcher (Lamb & Huttlinger, 1989). It also has the potential to promote honesty and transparency within the research process, thereby improving quality (Barry, Britten, Barber, Bradley, & Stevenson, 1999) and to present a clear picture of the complexities involved (Scott, 1997). Reflexivity thus raises the question of research credibility.

Avis (1995) argues that credibility should be judged by the usefulness of the research project. By furthering my own self-development I am able to help my clients further in their journey. Having said this, I am wary that recollections of experiences may be subject to distortions or unconscious falsifications, such as using selective memories, conferring my own meanings, views, values, and so on. It is, however, the truth as I know and understand it. The past history of words and deeds are inseparable from the interpreter. Subject and object are one. "Interpretation involves an inescapably subjective dimension . . . are neither true nor false, better or worse, more or less valid" (Freeman, 1993, p. 5).

Such a piece of autoethnographic research also has to face the accusation of self-indulgence (Koch & Harrington, 1998; Marcus, 1994) and "narcissistic preoccupation with the self" (Scott 1997, p. 134). It is virtually impossible to guard against this in this research approach. Waterman (1998) draws on the difficulty of developing self-awareness and understanding. While I carried the risk of compounding narcissistic beliefs obscured from my view by engaging in a self reflexive dialogue, failure to adopt a reflexive stance would compound such lack of self-awareness (Olesen, 1994). Exposing my work to a critical dialogue with my research peer group and tutor allowed confrontation of self-deceptions (Lamb & Huttlinger, 1989; Richardson, 1997; Soltis-Jarrett, 1997). Waterman (1998) also notes the problem of too much introspection leading to a lack of action, or loss of research objective. Indeed, I constantly needed to stop and trace back to the objective of the research during the endless cycle of reflecting upon reflections.

Conclusion

The research started with an overall aim to gain a confident *free* voice. Alongside this, to further self-understanding and professional development.

The trail of analytic reflections led me through a storm of anger to discover that my frozen/numbed self could have a voice. I find this voice being empowered and gaining a confidence, which I realize is self-developing now.

The trail halts at the discovery of the possibility of a divided self.

The very act of writing this paper is an attempt to voice myself, resulting in a more "voice embodied self". This raises the question: can the reader hear my voice?

Has my search for a voice been successful? It has.

References

Avis, M. (1995). Valid arguments? A consideration of the concept of validity in establishing the credibility of research findings. *Journal of Advanced Nursing*, 22(6): 1203–1209.

Barry, C., Britten, N., Bradley, C. & Stevenson, F. (1999). Using reflexivity to optimise teamwork in qualitative research. *Qualitative Health Research*, 9: 26–44.

Boothe, B. (2001). The rhetorical organization of dream-telling. *Counselling and Psychotherapy Research*, 1(2): 101–113.

Borman, K., LeCompte, M., & Preissle Goetz, J. (1986). Ethnographic and qualitative research design and why it doesn't work. *American Behavioural Scientist*, 30(1): 42–57.

Ellenberger, H. F. (1970). *The Discovery of the Unconscious: The History and Evolution of Dynamic Psychiatry.* New York: Basic Books.

Ellis, C., & Bochner, A. (2000). Autoethnography, Personal narrative, reflexivity: researcher as subject. In: N. Denzin & S. Lincoln (Eds.), *Handbook of Qualitative Research* (pp. 733–765), (2nd edn). London: Sage.

Ely, M., Anzul, M., Friedman, T., & Garner, D. (1998). *Doing Qualitative Research: Circles within Circles.* London: Farmer.

Freeman, M. (1993). *Rewriting the Self.* London: Routledge.

Freshwater, D. (1998). The philosopher's stone. In: C. Johns & D. Freshwater (Eds.), *Transforming Nursing Through Reflective Practice* (pp. 177–184). London: Blackwell Science.

Freshwater, D., & Rolfe, G. (2001). Critical reflexivity: a politically and ethically engaged research method for nursing. *NT Research*, *6*(1): 526–537.

Friedman, T. (1998). Feeling. In: M. Ely, M. Anzul, T. Friedman, & D. Garner (Eds.), *Doing Qualitative Research: Circles within Circles* (pp. 107–137). London: Farmer.

Greenson, R. R. (1967). *The Technique and Practice of Psycho-Analysis*. London: Hogarth.

Greenwood, D., & Loewenthal, D. (1998). Is therapy possible with a person diagnosed with dementia? *European Journal of Psychotherapy and Counselling Health*, *1*(2): 36–49.

Hawker, S., & Hawkins, J. (1999). *The Oxford Popular Dictionary & Thesaurus*. Oxford: Oxford University Press.

Hertz, R. (1996). Introduction: ethics, reflexivity and voice. *Qualitative Sociology*, *19*(1): 3–9.

Johns, C., & Hardy, H. (1998). Voice as a metaphor for transformation through reflection. In: C. Johns & D. Freshwater (Eds.), *Transforming Nursing Through Reflective Practice* (pp. 51–61). London: Blackwell Science.

Kalsched, D. (2001). *The Inner World of Trauma*. London: Routledge.

Koch, T., & Harrington, A. (1998). Reconceptualizing rigour: the case for reflexivity. *Journal of Advanced Nursing*, *28*(4): 882–890.

Kvale, S. (1996). *InterViews*. London: Sage.

Lamb, G., & Huttlinger, K. (1989). Reflexivity in nursing research. *Western Journal of Nursing Research*, *11*: 765–772.

Lindenfield, G. (1993). *Managing Anger*. London: Thorsons.

Livingstone Smith, D. (1991). *Hidden Conversations*. London: Routledge.

Marcus, G. (1994). What comes (just) after "post"? The case of ethnography. In: N. Denzin & Y. Lincoln (Eds.), *Handbook of Qualitative Research* (pp. 563–574). London: Sage.

Miller, A. (1989). *The Drama of Being a Child*. London: Sage.

Olesen, V. (1994). Feminisms and models of qualitative research. In: N. Denzin & Y. Lincoln, (Eds.), *Handbook of Qualitative Research* (pp. 158–174). London: Sage.

Reason, P. (1994). *Human Inquiry in Action*. London: Sage.

Richardson, M. (1997). Participatory research methods: people with learning difficulties. *British Journal of Nursing*, *6*: 1114–1121.

Schafer, R. (1983). *The Analytic Attitude*. New York: Basic Books.

Scott, D. (1997). The researcher's personal responses as a source of insight in the research process. *Nursing Inquiry*, *4*: 130–134.

Soltis-Jarrett, V. (1997). The facilitator in participatory action research: les raisons d'etre. *Advances in Nursing Sciences, 20*(2): 45–54.

Stengel, I., & Straunch, T. (2000). *Voice and Self*. London: Free Association.

Symington, N. (1986). *The Analytic Experience*. London: Free Association.

Totton, N. (2003). Bodywork. *Counselling & Psychotherapy Journal, 14*(4): 8–12.

Waterman, H. (1998). Embracing ambiguities and valuing ourselves: issues of validity in action research. *Journal of Advanced Nursing, 28*: 101–105.

Whitelaw, A. (2000). Feeling/knowing in research. *Journal of Free Association, 8*(2): 121–139.

CHAPTER ELEVEN

Multiple voices, multiple truths: creating reality through dialogue

Dawn Freshwater

Lost and found in translation

D ear Reader, have you ever had the experience of putting together an abstract for a conference, a proposal for a book, an idea for a paper, or even rehearsing a conversation in your head, so far in advance that when it comes to handling the situation or the event itself it bears little or no resemblance to what seemed so clear (and indeed inspirational) at the time? Somehow so much is lost (or gained) in translation. The translation of what to what is an interesting point to reflect on. From the internal thought to the external behaviour/action; from the cellular to the universal; the word to the reader; from the pen to the page.

As you read this chapter, and, indeed, as you have read this book, you may not be aware, but you will not have read what has been written. Well, at least, you may have read the concrete and literal words on the page. But this is not the sort of reading I am referring to; rather, I am interested in what you have done to the words you have read, how you have interacted with them, inter-preted and translated them. In this chapter, I want to emphasize the ways in which each one of us, in each and every moment of our lives, interprets and translates every interaction in order to enhance and validate our own personal narratives, experience, and truths. That is to say, we seek and create our own truths, and do so through multiple voices, representing multiple discourses and complex dialogues. At this point in the proceedings, I ask you to reflect on how you have participated in the process of this book and invite you to further that process through observing and attending to what I will call the participatory dialogue of the reader–audience (Freshwater, 2007).

One of the themes of this book has been that of multiple truths; these have been represented and presented through multiple voices. It is pertinent at this juncture, if you have not been stimulated to do so thus far, to pause. To look up in the act of reading. To pause, to breathe, and reflect upon how you have engaged with the text so far. Perhaps, you might feel that you have passively received the text, but even this seemingly passive act is an active choice, though not necessarily a conscious one. Of course, not engaging with the text is also a form of engagement, a type of relationship, a particular sort of dialogue. On each occasion that a text is read, another version of the truth is constructed. Throughout this chapter I aim to provoke you into reflecting more consciously and deeply on the process of reading and, importantly, the way in which this process *does* something to you. I do not mean to constrain reading to the literal act of reading text on a page, rather I would prefer to use a much looser description of reading to incorporate ways in which we read situations, people, places, spaces, and events (see Freshwater, 2007). I use the notion of dialogue in order to illuminate some of the concepts that I wish to explore, referring to the process that takes place between the reader and the read, the audience and the speaker, the writer and the paper. As with many of the chapters in this book, the use of metaphor and allegory is also employed; in contrast to the concrete and the literal, I prefer to evoke and provoke through the imagination and the use of symbolism and resonance. Westwood, Boyd, and Redwood provide elegant and creative examples of the ways in which metaphor and allegory can open up previously striated spaces, and in doing so, stimulate dialogue.

So, before going any further with this chapter, which, being the last chapter in the book, could be viewed as an ending, but may just as easily be seen as a beginning, I challenge you to let your heart be open to its natural resonance with all the energies of the present moment, thereby expanding, freezing, or pausing to allow one's self to be completely immersed in the present quantum moment. Maybe John and I "should" have "prescribed" this focus on yourself and your own natural resonance at the beginning of the book; it may have made a good preface and, indeed, could have been instructive. However, I believe it is more interesting, at least in the context of this book, to end at the beginning. That is, with a call to reflect back in the present moment of this chapter on what this text has done to you, or, in reality, what you have done to it.

In his chapter of this book, John writes about the process of ordering and structuring the text itself. He revealed that there was not necessarily any obvious order, instead, we relied heavily on what David Bohm (1980) describes as the implicate order, or what I and others might refer to as circumscribed indeterminacy (Freshwater, 2007). Hence, while in the first instance the text and, indeed, this exposition may appear fragmented, I would like to set out a fundamental principle (or guiding narrative) that underpins much of my own work. That is: everything is connected, everything is everything, and everything is also nothing (see Freshwater & Rolfe, 2004). In this sense, this chapter does not have the usual intention of final chapters of attempting to make connections for you, the reader; rather, it is about my connections. It is not necessary for me to make the connections for you; in fact it is a misapprehension to believe that I can do this, just as it is for the nurse to believe that she can heal the patient, or that the therapist can cure the analysand, rather than enabling the patient to access their own healing potential. You will make and create your own connections and meaning from what is written, and have been doing so already, even if that meaning is that this text has no meaning for you. In fact, this is one of the things that connects us: the yearning and quest for meaning and the ways in which we employ narrative understanding and participatory dialogue to achieve this. Participatory dialogue, as I propose it, is a way to further illuminate the epistemology of reflective practice that has been central to many of the chapters within this current text, importantly, the concept of practice-based research.

Dear Prudence . . .

I wish to write you a note or two regarding my current thinking around reflection, dialogue, and discourse. This has been stimulated by engaging with the authors, chapters, and process of this book . . .

Reflection

Reflection on practice provides an opportunity to enquire, to examine evidence, as does reflection in action and reflexivity. But reflection is not just about pausing, it is also a dialogue in itself; it not only requires something of you, it also demands some action or improvement, both locally, nationally, internationally, globally, and in the cosmos. In other words, it brings with it the "Burden of Prudence" (Freshwater, 2005).

Similarly, putting down words such as I am doing now is a Burden of Prudence. An idea, once committed to paper (or indeed reaching consciousness), begs to be developed; in fact, I might argue that it requires some action. Awareness of participation in a dialogue brings with it a heightened sense of responsibility and accountability, as Redwood alludes to when she describes the unconscious incompetence of unreflective ethics procedures. An author (and I include all of us in this definition of the author as we write our lives day to day and moment to moment) is faced with their accountability, whether the emphasis is on the personal or professional. What has this to do with practitioner-based research? Moreover, how is it related to the concepts of emancipation and transformation? (Those potent words used in the title of this book.) In common with the positions already outlined, I wish to emphasize the notion of *person*hood in the discussion about practitioner-based research and, naturally, to signify the importance of self-reflection in the production of reflective research texts. Hence, I am listening alongside you to my text, as the idea that has been called to action unfolds. I am aware of being in dialogue at an intrapersonal, interpersonal, and transpersonal level. The participation is both within myself and with other texts (through intertextual processes) and, of course, with you.

Having begun with the notion of reflection, and introducing the focus as one that requires action, it seems germane to refer to the idea of reflexive pragmatism. My process at this moment is one of wanting to create connections through bringing relevant perspectives to bear on the phenomena under scrutiny—practice-based research.

Having described in brief the concept of reflexive pragmatism, I outline the dialogic method, turning to the notion of dialogue and its relationship to relationality and resonance. Here, I will use a practical example of cardio-contemplation, drawing on cardio-energetics and musical rhythm as my guiding metaphors. Where I use musical metaphors, referring to harmonics and melodics, these are not used in an abstract sense, for our own bodies have their own natural harmonics, in common with clinical practice, healthcare practice, caring, research, and, indeed, the world, which, despite all it seems on the surface, is also searching for its own harmonic resonance. Finally, I turn to the idea of discourse—for what else is this chapter, no, this book, if not a discourse. A discourse set within multiple other discourses, guided and driven by political, ethical, and social discourses. It seems pertinent to end by inviting you, the reader, to reflect on how these contrasting and competing discourses collide and collude with your own personal discourse.

I have already mentioned the work of David Bohm (1980); in his cosmology he has begun to articulate a theory of the implicate order, a science of wholeness. Reflexive pragmatism, in my view, recognizes the implicate science of practice and in that practice-based research, the what-is-yet-to-be-known-and-articulated inherent in every moment of clinical activity. Several authors in this book have referred to the value of not knowing. Boyd muses on the value of not knowing the rationale for the title of her chapter, and Hunter and Lees point out the pitfalls of thinking that we know what we are doing, the seduction of expertise. Pragmatism as a philosophical act at least enables one to speculate on the value of not knowing and uncertainty.

Doing and being pragmatism

In order to develop the case for a reflexive pragmatism, I first need to sketch out the basic principles of pragmatism. However, I also wish to point out that I cannot do justice to the great philosophical debate that underpins the development of the movement in this short piece, and, as such, refer the audience to the original works of the main protagonists, most of whom will be recognized here. Pragmatism, as a philosophy, is distinct in that its emphasis is on practice. A tradition founded by three American philosophers: Peirce, William James, and John Dewey (known as the odd couple), one of the central tenets of pragmatism is that the function of inquiry is not to represent reality; rather, it enables the individual to act more effectively. It is a doing; however, it is also a way of being. The three philosophers emphasized different philosophical concerns (Peirce was a mathematician, James interested in religion, Dewey in education and politics) and accordingly each turned pragmatism into a significantly different doctrine (see Mounce, 1997). Nevertheless, each doctrine shared an opposition to the doctrine of correspondence of truth theories. Although the work of Dewey, James, and Peirce does not necessarily overlap, and despite the fact that the three "classical pragmatists" did not see themselves as an organized philosophical movement, an epistemology of pragmatism was born. In fact, pragmatism has been the subject of many misconceptions because it has never really been a unified movement (Anderson, 2001; see also James in Kuklick, 1987). As a philosophical tradition it lost its popularity in the 1930s and 1940s, but Mounce (1997) noted that it has regained its momentum in the latter half of the twentieth century, mainly due to such writers as Donald Davidson, Putnam and, of course, Richard Rorty. We might pause here and reflect upon the reasons for pragmatism growing in stature over the past four or five decades, when we have come to rely so much on technology and where relationships have become abstract and research driven by the desire for sanitization. (Readers might like to remind themselves of their responses to Chapter One at this juncture.)

Latterly, writers have distinguished two broad styles of pragmatism, these being reformist and revolutionary (Haack, 1993). In simple terms, reformist pragmatists seek to reform epistemology, abandoning foundationalism, but remaining concerned with epistemology. Revolutionary pragmatism, however, views the collapse of foundationalism as the end of epistemology altogether.

Haack (1993) notes that the early pragmatists tended to exhibit traces of both reformist pragmatism and revolutionary pragmatism.

However, in regard to this argument, I wish to make it clear that I do not align myself with revolutionary pragmatists, but do acknowledge that pragmatism *per se* was, and continues to be, revolutionary in its own right, and in so being has the potential for emancipation, revelation, and transformation. As an epistemology, pragmatism has more recently been developed and refined by such authors as Rorty and Davidson. Pragmatic epistemology is grounded in practice, and based on the premise that thought and action (in practice) are inseparable. This view is well rehearsed in the nursing and education literature (e.g., Gibbs, 1988; Rolfe, 1996) and is neatly summarized by Polkinghorne (2004, p. 5):

> Practice is sometimes differentiated from theory, doing something as opposed to thinking about something. However, the distinction is overdrawn. Action and thought (both conscious and unconscious) are interactive. Practices are grounded in understandings people have about the world, and these understandings are, in turn, influenced by the effect of their practices on the world. Contemporary practice theory refocuses on the point of interaction of people with the world and others.
>
> Practice theory and research come from the same energetic space; the point of interaction, where energy meets is dialogue.

Ahh . . . so now I begin to see the connections between dialogue, practice, and research, between participation and action, and, indeed, the implicate order. Pragmatic epistemology and the formal–informal continuum of knowledge provide a dialogic space within which all ways of knowing can be integrated (Bohm, 1996).

How a practitioner makes a decision about what to do in a particular clinical situation depends a lot on the individual: his/her assessment of the clinical situation/context, and his/her experience and exposure to different types of knowing. Thus, another important dimension of pragmatic epistemology is access to knowledge. For, if practitioners are not exposed (or more importantly do not expose themselves) to new knowledge and access to their own knowledge through reflection, then they cannot use it for their practice. Accessing knowledge requires, actually demands, dialogue at many different levels, interacting with multiple discourses, truths, and voices.

Many authors propose that one way of making this integrating dialogue more conscious and explicit is through the process of reflexivity (Freshwater & Avis, 2004; Rolfe, Freshwater, & Jasper, 2001); this is to say that one way of accessing new knowledge is through reflection. I have outlined elsewhere the subtle but significant differences between reflection, critical reflection, and reflexivity (Freshwater, 2006). But, in brief, reflection can be defined as thinking about practice, critical reflection as thinking about how you are thinking about practice, and reflexivity as thinking about how you are thinking about practice in the political, social, ethical, and historical context; reflexivity is essentially a constructivist activity and in principle is a process of inquiry/research activity that originates in the desire for social action, agency, and change. This is to say that it is closely aligned to emancipation and transformation, although this is not always explicitly referred to as an aspect or intended (and most often unintended) as an outcome of reflexive processes. Reflexivity is also an approach to research in its own right, and one that brings home the emphasis to the researcher/practitioner/academic/scholar.

The process of examining and recording the impact of researcher and intersubjective elements in research has a long history, spanning many decades and disciplines. Described as an assault on unity, reflexive research, then, is a humble and subjective *human* enterprise that is characterized as tentative and indeterminate. It is an approach to inquiry that means working with alternative lines of interpretation and vocabularies to balance endless reflection and radical scepticism with a sense of purpose and execution of results.

If reflexivity is, as I propose, one of the defining features of humanity, then inconsistency is certainly up there with it. As humans we are consistently inconsistent, rendering it nigh on impossible to secure validity and reliability in practice/research that often carries personal significance (which provides energy) and heightens both the meaning and sense-making experience of the individual's life (making it personal), as well as their conceptual and theoretical knowing (thereby creating evidence to be further tested through the process of participatory dialogue).

Thus, reflexive pragmatism:

- is concerned with questioning assumptions;
- focuses on the social rather than the individual;

- pays particular attention to the analysis of power relations;
- is concerned with democracy.

As Vince (p. 67) points out:

> reflection is not primarily an individual process, but a collective capacity to question assumptions means that it implies an ongoing inquiry into the nature and consequences of social power relations within organisations.

Speaking of ongoing inquiry and social relations . . . how is your heart doing at this stage? How are you engaging with the words on the page and to what extent are you aware of the dialogue that you are currently participating in? To what extent are you immersed in the quantum moment. Let us have a momentary pause; in other words, let us attempt to do what I am speaking about, better known as showing and telling the process simultaneously, something that many mental health practitioners and therapists live daily, often referring to themselves as facilitating parallel processes.

Pianist Artur Rubinstein described the power of such momentary pauses when he said that the notes I play like every pianist. But the pauses, ahhh, the pauses. The pauses are the places where the dialogue can become known, where voices can be heard and participation can be experienced.

Sensuous rhythms

In her paper "Musical meaning and the social reproduction: a case for retrieving autonomy", Lucy Green (2005, p. 78) considers the dialectical relationship between musical text and context. She notes,

> Sound is the raw material from which music is made. For music to come into existence and for musical experience to occur, this raw material must be organised in such a way as to have relationships which are perceived in the mind of the listener.

Rather like the organization/structure of practice (and indeed research) is in the eye of the practitioner. She goes on,

> Not only does music raise expectations for what might be going to happen next, it also causes us to make retrospective connections between present and past events, so that the present makes the past meaningful; and the musical past colours the present just as much as the present raises expectations for the future. [*ibid.*]

Using a reflexive approach and attending to the quality of the moment enables autonomy to be revealed, a concept that is critical in any attempt to manage and sustain change. Well, you might challenge me, we cannot just have pauses, they need to be organized in someway. Dialogue, I would argue, is one of the organizing principles of the self, of practice, of research, and of the world in which we locate the self.

Dialogue

Russian thinker and theorist Mikhail Bakhtin coined the term dialogism. All knowledge of the human subject, he argued, is formed through words, through language and in dialogue. This takes place in numerous ways and through infinite mediums; it happens whether we are questioning, listening, answering, agreeing, or challenging. For Bakhtin, all interaction tales places in the form of utterances, that is, the social form of dialogue. Bohm, our cosmologist, contrasts dialogue with discussion, which he suggests has the same roots as percussion and concussion, meaning to break things up, thus emphasizing the idea of analysis. However you interpret the term, dialogue itself does not necessarily mean a two-sided or even one-sided conversation; it means through language. It is through language that meaning emerges. Gordon notes that

> Language, in other words, is not mine. It belongs to, comes from and returns to the human community of which I am a part and in which I participate through language. This has profound implications for what it means to be a person. The dialogical principle insists that we are immediately and irretrievably social. [p. 66]

In fact, word is an interactive/energetic act. It is determined equally by whose word it is and for whom it is meant.

This dialogical principle reminds us that the process by which our selves are constituted is never finished, that dialogues are not something we can simply enter and leave, that life itself is dialogic. Dialogue, then, is "something more of a common participation, in which we are not playing a game against each other but with each other". The object of dialogue is not to analyse or to win an argument, or even to exchange opinions. Rather it is to suspend your opinions and to look at the opinions—to listen to everybody's opinions, to suspend them, and to see what all that means (Bohm, 1996). In this way, dialogue, closely aligned to the notion of reflexivity as earlier defined, is really aimed at going into the whole thought process and changing the way the thought process occurs collectively. It is also, in my view, clearly associated with the development and experience of multiple truths. Thus far, we have not really paid much attention to thought as a process. We have engaged in thoughts, but usually we only paid attention to the content, not to the process. Paying attention to the process of thinking is fairly demanding and not something that comes easily to any of us in our busy lives. And yet, it is that very process that determines how we interpret and create our lives and, indeed, how we interpret and create the evidence by which we create our lives. Pay attention now to your process of thinking as you read, translate, and dialogue with this text. Are you able to separate participatory thought from literal thinking?

Dialogical groups focus on participatory thought, rather than literal thought. Literal thought aims at being a reflection of reality as it is—it claims just to tell you the way things are . . . aims to be unambiguous and tells things as they really are. It focuses on a single truth and is more in tune with traditional approaches to knowledge development. Participatory thought sees that everything partakes of everything. It aims to bringing together and identify connections, rather than to fragment; deep cellular resonance, as you might suspect, is a fundamental element of this process (Beck et al., 2003). In Beck and colleagues' study, the methodology, dialogal phenomenology, was characterized by ongoing and open conversation. The conversation took place on two levels: "among the practitioner's researchers and between the practitioner researchers and the phenomenon; hence the name dialogal" (2003, p. 341). They go on to explain:

Faithfulness to the data is fostered through open dialogue among researchers in relationship to the data and through careful consideration of multiple perspectives rather than through adherence to a set of explicitly spelled out procedures. [*ibid.*]

They comment further that the essential dimensions of any genuine dialogue are structure and freedom. It is structure that provides the backbone for the conversation, and it is freedom that infuses the process with a spirit of exploration and discovery. It is the interplay between structure and freedom that creates the dynamic tension and creative ambiguity that make the dialogal process so exciting. Here we are seeing a lived example of circumscribed indeterminacy. Buber's dialogal philosophy consistently points to the relational core of all human existence. The well known and oft quoted, in therapeutic circles, notion of the I–thou and the I–it relationship is a science of relationality, of intentionality and of truth. It could be argued that, "Conversation, dialogue, is necessary for the truth itself, which by its very nature opens to an individual only in dialogue with another individual (Jaspers, 1957, p. 16).

Structure, freedom, and truth are all constructions with their own inherent discourses, but it is also interesting to note that both structure and freedom are integral aspects of the construction of a discourse itself.

The discourse of truth telling

Psychology and psychotherapeutic practice have become ideologies and the language of qualitative research has increasingly become psychologized dialogues; this has significant implications for the understanding and experience of responsibility and power in relation to practice-based evidence and, indeed, for the processes of emancipation and transformation.

Discourse is used as an umbrella term to capture a variety of different approaches to understanding and going beyond language to apprehend organized meanings on a given theme. Discourse analysis is described as a detailed exploration of political, personal, media, or academic "talk" and "writing" about a subject, designed to reveal how knowledge is organized, carried, and reproduced in particular ways and through particular institutional practices (Muncle, 2006) (such as the way in which this book has been organized and has reproduced knowledge). The term itself covers a number of theoretical approaches and analytical constructs derived from linguistics, semiotics, social psychology, cultural studies, post-structuralism, and postmodernism.

Discourse analysis challenges the authority of the expert writer and replaces it with the authority of the reader, something that I began to articulate at the beginning of the current chapter. From a research perspective, it is primarily a method of reading text, documents, and conversations, and explores the connections (or dialogue) between language communication, knowledge power, and social practices. In short, it focuses on the meaning and structure of acts of communication in context, both hidden and overt. As I have already alluded to, language is viewed as active and facilitating action and as having the power to "do" something; it also has the capacity to simultaneously repress and express. In other words, there is more to textuality than text; in this sense, discourse analysis examines the relationship between the word and the world. Naturally, discourse analysis is also part of that relationship.

The broad appeal of discourse analysis to social researchers lies in its ability to reveal how institutions and individual subjects are formed, produced, given meaning, constructed, and represented through particular configurations of knowledge.

Three key characteristics of the research practice of discourse analysis are:

- locating talk and text as a social practice;
- identifying processes of action, construction, and variability;
- reorganizing the rhetorical or argumentative organization of talk and texts.

(For further elucidation, see Potter and Wetherall, 1994.)

Perhaps we could think about these characteristics in relation to the practice of discourse analysis itself, but I am more interested in what they can reveal about the practice of research, the nature of truth, and, indeed, of dialogue and transformation in the research process: specifically, the discourse of responsibility and power inherent within the theory and practice of qualitative research. And, more contextually, the discourse we are privileging—that of practitioner-based research. Taking a Foucauldian perspective, discourse analysis is deeply concerned with power, and the complex ways that power and ideology can permeate society and social practices . . . and create power imbalances . . . Foucault then advocated a necessary problematization of commonplace presupposition concerning social life.

In Foucault's *The Archaeology of Knowledge*, the concept of discourse was used to counter positivist and scientific claims to truth and to identify mechanisms whereby some versions of the truth came to be accepted and other readings were marginalized, discredited, and discarded, such as those voices of practitioners. Discourses can dominate and overthrow other dominant discourses; they can, of course, be refused, contested, critiqued, and resisted. However, when this is related to power and marginalization, the people that challenge them are not always the marginalized, rather some other authority that seeks to empower and emancipate. This is often one of the aims of qualitative research and, although it is not always explicit, it can be an unintended outcome.

This conceptualization of discourse views language as social action, language is used to "do" things as well as be things. Critical discourse analysis aims at exposing power imbalances, has a political and ethical intention, and emphasizes social action. It also sees language as social action. We might ask: what are the covert political messages that we as academics, practitioners, and researchers pass on; what of the research literature? What are the covert messages that this book, and this chapter, sublimate? This is an interesting turn in terms of the psychologizing of research and writing processes and, in particular, the link between this and responsibility for truth-telling.

Power and responsibility are important aspects of research, also important aspects of discourse around research and, indeed, writing; not least because they provide a framework for apportioning blame! Labov and Fanshel (1977), for example, formulate their discourse rules as "if . . . then": the rule for assigning blame (read responsibility):

Quantitative research is often blamed, one might argue scapegoated, for being too rigid, too objective and dehumanizing. To a certain extent, I agree, and have criticized positivists myself in this vein. However, qualitative researchers also need to take their share of the blame, or rather, responsibility.

The discourse of qualitative research was developed partly out of the move against discordant theories and techniques leading to the fragmentation of human experience; however, it could be argued that the psychologizing of qualitative research practice also leads to discordant theories and techniques: not surprising, for, as Levinas points out, the very search for intelligibility that dominates western philosophy implies reducing difference and otherness to the same. But we cannot escape the need for dominant discourse or the need to understand.

Levinas proposes an alternative ethic of responsibility to the other, whom he argues is radically unknowable. He urges us to seek a new relationship between ethics and psychology that inform our best efforts to be in relation, that is, to be in dialogue, despite competing and colliding discourses. As qualitative researchers we must strive to grasp the complexity of seeking to understand another person. How have we, as qualitative researchers, done that? Through responsibility? Has this been a conscious movement, or one driven by the psychological society that we inhabit?

Jones and Hill (p. 13) outline the tension between "doing to" and "being with" in the spirit of co-operative inquiry, asking the question: "How can I be in relation with my clients in a non-oppressive way that nevertheless does justice to my knowledge and understanding?". This tension between doing to and being with deserves more attention: Doing to can be aligned to technical competence, problem resolution, evidence of effectiveness, and the researcher taking significant responsibility for the effectiveness of the research.

Being with relates to the dynamic nature of the relationship, expectations and assumptions about issues of accountability and responsibility that must be reflected upon and made clear at the start, together with the means by which they will be enacted, so as to facilitate shared responsibility. Language can be used to describe responsibility, and ascribe responsibility; it is also, in itself, responsible and irresponsible. This is particularly noticeable in the language of research ethics, but could easily be a question that you, the reader, pose in regard to this text. Have we written responsibly and truthfully?

Truth and power

All research entails responsibilities, and therefore power must be exercised ethically. There is, of course, a distinction between responsibility for and to; this is both a political act and involves reflective positioning. Guggenbahl Craig points out that in general the power drive is given freest rein when it can appear under the cloak of objective and moral rectitude. He speaks of:

Role Power (ascribed by society and the context of the practitioner);
Societal Power (such as those from structural positions such as age, sex, culture);
Historical Power (including each persons experience of power in their own relationships).

The exercise of role power to help another, to empower (perhaps here I could use the term emancipate), is a benevolent exercise of power often used and discussed in the context of qualitative research. However, Proctor cleverly observes that power is something that is present in the relationship rather than being the possession of one person; a bi-directional experience, influenced by outside relationships, is inescapable and potentially both positive and negative.

Social power and historical power are particularly complex as they vary within individual relationships and context. Both role and social power have a historical dimension. All three levels of power are at play in the researcher and, indeed, practitioner relationships. A distinction needs to be made between responsibility to, which accounts for the autonomy of the other, and responsibility for, which may devalue it. So, in the context of this chapter, and this book, we have a responsibility *to* you, the reader, but we cannot be responsible *for* your reading or interpretation of the book.

Neither can we simply suggest that practitioner-based research is the answer to the ills of research; instead we need to look carefully at how we construct the concept of PBR and, in that, the language that is used to describe it, for, while it is likely in reality to become another dominant discourse (this cannot be avoided), it could also potentially become a discourse of openness, of participatory dialogue, multiple voices, and multiple truths.

In this sense, my position on practitioner-based research is not concrete and static; rather, it is transient and dynamic, it is moveable, changing, and fluid, and perceives data as a series of moments, fragments knitted together through narrative time and space.

The political voice of many practitioners, researchers, writers, and academics is often denied; although many postmodernists and post-structuralists write about it, the sense of multiple truths is lacking in form and content. Quite often you may read about being true to the data and representing closely the narrative, or perhaps staying close to the emerging themes, but where is the responsibility here? The text is co-created; each individual is both responsible and yet also reliant on the truth being out there waiting to reveal itself.

Good practitioner research?

What, then, is good practitioner-based research, how will I know a scholar when I meet one? Of course, in one sense, good practitioner research cannot be known in its entirety, only a partial view can be articulated. But, of course, there also needs to be some guidance, some signposts, perhaps a guiding fiction as opposed to a discourse.

Garman et al. (1997) outline criteria for "good" research, which I believe to be salient in our conversations regarding practitioner-based research. These are:

Verity:	Does the work ring true? Is it intellectual and honest and authentic?
Integrity:	Is the work structurally sound, does it hang together, is it rationale, logical?
Rigor:	Is there sufficient depth of intellect?
Utility:	Is it useful and professionally relevant?
Vitality:	Is it important, meaningful, and vibrant, is there excitement, is there discovery, use of metaphors, images and symbols?
Aesthetics:	Is it enriching, touch the spirit?
Ethics:	Is there privacy and dignity of respondents?
Verisimilitude:	Is this a truly conceivable experience?

INDEX